Spiritual Capital, Natural Law
and the
Secular Market Place

Spiritual Capital, Natural Law and the Secular Market Place

W. Duncan Reekie

Civitas: Institute for the Study of Civil Society
London
Registered Charity No. 1085494

First Published January 2007

ISBN (10) 1-903386-55-1
ISBN (13) 978-1-903386-55-2

Typeset by
Civitas

Printed in Great Britain by
The Cromwell Press
Trowbridge, Wiltshire

Contents

Author

Duncan Reekie is Emeritus Professor of Industrial Economics at the University of the Witwatersrand, Johannesburg. He was previously lecturer and subsequently reader in Business Economics at the University of Edinburgh, 1969-83. He was Dean of the Faculty of Commerce in his current university from 1989-94, and of the combined Faculty of Commerce, Law and Management in 2002 and 2004. Educated at the Universities of Edinburgh and Strathclyde, he has held visiting professorships in the USA, Canada and the UK. Author or co-author of several books, he has published papers in, among others, *The Economic Journal, The Scottish Journal of Political Economy, The Journal of Industrial Economics, Applied Economics, The South African Journal of Economics* and *The Australian Economic Papers*. He founded, and for ten years edited, the journal *Managerial and Decision Economics*. From 1995-97 he was the President of the Economic Society of South Africa.

Acknowledgement

This publication is supported by a grant from the Templeton Foundation. The opinions expressed in this report are those of the author and do not necessarily reflect the views of the John Templeton Foundation.

Preface

Maynard (Lord) Keynes once remarked that for some centuries Europeans had kept religion and business in 'different compartments of the soul'. He may well have been correct. One purpose of this essay is to suggest why a separate treatment of the two is inappropriate and what we can do about it. For some, the word 'capitalism' carries emotional and moral baggage. It should not. 'Capitalism' has been seen as an alternative moral and economic 'system' to ideologies such as socialism and communism. This is misleading. Capitalism is strictly an amoral word. It implies merely deferred gratification. That is, if one foregoes consumption today one can become better-off at some future date. This morally neutral truth applies in the economic world, in education, and also in the compartment of religion.

Thus, in economic affairs we can save today and invest in physical capital (tools, equipment and infrastructure) that will enable us to produce more for tomorrow's consumption. By means of education we can build up stocks of human capital. All else being equal, a person who prolongs his schooling defers earning immediate income in order to pursue education, but he will generally earn a higher total life-time income in his chosen vocation. He will also be better prepared more readily to appreciate and enjoy some of the finer elements of life such as art, literature and music. But high stocks of physical and human capital are not enough. For humanity efficiently to build and use such stocks, moral or spiritual capital is also required.

An understanding of the individual rights humans can exercise and the duties they must fulfill when interacting with others is necessary. This facilitates economic interchange (e.g. the spiritual assets of trust, honesty and reliability lower the costs of trading) and so encourages a further build-up of economic assets or capital. But such understanding also enhances our awareness and sensitivity as to what is morally beautiful and what is spiritually ugly. In turn this increases our sensitivity as to how our relations with our fellows can be adjusted better to enhance the quality of their lives, and, by implication, our own. Spiritual capital is acquired over time through the training given by and the environmental habits learned in families, faith-based organisations, social groups, clubs and the wider culture. Gratification of immediate wants and desires is deferred as we learn (by teaching and example) to love our brother, sister or neighbour as ourselves. The result, both for our neighbour and for ourselves, can be a positive net gain.

And this is where morality can be linked to capitalism. When and why do we choose to defer gratification? Is it right (or wrong) to do so? How much deferral is 'correct'? When is it economically and morally justifiable to assert: 'I want this and I want it now'? Is it right (or wrong) to encourage others to agree? Are we accumulating or maintaining a sufficient stock of spiritual assets to help us judge these moral issues? If not, what can we do about it?

This book expands on these questions, on the issues of our rights and duties as human beings. I do so from a broadly Christian perspective although I am not a member of either the Established Church (of Scotland) or of the Anglican or Catholic communions.

The idea for this book came during an interchange with David Green. Without that initiative and his encouragement the idea would have remained just that, concept without substance. The Templeton Foundation generously provided the resources which made the project possible in a practical manner. The University of the Witwatersrand, Johannesburg furnished the necessary research time and library facilities. Robert Whelan not only provided on-going encouragement during the time of writing, he was fastidiously accurate and helpful in his editorial capacity. Thanks are also due to Henry Kenney, Robert Vivian and to those who participated anonymously in the refereeing process. They helped enormously to improve earlier versions of the manuscript. Philip Booth of the IEA was kind enough to provide me with sight of a then-unpublished lecture delivered in 2005 at a seminar on 'Economic Issues for Christians in the Modern World'.

The usual disclaimers apply. The responsibility for remaining imperfections is mine alone.

W. Duncan Reekie

1

Introduction

The lex naturalis... has for its proximate principle the essential nature of man. It is a judgement of reason concerning the conformity of moral action and nature. God, who fashioned the essential nature of man with reason and will, is simultaneously regarded as Lawgiver, too.

Heinrich A. Rommen, 1998[*]

This division of work is not however the effect of any human policy, but is the necessary consequen(c)e of a naturall disposition altogether peculiar to men, viz the disposition to truck, barter and exchange... Man continually standing in need of the assistance of others, must fall upon some means to procure their help. This he does not merely by coaxing and courting... A bargain does this in the easiest manner.

Adam Smith, 1766[†]

We entirely repudiated a personal liability on us to obey general rules. We claimed the right to judge every individual case on its merits, and the wisdom, experience and self-control to do so successfully. This was a very important part of our faith, violently and aggressively held, and for the outer world it was our most obvious and dangerous characteristic. We repudiated entirely customary morals, conventions and traditional wisdom. We were, that is to say, in the strictest sense of the term, immoralists. The consequences of being found out had, of course, to be considered for what they were worth. But we recognised no moral obligation on us, no inner sanction, to conform or to obey. Before heaven we claimed to be our own judge in our own case.

John Maynard Keynes, 1949[‡]

In a post-Christian era surely there is no place for 'natural law'? Certainly private property is still granted a role. It is a prerequisite for a market economy. But markets only receive acceptance because they generate material wealth. Once appropriately redistributed, wealth permits modern voters a freedom of behaviour and supports their lifestyle choices. Hedonism has no need for a moral yardstick. The age-old tension between

---

[*]   Rommen,H.A., *The Natural Law*, Indianapolis, 1998, p. 56.

[†]   Smith,A., *Lectures on Jurisprudence* (1766), Oxford,1978, pp. 347-48.

[‡]   Keynes, J.M., *Two Memoirs*, London, 1949, p. 97.

Apollo and Dionysus, in a rich and modern welfare state in a post-Christian world, has not only been resolved: it is redundant.

This essay disputes these premises. The pursuit of happiness certainly requires freedom and some degree of material welfare. But the ethical standards of Christian caritas complement and reinforce many of the workings of the market economy. It will be argued that such mores are necessary preconditions for its success. It will also be argued that many *dirigiste* interventions in the market economy, including the financing of policies such as health, education and welfare on grounds of wealth redistribution, are not, first appearances to the contrary, necessarily in line with the underlying principles of caritas. Robert Fogel, the Nobel Prize-winning economist, claimed (2000) that there is indeed a dysfunctional and inequitable distribution of assets in modern societies. But the mal-distribution is spiritual, not material. The argument put forward in the following pages is that entrepreneurial alertness to gain (profit) is required to start up the market process. Once the process begins, transfers and exchanges occur and total wealth increases. In an analogous manner caritas triggers entrepreneurial alertness and subsequent actions to transfer spiritual assets. But spiritual assets, like public goods, suffer no diminution in their stock when others are given access to them. Nevertheless, in a Fallen World, the actual and latent demands for such redistribution will never reach their full potential. Some will always opt for Dionysus.

Why do people engage in market exchange? Why do we 'truck and barter'? In the *Wealth of Nations* Adam Smith (1776, p. 25) noted how human specialisation and hence trade leads to the provision of 'many advantages', including 'general opulence'. Reciprocal bargains help us improve our condition and satisfy our wants. What, if any, are the natural or institutional rules that can facilitate or hinder mutually beneficial and voluntary exchanges? Economists spend much of their working lives pondering these issues. And philosophy? Aquinas claimed we wish to explore the 'ground', or explanation of everything (Scruton, 1994, p. 8). Obviously 'everything' includes the natural propensity to trade, truck, barter and exchange. A religious believer, more specifically, would ask: Why do we desire to understand more about God? Does a fuller under-standing of the 'ground of our being', of God, help us better to know the underlying rules of trade? Can we thus better achieve and more fully appreciate the opulence and advantages to which we aspire and to which truck and barter contribute? How appropriate are these aspirations? Theologians and philosophers focus on these questions.

Yet this traditional division of intellectual labour may be counter-productive. For example, if we trade to improve our condition this implies not only differing marginal valuations of the traded good by the traders (the narrow economic view), but also that there are some overall standards of value by which we live and judge 'our condition'. Change our values (in economic jargon, re-order and re-shape our various utility functions for all goods) and whatever particular exchange could lead to an improvement of condition may no longer do so. God and Mammon, however defined, compete for allegiance to differing standards of values. Philosophers and economists working together might provide a more meaningful under-standing of the ordering and shaping of our utility functions than they can do in isolation. In vulgar terms, man does not live by bread alone. But economists usually measure changes in man's condition as though he did. Philosophers and theologians, to the contrary, often ignore the economic truth that if the living of life is to be made more worth the living, then some bread will have to be baked.

For example, it may be operationally possible to 'repudiate general rules', but the real question is: At what cost? Trade and exchange have as general prerequisites the institutions of private property rights, freedom of contract and trust. But these requirements are not indivisible absolutes. Keynesian freedom of lifestyle choice, without 'inner sanction', is increased the lower is its cost to the individual. The growth of state-funded welfare and entitlements has improved that freedom dramatically. But the consequence has been a reduction in private property, in market freedom and in interpersonal trust. Private trading in general has shrunk due to the levying of taxes across the board to fund the so-called entitlements. Private sector providers have withdrawn from trading, or otherwise adjusted their behaviour in specific areas where state provision is 'free' and where they cannot therefore commercially co-exist. Is this reduction in trading activity disadvantageous? Are there offsetting gains in quality of life?

Private contractors, individual and corporate, act in order to better their condition. They do so subject to rules and mores laid down by convention and by governments. For good or ill these laws and practices may be more or less followed or rejected. This essay explores the implications of man's natural propensity to engage in market-based activity. It examines the advantages of spontaneous trading both in the presence and absence of spiritual capital, and also when subject to greater or lesser external legislative control. To do so it draws on economists, philosophers and theologians. More insights are gained than if only one discipline were relied upon in isolation.

Chapter 2 notes that private property is a divinely inspired (or First Cause) institution. It has been regarded as derived from Natural Law, by Catholic and Protestant thinkers, by deists such as Aristotle, as well as by agnostics such as Hume. Its existence satisfies our propensity to trade and exchange and provides us with our material welfare. It coexists with self-interest 'properly understood' and is an essential component of individual freedom. Our 'moral sense' and the 'impartial spectator', our consciences, constrain selfishness, permit and induce appropriate care of others and create the spiritual capital of mores and behavioural norms which can be passed through the generations.

Alongside this tradition there have also always been those with alternative views of property and morality. Some have seen property as merely the result of either utility or expediency, or of self-interested action, or as the product of human reason. If so, it is not a First Cause institution. Indeed if reason itself is exalted as a First Cause then common rather than private property may be advocated as the institution of choice to maximise utility. A Platonic Republic governed by benevolent Guardians provides an early example. Later (as we will see in chapter 4) some even saw Natural Law as the *product* of reason. But to them, as with Plato, the reason in question was that of the 'enlightened despot', or of the 'man of system', with whose laws individuals had to comply.

Chapter 3 records that by the nineteenth and early twentieth centuries leaders of both Protestant and Catholic churches, perhaps influenced by the impact of industrialisation, perhaps by the unemployment observed during times of economic depression, were expressing moral doubts about the justice and workings of markets based on the institution of private property. This was a time when the Social Gospel movement was influencing not only churchmen but economists as well. Some market economists, in reaction, and in defence of the benefits of trade and exchange, attacked in their turn the principles of Christianity. They believed Christianity was self-degrading and that Christian love was 'mush'. The views of some church leaders on economics were misguided, but the market economists were no better. They misinterpreted both Christianity and the meaning of *caritas*. By the end of the twentieth century Christian thinkers appeared who could reconcile the materialistic wealth-creating aspects of private property with the spiritual-capital-creating benefits provided by our 'moral sense'.

4

This dichotomy was epitomised by the 'two Enlightenments'. The Scottish Enlightenment stressed subsidiarity. Because it acknowledged that love and concern for others could and should vary by distance, the principle of solidarity was seen as necessary but spontaneous. It was not loaded with more baggage than it could accommodate. The role of Natural Law and the Creator was prominent. To the contrary, members of the French Enlightenment saw Natural Law as the product of 'reason' and the 'general will'. The group, represented by the benevolent despot, not God, was the First Cause. And by the time of Comte, solidarity-by-compulsion had become a formal religion. Chapter 4 describes how these developments influenced social thinking in Britain, France, Germany and America. When coupled with periods of economic depression or stagnation they resulted in policies that came to their fullest fruition in the corporatist and welfare state.

The growth of state welfare may have undermined what Smith termed 'benevolence'. A worrying paradox has also emerged. Individual freedom of a kind can be maximised in a collectivist, welfare society where others pay the direct costs of one's own lifestyle choices. A desire for moral autonomy, for a right to opt for a hedonistic way of life, has not only become pervasive, it has become affordable. Yet the Natural Law cannot be repealed and economics reminds us there is no free lunch. The actions and behavioural choices prompted by unrestrained self-interest do not justify a 'repudiation of personal liability'. To be 'our own judge in our own case' (to cite Keynes) imposes costs on others. Not only must others bear the financial costs, the wider community also then suffers from widening 'inequalities in endowments' of spiritual capital. Spiritual assets, although privately and unevenly held, potentially possess large external benefits. They are like public goods in that they are costless to transfer, the stock held by the transferor is undiminished, the transferee's quality of life is enhanced, and there are positive spillovers for others. (The whole community benefits when individuals themselves somehow become 'better citizens'.) These unevenly distributed assets include: a sense of purpose, a strong family ethic, a capacity to resist the lure of hedonism and a sense of community. But how can *voluntary*, mutually beneficial trade in spiritual assets be initiated?

A major problem is that for politicians there is more to be gained from trading in political than in spiritual assets. The logic of trade also operates when extended from commercial to political entrepreneurs, and not necessarily with such benign outcomes. Political assets can be traded between voters, sections of an electorate, politicians and bureaucrats because of the potential electoral gains spotted by a political entrepreneur. The opportunities for political entrepreneurship may increase in number and attractiveness if impinging on private property rights and contractual freedom can be demonstrated to be beneficial to sectional interests with sufficient electoral or bureaucratic clout. This appears to have happened when social welfare policy changes coincided with economic recessions. And it did so against a background of a change in the intellectual climate towards 'reason' and the 'men of system'. There was a shift away from Natural Law, the spontaneous market order, the individual conscience and 'moral sense'.

The presence of political activity is ubiquitous in the field of healthcare. Compassion for the sick, injured and ailing, so the arguments go, cannot be left to the cold logic of trade. Hence we must turn to government to provide and obtain for us the care that at some time in each of our lives we will all depend upon. Social cohesion is never more necessary than when we are helpless. And our individual primacy is never held in higher esteem than when we are the focus and the object of the attention of professional healthcarers. So runs the conventional wisdom. Chapter 5 challenges this by examining the economics of the financing and provision of healthcare. A lengthy list of reasons why markets 'fail' patients is examined. But what may be surprising is how few of the arguments are valid. They are either wrong, or hold only in instances where regulations introduced by politicians have already distorted the market place. In fact, markets appear to be able to provide and finance more appropriate healthcare at lower costs, in different ways, and better tailored to individual requirements, than the alternative. The one area where markets appear to be inadequate is in the provision of time or money for care of the poor. But this is not a problem unique to healthcare. As with any poverty relief, the dilemma is that government provision raises any shortfall between need and altruism. And it does this while simultaneously distorting some of the lifestyles and certain of the values of the population.

Is this a cost worth bearing? Are we yielding to the temptation to turn stones into bread, and grasping at the political and regulatory powers of the world to do so? Successful political entrepreneurship is 'crowding-out' voluntary and consensual market-based exchange. But there is worse. It is also diminishing the stock of, and increasing the inequities in, the distribution of spiritual capital. Words like 'compassion' have been arrogated for their own political use by collectivists. Concepts such as family- or self-responsibility have been shunned for hedonistic reasons by selfish individualists. Each has struck a political bargain with the other. Votes are traded in exchange for the promise of collective provision. In the market place for ideas statism received a setback after the collapse of communism. But, as chapters 4 and 5 illustrate, that setback passed virtually unnoticed in the areas of healthcare and welfare.

Chapter 6 examines a sector of the economy where ideas are the unit of currency: university education. Again, economic analysis can be applied to ascertain if the sector is providing what its consumers want, and if it is doing so in the most effective way. Is the sector innovative, competitive and dynamic? Or is it constrained by a combination of regulation and self-interest? Is the sector attracting those students who most value its output? Or is it compelled—or worse does it opt—to provide post-secondary teaching to all who think, in some 'positive rights' fashion, that they 'should' be awarded admission? As with welfare and healthcare, the paradox is again apparent, of individual license, largely unfettered by any price to be paid or responsibility to be carried, coexisting with, or resulting from, centralised provision. This paradox is observed in both producers and consumers, both staff and students. Economics can help us understand how better to write voluntary exchange contracts in the sector. Property rights can be properly specified, for both academics and for students, so that the academy is unencumbered by unjustifiable, centrally imposed, positive laws and regulations favouring vested interests.

Accordingly there is much less economic justification for the heavy emphasis we see in practice on high levels of state funding and provision of healthcare, welfare and education. Moves towards what we observe have (understandably) been most popular in times of economic downturns. Then, appeals to permit spontaneous market forces to operate to allow us to reap the moral and material advantages of mutually beneficial exchange are often apparently at their least attractive. Worse, the Natural Law itself can come to be misunderstood, and be deliberately and mistakenly attacked by those who should be its advocates. In this way chapter 7 concludes the discussion. The tendency to act in breach of Natural Law is universal. Failure to understand the place of freedom of exchange and private property rights within the framework of Natural Law remains widespread. Most importantly, for the benefit of all, the latent demand for a removal of the maldistribution of spiritual capital must be cultivated and then met. An entrepreneurial gain from rectifying the inequity is available. One's own stock of spiritual capital is not reduced if one shares it. Yet both parties gain if the stock is spread more widely. The proximate gain can be defined in material and utility terms since a safer, happier and more productive society will result. And what switches on the alertness to that gain? That question remains unanswered even in the commercial market. (There, profit is certainly the reward. But why is one person alert to a given profit opportunity while, at the same time and place, another is not?) In the spiritual asset market place, however, entrepreneurial alertness can only be caritas itself.

2

Natural Law and Property Rights

Property rights are at the heart of the incentive structure of market economies. They determine who bears risk and who gains or loses from transactions... they spur... investment, encourage careful monitoring ... promote work effort, and create a constituency for enforceable contracts. In short [when well specified, they promote] economic growth and wealth creation. In addition [their] wide distribution... counteract[s] concentration of [political] power... and contribute[s] to social stability.

World Development Report, 1996*

From each as they choose, to each as they are chosen.

Robert Nozick, 1974†

Property... has no purpose where there is abundance.

Arnold Plant, 1934‡

Between 1917, the year of the Russian Revolution, and the final decade of the twentieth century, some one-third of the world's population lived in countries whose government's had 'seceded from the market economy'.[1] The experiment of abolishing private property failed, and did so at a high cost. There was large-scale loss of life as Stalin and Mao attempted to foist their policies on recalcitrant populations. The foregone economic benefits have been immeasurable. Moreover the costs of transition back to the path from which these economies mistakenly diverged continue to be immense. In addition, on both sides of the geopolitical divide, the resulting 'Cold War' diverted resources from preferred alternative uses. But the 1917 experiment was not based on a novel idea. Nor has that idea, the notion of the beneficial effects of common property, been totally discredited by the disasters of the twentieth century. The debate over whether the Natural Law implies common or private property, whether it exalts the individual or the collective, and whether it is discovered by reason or is designed by

---

* World Development Report 1996, *From Plan to Market*, World Bank, Oxford: 1996, pp. 48-49.

† Nozick, R., *Anarchy, State and Utopia*, New York, 1974, p. 160.

‡ Plant, A., *Economica*, February 1934, p. 30.

reasoning, extends back in time to Plato and beyond. The purpose of this chapter is to study the ultimate nature of the institution of private property. We examine the development of the understanding of property, from the earliest philosophers to the mediaeval and post-Reformation writers in Natural Law. It has been alleged that some of the latter, and in particular economists and philosophers of the Scottish Enlightenment, overturned or denied the Natural Law tradition. We reject this view. Rather we show how they resolved the tensions surrounding the Natural Law. Grotius and Locke explained the natural origin and rights of private property. Pufendorf explained how and when common property was a natural phenomenon. The Scots showed how the moral sense was innate, but also how it could be cultivated and refined by habit and discovery. And they demonstrated how a society based on private property and consensual exchange could better increase welfare than one governed or designed by what Plato called a Guardian, or Smith a 'man of system'.

2.1 Plato and Aristotle

The concept of a Golden Age, past or future, is common to many religions. Eden precedes the Fall in each of the three Abramic faiths. Around 700 BC the Greek poet Hesiod, convinced he was living in the more miserable Age of Iron (the happier Ages of Gold and Silver being irrecoverable history), argued that worship of the Goddess of Justice was the only solution to mankind's plight. Rules for life were laid out in his poem *The Works and Days*, including the assertion that: 'Before success the immortal gods have placed the sweat of our brows'. In Hesiod's Golden Age all property had been held in common. Rules of behaviour relating to private property were required only after Pandora (the first woman) opened her jar releasing evils and miseries into the world.

Plato (perhaps articulating the views of Socrates) in *The Republic* looked forward to, rather than back at, an ideal state. In Books IV and V he argued for common ownership of property and the dissolution of the family. Private property, he asserted, leads to quarrels and divisions. In Book V Socrates suggested 'individuality' was a 'dissolving force' resulting from the use of 'such words as "mine" and "not mine"'. Plato's basic premise was that 'the highest unity of a state is its highest good'. The concept of 'one's own' must thus be shunned and communism embraced in order to promote harmony within the state. In the *Laws*, however, Plato was more realistic. The demands made on human nature were not so high. The communism of the *Republic* was dropped. So too was the notion of holding wives in common. Rather monogamous marriage, coupled with fidelity, was the rule. The *Laws* were intended more for contemporary Greeks than for those in some idealised future. The beginnings of Natural Law were visible. In both works Plato taught that the state is supreme and that individuals had no role except as parts of, or servants to, the state. He advocated a caste society without social mobility. The (elder members of the) ruling, military caste would possess a concentration of political power. But even they would have no personal freedom.

> The greatest principle of all is that no one of either sex should be without a commander; nor should the mind of anyone be accustomed to do anything, either in jest or in earnest, of his own motion... he should look to and follow his leader, even in the least things... he should stand or move, or exercise, or wash, or take his meals...when he is bidden...in a word, not teach the soul or accustom her to know or understand how to do anything apart from others.
>
> Plato, *Laws* 942.

This refers not only to the servile castes, but also to the rulers. Presumably somewhere there is someone who does act with initiative and gives instructions. But Plato is coy about this. It is clear that such a real ruler would at least pretend that initiative was not being exercised, but that he was merely administering pre-existing laws or customs. How did the authority of the ruler, the Guardian, achieve its legitimacy? It was not gained by force, nor was it awarded by traditional aristocratic privilege. Rather, Plato's Guardians based their claim to rule on the basis of superior knowledge that fitted them to rule for the 'happiness of all'. Further, the Guardians ruled as trustees, charged with the collective welfare of the state. The problem is that Plato proposed no safeguards or sanctions to ensure that the Guardians would in fact act as he intended. If they were so 'insensate and childish' as to abuse their positions and attempt to achieve more happiness for themselves than their 'moderate and secure' lives supplied, then they would be compelled to learn the wisdom of Hesiod that 'the half is greater than the whole' (*The Republic*, V 467).

There are two main lessons to be learned from the teachings of Plato. One is to note the naïve idealism. He saw little, if any, value in the individual citizen except as a member of the greater community. His belief that a Guardian class would be benign and benevolent, or be well informed, is, from a historical vantage point, mere wishful thinking. His stress throughout on the 'happiness' of the state, not on the freedom of the person, is unattractive. To a modern philosopher like Karl Popper, Plato's laws, if put into practice, would result in tyranny, and an unsuccessful tyranny at that. Popper in his two-volume book *The Open Society and its Enemies* (1942), identified Plato (along with Hegel and Marx) as enemies of personal freedom and democracy. Popper writes:

> I demand that the fundamental purpose of the state should not be lost sight of; I mean the protection of that freedom which does not harm other citizens. Thus I demand that the state must limit the freedom of the citizens as equally as possible, and not beyond what is necessary for achieving an equal limitation of freedom.

Vol. 1, p. 110.

> The individualist must maintain that the morality of states (if there is any such thing) tends to be considerably lower than that of the average citizen, so that it is much more desirable that the morality of the state should be controlled by the citizens than the opposite.

Vol. 1, p. 113.

A second, more positive way to interpret Plato is to see him (or Socrates) as one of the original codifiers of Natural Law. Certainly Popper's critique, that Plato allowed no individual to have a goal that was superior to the ends of the *polis*, was correct. And given Popper's premise of the value of the individual, the resulting tyranny is evil. Nevertheless the Socratic dialogues showed how virtue consists in knowledge. Plato (through Socrates) demonstrated that there is an objective, knowable world of values such as goodness, beauty and justice. Therefore no one knowingly does evil for its own sake, unless he is either ignorant of these values or errs culpably in believing that his evil action is good. Knowledge, in turn, involves the contemplation of concepts such as justice. As a result, Socrates regarded the individual's 'daimonion (*sic*), conscience and its voice... as a reflection and testimony of these ultimate values and of the divinely instituted order of the world' (Rommen, 1998, p. 11).[2] By laying hold of the ideal in literal terms we can strive to understand the essence. We can then move to concepts such as the true judge and the true law. Plato contrasted the true and proper law, the Natural Law, whose essence is invariant and abides in the realm of ideas, with the positive (or posited) law of the 'party'. Thus in the *Laws*, IV, 715 the Athenian states:

> That when there has been a contest for power, those who gain the upper hand so entirely monopolise the government as to refuse all share to the defeated party and their descendants... such governments are not polities at all, nor are laws right which are passed for the good of particular classes and not for the good of the whole state. States which have such laws are... but parties, and their notions of justice are simply unmeaning.

12

In this way Plato groped towards identifying the elements of what we now term Natural Law. Likewise, St Thomas Aquinas in *Summa Theologica* defined Natural Law as a participation in the eternal law by rational creatures (I-II q. 91 a. 2). And, in the *Oxford Compendium to Christian Thought*, Adrian Hastings (2000, p. 465) amplified this, saying it:

> signifies the very functioning of a person's practical reason with its inbuilt commitment to seeking good and avoiding evil...the intellect is enlightened by the divine law which it can reject but not escape. From this first inbuilt quest follow other primary principles of natural law relating to truth, justice and the like.

So although Aristotle is often held to be the Father of Natural Law (*vide* Rommen, 1990, p. 14, and Hastings, 2000, p. 465), the honorific is a misnomer. In *Politics*, however, Aristotle did challenge Plato's views on property. He explained that common property is not a source of social unity but rather of disagreement (*Politics*, Book II 1263a). It is only private property that permits the giving of personal assistance and aid to one's fellows (1263b). While, with private property, because 'everyone has a separate interest, one main source of disagreement is removed, and work will prosper all the more because each man will be occupied about his own business' (1263a). Self-interest results in greater care being taken and more productive use being made of property that is privately rather than communally held. The inevitable grudges against those who consume a great deal but do little to produce are dissipated if private property is the rule. The perceived evils of private ownership are due less to the nature of property, and much more to the selfish desire for it inherent in the 'wickedness of human nature' (1263b). Private property could in theory be abolished, but it would be impossible to eliminate the desires of human nature. So Aristotle is a realist compared to Plato. '[I]f the methods advocated by Plato's *Republic* were sound, they would not have gone unrecognised by so many generations' (1264a).[3]

Plato and Aristotle also saw reason itself from alternative perspectives. For Plato, reason had the perfection and essence of values as its end. To Aristotle these were causes initiating reason. From Aristotle's teleological view, disciplined reasoning is the key to knowledge. Pure thought is the most God-like activity. How should one then live? Certainly one should not strive exclusively for material wealth. 'The life of money making is one undertaken under compulsion, and wealth is evidently not the good we are seeking' (the *Nichomachean Ethics of Aristotle*, hereafter *Ethics*, I.6). Aristotle maintained that the ultimate human goal is happiness, and that the

13

happiest life is a well-rounded one, guided by virtue, learning and habituation (*Ethics*, I.9). The generalised virtue of the mean is determined by reason to lie somewhere for any given quality between the positions of irrational excess and parsimony. Time and experience are required if special virtues such as liberality, courage, justice, temperance, veracity and the appreciation of beauty are to be gained. Intellectual virtues are acquired by contemplation. Moral virtues are gained by habit. They are not innate. Nevertheless 'we are adapted by nature to receive moral virtues, and are made perfect by habit' (*Ethics*, II.1). Further, just as doctors have continually to adjust their prescriptions to meet changing circumstances and diagnoses, so philosophers have to be adaptable in the courses of action they recommend:

> ... the whole account of matters of conduct must be given in outline and not precisely; matters concerned with conduct and what is good for us have no fixity, any more than matters of health.
>
> *Ethics*, II.2

This is not, as it might first appear, a lifestyle charter for a youthful libertine. Learning and habituation require time and experience in order to develop the prudence and 'practical wisdom' that can direct behaviour to secure the ends of human life:

> ... [only] the man who is capable of deliberating has practical wisdom...[and] no one deliberates about things that are invariable...[practical wisdom provides] a true and reasoned state or capacity to act with regard to the things that are good or bad for man.
>
> *Ethics*, VI.5

> ... it is thought a young man of practical wisdom cannot be found...[since] such wisdom is concerned not only with universals, but with particulars.
>
> *Ethics*, VI.8

Aristotle's approach to Natural Law runs in parallel to this approach to moral conduct. There is a natural justice 'which exists everywhere, has the same force and does not exist by people's thinking this or that' (*Ethics*, V.7). But he also notes there is a 'legal justice' whereby laws are administered in the real world. These are constantly being adjusted and so it becomes difficult to ascertain which particular rules are natural and which legal or conventional. Natural Law has its source in the essence of the just. It is everywhere and always unalterable, carrying with it the same force. However, statute laws have their origins in the assemblies or in the parliaments that posit them. These positive laws will more or less correctly embrace the Natural Law. They will and should, as a matter of practical wisdom, reflect in their detail immediate social circumstances or constitutions (*Politics*, Book IV, 1289a). When they fail to do this in detail then Aristotle argues that the principle of 'equity' be applied by the judge as a corrective:

> When the law speaks universally…and a case arises…which…is not covered by the universal statement, then it is right, where the legislator…has erred by over-simplicity, to correct the omission—[for the judge] to say what the legislator himself would have said had he been present.'

Ethics, V.10

But what of the actual content of the Natural Law, particularly as it applied to property? Plato and Aristotle had really very little to say. This is only partly explained by their differences of opinion on the value and place of private property in society. Both tended to assume that positivist legislators would conform to the principles of Natural Law when dealing with property or any other issue. If legislators produced flawed laws, it was rather because of gaps in detail than in deviations from principle. The lacuna in their discussion can perhaps be better explained by recalling that private property implies important rights of the individual owner. But individual rights were not of prime consequence, even to Aristotle. Rather Rommen notes (1998, p. 17) that for both Plato and Aristotle 'the *polis* or city-state was the great pedagogue, against which…no natural, subjective right of the citizen could be admitted…They remained state socialists.'

It was not until the Stoics, the earliest of whom was Zeno (*c.* 336-224 BC), that the importance of the individual personality was emphasised. For the Stoics, it was the individual soul that transformed impressions into intelligent perceptions. And it was these perceptions that resulted in reasoned action. Only rational action could raise the individual above the confusions and complexities of his environment. The highest good, apathy towards life's experiences could thus be attained through the application of reason. Only the wisest of men could achieve this indifference. Most remain slaves to their emotions and ignorance. The sage, however, carries his happiness within, and has more in common with similar individuals from other states than he does with so-called fellow citizens. The Stoic, through reason, could discover the natural, universal law, since nature and God and cosmic reason are one. (Compare Jn. 1:1: 'In the beginning was the Word, and the Word was with God, and the Word was God.' The 'Word' as used in John is the translation of the Greek *logos*, meaning reason.)

2.2 Roman and Mediaeval Approaches

Stoic thought has come down to us mainly through the writings of Cicero, the Roman lawyer, politician, orator and philosopher. Educated in both Rome and Greece, he was a staunch upholder of the values of the Republic. He favoured none of the other forms of governance prevalent prior to that era: neither oligarchies, nor kingdoms, nor democracies. He held that man has an inborn sense of right and wrong provided or derived from innate ideas. Since these are naturally imbued and not dependent on the whim of a ruler, or the will of the masses, or abstracted from the legislator's edict, they will be identical with divine (pantheistic) right reason. And since divine reason is universally valid, the Natural Law is unchangeable and invariant. Indeed, Cicero emphasised that while evil men might ignore it, it would be sinful for others to attempt to repeal it.[4] Natural Law was not simply a listing of prohibitions, but also of obligations concerning how life should be lived.

Like Plato and Aristotle, however, Cicero would have been unhappy in the modern economic world. Aristotle held the aristocrat's view that some were born to rule and others to obey, that manual labour was the work of slaves, that engaging in commerce was little better, and certainly not the work of a free man qualified for full citizenship. If anything, Cicero outdid Aristotle in these views. The son of a wealthy businessman, he wrote that the gains from hired labour were dishonourable, that retailing involved inevitable lying and huckstering and that the work of the artisan is sordid.

The Greek city-states were disappearing. The Roman Republic, subsequently the Empire, was soon to cover most of the known world. Rome was absorbing other peoples within its boundaries, and meeting still others at the edges of Empire. This provided practical problems for Roman jurists. The Natural Law had been handed down to the Roman world from Greek philosophers. It had its roots in reason applied to some ideal Golden Age, now or in the future, since, as Sumner Maine (1861, p. 45) put it, to 'live according to *nature* [was] the end for which man was created and which the best men were bound to compass' (emphasis in original). The Greek city-states administered their positive or civil laws with deliberate equality— equality, that is, among citizens. This excluded the bulk of the population and the despot. The Romans, to the contrary, also applied the concept of 'equity' or *aequus*, but to them equality of administration applied also to foreigners, and sometimes even to slaves (Sumner Maine, 1861, p. 47). This greater tolerance of the Romans was epitomised by Marcus Aurelius, the second-century emperor and, like Cicero, a student of the Stoics, when he

16

said: 'My city and country, so far as I am Antoninus, is Rome, but so far as I am a man, it is the world.'[5] Of course this attitude was also a pragmatic response to growth of Empire. Populations and hence legal, behavioural and religious traditions and practices were colliding and merging as never before. The Roman authorities had to adjudicate and apply laws across the Empire and between peoples of different origins even in the same areas. The problem might seem to have become particularly acute by the year 212, when all free inhabitants of the Empire also became Roman citizens. Yet the Roman lawyers had already discovered that in many instances the collisions were not as traumatic as might have been predicted. They found over the years that the behavioural mores and expectations of the different subject peoples were often very similar. This similarity, or even identity, was termed by the jurists as *ius gentium*, the Law of Nations. The *ius gentium* was unwritten and arose out of actual practice. The Law of Nations, together with the Natural Law of the Greeks, based on reason, were ultimately conflated. The sixth-century emperor Justinian, in his *Institutes* commented:

> All nations who are ruled by laws and customs, are governed partly by their own particular laws, and partly by those laws which are common to all mankind. The law, which a people enacts is called the Civil Law, but that which natural reason appoints for all mankind is called the Law of Nations, because all nations use it.[6]

Natural Law as seen by the Romans therefore displayed a significant advance on how it had been viewed by the Greeks. Now every member of human society was possessed of certain natural rights. (Slavery was seen as a positive law institution only.) The Greeks, on the other hand, in terms of Natural Law saw the *polis* as supreme, and divided mankind into 'Greeks and Barbarians, freemen and slaves'. However this Roman approach, where Marcus Aurelius could argue for citizenship of the world, the *civitas maxima*, still begged the question as to the relative roles of individuals and the greater society. Christianity, from its beginnings, and prior to its dominance as the religion of the Empire, has laid a stress on Natural Law. Paul, the Apostle to the Gentiles, emphasised that it was written on the hearts even of those with no access to the Decalogue of Sinai. It was made known through conscience and thought (see Rom. 2:12-16). Following this Platonic line of argument, St John Chrysostom, the Early Church Father, wrote:

> We use not only Scripture but also reason in arguing against the pagans...They say they have no law of conscience, and there is no law implanted by God in nature. My answer is to question them about their laws concerning marriage,

homicide, wills, injuries to others, enacted by their legislators. Perhaps the living have learned from their fathers, and their fathers from their fathers. But...the first legislator! From whom did he learn? Was it not by his own conscience and conviction? It is evident that they derived their laws from the law which God ingrafted in man from the beginning.[7]

St Augustine, Bishop of Hippo, also wrote on Natural Law. Born in the year 354, and dying in 430, he was converted to Christianity in 386. He was heavily influenced by the writings of Cicero. He encountered them as a student in Carthage when he was 19 years old. (Petrarch said of Cicero's writings: 'You could sometimes fancy that it is not a pagan philosopher but a Christian apostle who is speaking.'[8]) Like Plato, Augustine argued that the human teacher could only assist his pupil to make valid judgements. Moral values are not the products of a teacher's, or a pupil's individual mind, but are accepted universally by all. The job of the teacher is properly to formulate true values so that they can be recognised by the pupil. To Augustine the individual finds or discovers the truth because Christ, the Word of God, the *magister interior*, reveals it to him. In the *City of God* he restated the view that conduct is properly directed at happiness. He redefined the Aristotelian virtues required to attain happiness in Christian terms. Temperance keeps the self incorruptible and complete for God's service. Fortitude helps one bear all things cheerfully for God's sake. Justice is the service of God alone to the exclusion of all else. Prudence (or practical wisdom) is the ability to discriminate between what helps and what hinders God.

We noted Aristotle's view that rules of conduct could not be precise and that they might be interpreted as license for a libertine. Notoriously, Augustine may have been just that. Prior to conversion to Christianity he had sown his share of wild oats. His subsequent prayer—'O Lord, make me chaste, but not quite yet!'—is a classic. Aristotle's solution was to emphasise prudence and the acquisition by habit and learning of practical wisdom. Augustine's post-conversion answer was to expect adherence to a scale of values. Man acts according to the dynamic of love (*amor*). But only if this instinctive desire is rightly directed will man stick to the appropriate ordering of values. Lesser goods should be used, not for their own ends, but only as means to achieve, attain and enjoy the ultimate end on which the heart is set. This supreme good, true happiness, the enjoyment of God, is caritas (see chapter 3). God then will have given himself to man, and man will have the ability to fulfil the two New Testament commandments of loving God and loving others as himself. As with the Stoics, the highest good is attainable provided the appropriate level of indifference to the passions is achieved. Supreme reason and eternal truth is identical with God's reason, and God's reason is the appropriate ordering of values. Bad acts disturb this natural order. A lawmaker can prohibit such acts because they constitute a disturbance of that order. They breach Natural Law. They are evil, in and of themselves, not because a legislator has defined or posited them as such.

Augustine, like Hesiod a millennium earlier, saw a Golden Age existing prior to Original Sin. Augustine taught that life preceding Original Sin would have been governed by a primary Natural Law anterior to a secondary Natural Law suitable to a post-Fallen world. Eve was merely the Biblical equivalent of Pandora. First ladies aside, the opinion that perhaps there were 'Two Natural Laws' was not laid to rest until St Thomas Aquinas examined the issue. For the particular purposes of this discussion, from Hesiod to Augustine and beyond, common property was seen to be an ideal, even if it remained an unrealised one. Private property ownership was accepted, but as a 'natural', post-Fall institution (Augustine's view); and while conducive to social peace and productivity, its abolition as a step back to the Golden Age could only happen if the inherent post-Fall desires of human nature could be abolished (Aristotle's view). It was left to the Calvinist, Hugo Grotius, fully to develop the place of private property in Natural Law; and to the Lutheran pastor's son, Samuel Pufendorf, fully to articulate and to explain the exceptional and different place of common property in that same framework. But first we have to examine Aquinas' dismissal of the 'Two Natural Laws'.

Under St Thomas Aquinas (1225-74), and in his *Summa theologica*, the Christian philosophy of Scholasticism reached its zenith.[9] Aquinas began by noting the difference between man and every other creature. It is the very presence of his intellect and free will that show that man is made in the image of God. The essence of the entire created world is that it conforms to the will of the Creator. This conforming 'oughtness' is the eternal law. It embraces the natural sciences as they pertain to the lifeless and inorganic world around us; the laws of biology, evolution and growth as they pertain to animals and plants; and thirdly, the laws of reason by which a free and rational man 'ought' to live if he wishes 'to perfect or fulfil...the potentialities of his being...as he perceives them in virtue of his reason and becomes conscious of them' (Rommen, p. 41). Aquinas also arrived at this conclusion by another route. Given free will and reason, all men act for an ultimate end or purpose. But only a worthwhile and good end will induce an act. Goodness is that which is worth striving for. 'Hence this is the first precept of the law, that *good is to be done and promoted, and evil is to be avoided*. All other precepts of the natural law are based upon this…' (cited from the *Summa theologica* in Rommen, p. 42). The question as to what is good and evil remains unanswered, of course. Acts are good, moral and just if they correspond to the essential nature of man. This essential nature, as a measure or yardstick of what is good, must itself be immutable, just as the essence of man, the image of an unalterable God, is unchangeable. In this way Aquinas emphasised it is the intellect, the reason, which is supreme, not the will or the passions, when assessing whether actions are in compliance with the Natural Law.

When it comes to practical cases Aquinas recognised that reason (other than speculative axioms) could be at the mercy of the passions. The inferences of deductive or practical reason could be less than clear if influenced by the will. This did not mean Aquinas saw no need for a positive law, rather the reverse. The positive law should be designed precisely because the Natural Law is general, and because the Natural Law can be overwhelmed by corrupt habits and evil practices. Positive law may not conflict with Natural Law, rather it should be there to aid a citizenry to achieve perfectibility in its day-to-day life. The Natural Law is then the yardstick against which any positive law must be assessed. But for Aquinas, the Natural Law was more than doing good and avoiding evil, it was also more than the two New Testament commandments of loving God as well as one's neighbour. Explicitly Aquinas argued also that the Decalogue contained the most essential conclusions of speculative reason (Rommen, p. 46). Aquinas did not need to appeal to a 'Secondary' natural law, applicable to a post-Fall world, preceded by a Golden Age, when a 'Primary' natural law only was required. If man is indeed free and rational, fallen or not, the fundamental distinction between good and evil remains the same. Thus:

> …the precepts of the Decalogue contain the very intention of the lawgiver, who is God. For the precepts of the first table, which direct us to God, contain the very order to the common and final good, which is God; while the precepts of the second table contain the order of justice to be observed among men, namely, that nothing undue be done to anyone, and that each be given his due; …the precepts of the Decalogue admit of no dispensation whatever.
>
> *Summa theologica*, IIae, q.100, a.8.

So the Eighth Commandment, 'Thou shalt not steal', with its clear corollary acknowledging the concept of 'one's own', namely private property, is part of the Natural Law. It is part of the essence of God and the conscience of man emanating from divine reason. There was no longer cause to see the institution of private property as simply the making of the best of a bad job in a fallen world. Nevertheless, to Aquinas the general issue of property was something of an aside.[10] The next step in the development of a theory of property and its place in Natural Law had to await the thoughts of the Dutch Calvinist, Hugo Grotius (1583-1645).

2.3 Grotius and Locke

Grotius, or Hugo de Groot, is sometimes called the Father of Natural Law. As the last several pages have indicated, this is clearly untrue. What he did do, however, was to continue the intellectual tradition of attempting to discover the Law of Nature, while doing so from a rational rather than necessarily a metaphysical base. Grotius, although far from atheistic, has consequently earned the perhaps unmerited disapproval of Roman Catholic and Protestant Christians alike. Rommen (p. 62), a Catholic, while worrying that Grotius started a process which would ultimately attribute Natural Law to an *ex nihilo* system, further suggests Grotius made no significant 'intellectual contribution of his own'. Rushdoony (1973, p. 688), a Reformed Protestant, saw the end of that process which so concerned Rommen as 'the humanism of the Enlightenment which developed natural law philosophy as its *alternative* to the sovereign, predestinating God of Scripture' (emphasis added). It will become clear, *ambulando*, that these assertions are not well grounded. Nevertheless Grotius (and a little later Samuel Pufendorf in Germany) did develop a non-theological theory of Natural Law, particularly as it related to property. Buckle (1991, p. vii) argues that Grotius and Pufendorf understood Natural Law as a science of morals grounded in human nature. Private property is part of the moral framework within which we live. It is a natural response to increases in the sophistication of human relationships. It arises necessarily and through peaceful processes from the elemental moral realm of what is 'one's own'. Private property thus, for both Grotius and Pufendorf, is seen as an area of moral inviolability which it is the purpose of society through the positive law to protect, and which further depicts the importance of the individual in the social order.

To Grotius property is a key element of the whole of Natural Law. Other issues cannot be treated independently of it. This assertion (Buckle, 1991, pp. 2-3) rests on the logic that property, 'one's own', is the first element of justice, on which in turn society rests. Society and individual interdependence in its turn is necessitated by the characteristics of human nature. Grotius, like Hesiod, saw an original Golden Age when only Natural Law existed, and private property was not present. Only the increasing 'sophistication' of human activities outside of the Golden Age required the institution of property and a positive law that could govern its moral and legitimate exploitation. That could only be the case if the positive laws were not contrary to the Natural Law. Grotius (cited in Buckle, p. 9) goes further: 'The present-day concept of distinctions in ownership was the result, not of any sudden transition, but of a gradual process where initial steps were taken under the guidance of nature herself.' And this was inevitable, and 'patterned after nature's plan' (p. 13), since ownership of resources often became inseparable from use or occupation. And if 'use' is the equivalent to 'using-up' then we have *de facto* ownership.[11] Buckle continues: 'The very practice of exercising the original universal use-right thus gives rise to a form of natural private property.' The creation of a positive law to recognise this must 'mirror nature itself'. Grotius thus depends on the increasing sophistication of the human economy to justify his arguments. He anticipates Adam Smith's theory of the four stages of growth. In his *Lectures on Jurisprudence* (hereafter *LJ*, 1762-63, i.27) Smith identified four states which mankind must pass through: the ages of hunting, herding, cultivating and commerce. In these several stages the laws with regard to property will, and have to, vary significantly. In the hunting stage, property is generally an unimportant concept. Theft is relatively unlikely; only relatively small injuries can be inflicted on another. The scope for injury to others and hence the need for property protection laws is much greater when flocks and herds are being bred and grazed. Once land is permanently occupied for cultivation over time, rules and regulations require an increase in complexity. When commerce arises with a multiplicity of independent exchanges of varying goods and services, the laws of property must be further multiplied to protect the underlying human activities of trade and exchange (*LJ*, i.33-35).

Grotius, unlike Aquinas, is therefore implicitly suggesting that there is an anterior and posterior Natural Law. An organised social life, however primitive, has as basic requirements in a Fallen World the main elements of Natural Law. To Grotius (cited in Buckle, p. 20) these are:

- abstaining from that which is another's

- the restoration to another of anything of his which we may have, together with any gain which we may have received from it

- the obligation to fulfil promises

• the making good of a loss incurred through our fault.

These qualities of the Natural Law emphasise the importance of 'one's own'. It is the protection of individuals within society that is crucial, not some amorphous social whole, such as a Greek *polis*. Further, these elements of the Natural Law are rational and can be justified or discovered by reason. They are neither founded on the passions, nor on expediency. Certainly (Buckle, p. 21) the Natural Law, and the social order that flows from it, are expedient. The elements of the Law concur with the instinct of self-preservation. From this stems individual and collective action for self-defence which encourages positive sociability. Buckle (p. 28) asks what does this 'essential trait of sociableness require?' Grotius' answer is that society must provide its members with protection for each other's rights. What is 'one's own', the *suum*, or property, is prior to positive law. For Grotius (almost anticipating Locke) the Natural Law protects 'life, limbs and property', which cannot be removed without injustice. As the *suum* is extended by the appearance of use-rights, so the scope of the Natural Law is extended in its defence. 'Use-rights' in their turn tend to become exclusive rights, not only because of the 'used-up' factor, but because as our economic activities increase in complexity, sub-division of property and its legitimate transference, trade, becomes commonplace. Grotius used the Biblical example of Genesis 13 to illustrate this. The passage records how Abraham and Lot subdivided what had previously been their common land to avoid the costs of disagreement between their herdsmen.

Grotius mentions moral aptitudes such as generosity and compassion. To him these are not part of the binding Natural Law, however desirable these qualities may be for helping the needy. Private ownership and original use-rights have as their purpose the efficient meeting of needs (Buckle, p. 37). They guarantee that 'whatever each had thus taken for his own *needs* could not be taken from him except by an unjust act' (emphasis added). This argument, of course, does not preclude the service of additional ends such as charity, but the original purpose of private property is need satisfaction. Property as such does not have duties in Grotius' eyes. Nevertheless the ability to subdivide property, once self-preservation needs are met, permits the exercise of affection to others.

Samuel von Pufendorf (1632-94) held the first academic chair in Natural Law in a German university. His conclusions were closer to those of Aristotle and less individualistic than those of Grotius. Natural Law arises as part of our 'social training' (Buckle, pp. 65-67). It comprises those precepts inevitably acquired through social training because social life requires them. Certainly 'social trainings' differ (not least through Smith's four stages of economic development). Certainly self-love, love of the *suum*, is a prime motivator. And as Pufendorf emphasises (cited in Buckle, p. 71): '...surely there is no one to whom the clear and special care of myself can more fittingly fall than upon myself'. Natural Law is therefore expedient. But there is more. Man must cultivate sociability, and do so beyond Grotius' position of simply respecting the rights of another. There are mutual obligations of kindness. To Pufendorf rights are secondary phenomena (Buckle, pp. 80-83). They arise not as use-right extensions of the *suum* but as express or implicit social agreements to avoid quarrelling in the presence of relative scarcities. Buckle cites Pufendorf thus:

> ... man has by nature a faculty to take for his use all inanimate objects and animals. But that faculty [is not] a right, both because such things are under no obligation to present themselves for man's use, and because, by virtue of the natural equality of all men, one cannot rightfully exclude [others] unless their consent, express or presumed [is given]. Only when this has been done can [one] say that he has a proper right to the thing.

Pufendorf, therefore, lays an emphasis on the requirement not to exclude others from the ability or opportunity to use their natural faculties. Only after others have consented, for whatever reason, to be so excluded can one attempt to grasp an opportunity oneself to create an ownership right. This certainly ensures that charity towards those unwilling or unable to grasp opportunities is not overlooked. But it does so by relegating use-rights from a primary position in Natural Law. And this is done on the grounds that that which can be used (inanimate objects and animals) is without 'obligation' to present itself as an opportunity for use. Once that which can be used is used (and the opportunity grasped) property exists and rights and duties arise. Consent to exclude another from the actions necessary to create a conditional right is thus obtained by a hypothetical promise to carry out a conditional duty if one is oneself successful in taking the opportunity to create a conditional right. This is an improbable social contract. All human actions are dependent on alertness to opportunities that provide net benefits. It is only those who are sufficiently alert, those who perceive the existence of the benefits, who take the decisions to act. Those who are not alert to the opportunities simply have no consent to give. They are unaware that there is an opportunity out there either to be taken or to be created. Contracts (even conceptual ones) can certainly be entered into between those who know what they are exchanging. If contractors do not know what they intend to trade or exchange, conditional contracts or contracts which are not fully specified are feasible. The obligations of both parties can be decided in detail on contract execution. But in most cases it is not even conceptually possible for a hypothetical Pufendorf-style of consensual contract to be entered into. *Ex ante*, before someone becomes alert to and acts on a novel or innovative opportunity (using inanimate objects or animals), the parties to such a contract would not even know they did not know they are about to exclude or be excluded, *ex post*.

John Locke (1632-1704), a contemporary of Pufendorf, resolved this issue. They both, along with Grotius and other Protestant philosophers, were described by Schumpeter (1954, p. 116) as following in the Scholastic tradition of Aquinas. Unlike Grotius, Locke did not view Natural Law as the product of reason, and so something which could exist with or without the presence of God. He rather saw the role of reason as one of discovering and investigating the Natural Law as laid down by the higher power. Locke did not see charity as a duty agreed to between rational agents. Nor did he view property as a secondary right, as did Pufendorf (1735, p. 129), dependent on the principle of 'previous Consent, or... a tacit Compact of Man'. Rather he saw private property as established by Natural Law. Each man has common access to God's earthly resources; each man, created equal with all other men, has the right of self-ownership; and these, 'combined with man's right and duty to survive, permitted him to create property where none previously existed' (Vaughn, 1980, p. 82). Locke's theory of property rested on two pillars: self-preservation and self-ownership. The former is an instinctive priority built into us by the Creator, who in turn has provided all men with the means to maintain themselves. Self-ownership is axiomatic. Each individual has a right or entitlement to the labour services he performs using his human capital. All other rights are the consequences or corollaries.

Self-ownership is not a 'right to life'. The right to life, as Nozick pointed out (1974, p. 179), could imply the right to certain physical things necessary to sustain life, but if other people have rights over these physical things then their rights are violated. But this is to get ahead of our argument. According to Locke an individual obtains an entitlement to a previously unowned gift of nature by being the first person to mix his labour with that piece of land. (The word 'land' is here used as part of the triumvirate of land, labour and capital that, together with entrepreneurship, form what economists call 'factors of production'.) The right to (unowned) land arises by mixing it with what is owned (the self, one's own labour), thereby

25

removing the gift of nature from its original state and putting it into a state more serviceable to human wants (i.e. into capital or even into a consumable good). Some, of course, may voluntarily agree to hire out their labour services, trading their title to any resultant (uncertain) property in exchange for a (certain) wage. In essence Locke is arguing that property is primarily a natural right in a state of nature. It is not simply a pragmatic concept based on the rationale that we take better care of what we own, nor is it a symptom of the Fall. Buckle (p.169) notes that, like Grotius, Locke sees property as part of the *suum* and its extensions, namely Life, Liberty and Estates. For most cases this would be a sufficient theory of property and of property rights. But how are extremes or exceptions to be handled? There are two issues here. First, do property rights also imply duties and obligations? Second, would the presence of monopoly be a special case? Locke's answer to the first is as follows:

> As *Justice* gives every Man a Title to the product of his honest Industry…so *Charity* gives every Man a Title to so much of another's Plenty, as will keep him from extream want, where he has no Means to subsist otherwise.

Two Treatises, i. 42

Self-preservation has priority, but there is also, on occasion, a duty to preserve others. And thanks to the productivity increases which private property and its exploitation by labour permits, there is more available for all, even the worst off. This again is more realistic than the view that property rights are awarded by agreement to avoid:

> … Quarrels; and for the sake of good Order…whence it follows, that we may at our own Pleasure dispose of these Things which are our Property, and hinder all other People from the Use of them… unless by Agreement…

Pufendorf, 1735, p. 129.

On the second (monopoly) point Locke delivered his famous proviso. Once a man has mixed his labour with part of the common pool of land no one but he can have a right to what he has attached his labour to, provided that 'there is enough and as good left in common for others' (*Two Treatises*, ii. 27).

Pufendorf on Common Property and Public Goods

There are two alternative ways to explicate the proviso. One is to accept it as a problem and draw on the economic theory of public goods to help resolve it. The other is to reject the proviso as economically and philosophically unsound. The public goods approach has its roots in Pufendorf's discussion of common property.

In the jargon of economists public goods have three characteristics. They are non-rival, non-excludable and are liable to abuse by 'free-riding'. That is, they can be consumed by an increasing number of people without any diminution in the amount available to others (the non-rivalry quality). They are available to everyone in a given catchment area, independently of the level or presence of a price (non-excludability). And since they cannot be withheld from non-payers, the free-rider problem, they must necessarily be financed by centralised, collective payments, legally enforced, since a private monopoly or single seller would be unable to levy and collect the charges necessary to cover the costs of the benefits provided. Pufendorf (1735, p. 130) put forward much the same argument:

> … *some Things may, and some Things ought to continue, as at the Beginning, common to all…* since they are *inexhaustible* [non-rival], so that every Man may have the Benefit of 'em, and yet no single Person can have the less Use of them, it would be … to no purpose … to enclose or lay claim to 'em [they are non-excludable]… where a Thing is of that Nature, it is not only in vain [because of free-riders] to divide or lay claim to it, but it is apt to give Occasion for insignificant Quarrels.
> (Original emphases.)

The only differences between Pufendorf and the modern public goods approach is that he concludes that private property is redundant for such goods since by their nature they are not a source of the major quarrels he wished to avoid. Also he was uninterested in, or unaware of, the possibility of their funding by collective provision. (The examples he gives of the light of the sun, the air, running water, and the oceans far from land, help explain his lack of concern on this issue.) Today, however, many of his examples would indeed be regarded as problematic, and sources of 'quarrels'. Clean air and unpolluted water are not inexhaustible. But their use can be metered and charged for, and by the late twentieth century both national and international law had developed methods both of awarding and of trading the rights to such usage. Pufendorf's analysis was sound. His lack of concern on the breaching of the proviso in the case of what we now call public goods was appropriate. Industrialisation and population growth, however, have resulted in his examples being somewhat less benign than when he wrote. Nonetheless modern institutional develop- ments (e.g. markets in pollution permits; the trading of riparian rights between upstream and downstream farmers) have better enabled the specification of private property rights in many apparently public goods.

These developments confirm the correctness of his low level of concern on the issue of principle. They also validate the worth and utility of specifying private property rights in hitherto unwonted places.

Is the Lockean Proviso a Non-Issue?

The second approach to dealing with the proviso is more comprehensive. While many goods have one or other of the properties of public goods, few have all three attributes. National defence may be one such good. But most goods provided collectively actually tend to have private property attributes. For example education results in increased earning power or a better appreciation of life for the educated individual. Healthcare results in improvements in individual health. Both the activities of education and of healthcare provision use inputs that are limited in supply. So neither activity is non-rival or non-excludable. If there is a problem raised by the proviso, it may be that of monopoly (single seller) organisation and refusal to supply except under conditions regarded as 'unfair', which is not the public good issue.

Nozick (1974, p. 175) argues that 'the crucial point [of the proviso is] whether appropriation of an unowned object worsens the situation of others'. He cites (pp. 175-82) several 'monopoly type' examples: a castaway arriving at a desert island which someone had already appropriated would apparently have no right to crawl ashore; an owner of the only water hole in a desert can apparently charge what he will to thirsty travellers; a man who, in Lockean fashion, mixes his labour with the ocean by pouring into it a glass of tomato juice becomes the apparent owner of the ocean—or has he simply wasted a perfectly good glass of juice? If the crux is 'worsening the situation of others', then the juice is certainly wasted, the castaway cannot be turned away, nor can the water seller charge what he likes. Pufendorf-style obligations arise from property rights but they dilute the concept of rights, or at the least temporarily over-ride them. This is conceptually untidy but Nozick suggests the likelihood of running foul of the Lockean proviso is small. Underlying Nozick's view is the chain of title in property through history. If individuals with property rights engage in non-coerced trade, absent fraud, then property rights are legitimately transferred. Both parties will be better off, and if there are no third party costs (externalities), breaches of the proviso will be rare. Certainly a given natural resource, say coal, originally accessible to all at the dawn of history, may today have been wholly appropriated as private property. No one can start a new coalmine merely by mixing his labour with un-owned, coal-bearing land.

28

But, Nozick would argue that this does not breach the Lockean proviso provided all owners of coal-bearing land today justly acquired title to that land either originally in Lockean terms or through a sequence of voluntary exchanges. Non-owners of coal-bearing land today are not worse off as consequence of this process, indeed they are probably better off due to the utilitarian benefits of the sequential trades. Nozick's interpretation of the proviso (p. 181) is *not* that it refers to today's 'end state' in terms of coal-bearing land, but rather that it applies to each stage of the chain of entitlements in such lands generated by voluntary exchanges from the dawn of history. Although the Lockean view would still be that a catastrophic need by others would continue to override rights of property, Nozick's emphasis on *process* suggests the proviso would apply infrequently.

Israel Kirzner (1979, pp. 200-24) was less sure that this exposition of the Lockean proviso covered most cases. He added the gloss that *all* trades between willing buyers and sellers (again absent fraud) occur because an entrepreneur has discovered that differing valuations exist between two parties. All trades therefore contain an element of valuation error. 'Those who paid the higher prices were clearly unaware of the sellers who were prepared to accept, and in fact did accept, lower prices', and *vice versa*. Since most market transactions depend on this type of 'error', how can their 'voluntariness' and hence the 'justice' of the outcome be defended? (The glass of water in the desert is simply an extreme case of such error in that the prudent traveller no doubt first ascertained that there were ample oases available: he simply had no inkling when he began his journey that, for whatever reason, his projections were wrong. Similarly the value the castaway placed on being allowed to set foot on the desert island when he commenced his original and apparently secure sea voyage would be very low, or even zero, if he was unaware of the island's existence.)

How can natural property rights be disentangled from obligations? Kirzner's point is that the Lockean proviso, not making others worse off, is apparently breached in *all* trades. Even the condition of voluntariness is apparently absent in *all* exchanges. On the face of it no trades would be made if all parties were fully informed about the true valuations of the other. All transactions depend on an entrepreneur uncovering valuation differences (errors or mistakes) and hence buying low and selling high. Kirzner (1979, p. 218) thus points out that Nozick's conclusion that the Lockean proviso is rarely breached is defective. Nozick (1974, p. 151) claims that his entitlement theory is 'exhaustive', apart from a few exceptions such as those already mentioned. It is based on just acquisition from nature and just acquisition by transfer. Kirzner (pp. 218-19) interposes a third and intermediate acquisition category of 'finder-creator *ex nihilo*-keepers', and properly to explain and to:

> ...introduce plausibility into [this] notion...[one must] adopt the view that, until a resource has been discovered, *it has not*, in the sense relevant to the rights of access and common use, *existed at all*...the discoverer...in the relevant sense [is] the creator of what he [has] found.

Kirzner, 1979, p. 218. (Emphases in original.)

Entrepreneurial alertness to a profit opportunity or a price differential 'constitutes the discovery of hitherto unknown and non-existent value' (p. 219). This alertness to valuation differences can range from alertness to price differences for the same good in two different places or at two different times. More completely it can embrace the realisation that a mixture of resources, if brought together, can result in a final product with a much higher time-discounted price than has the original resource bundle. Entrepreneurs not only arbitrage across space but also across time. They help 'construct the future'. The entrepreneur creates value where none existed before (if he guesses correctly) and profits thereby. If he guesses incorrectly and fails to create value, only he, the entrepreneur, loses. The Lockean proviso is thus never violated if the finder-creator-keepers ethic is attached to Nozick's entitlement theory.

How would this apply to Nozick's exceptions? The owners of the water hole and the desert island have undoubted property rights over them. They were more alert than the sea voyagers or desert travellers when they acquired them. The latter are no worse off due to the acquisitions. In fact subsequent travellers may now be better off if, in the event of a disaster, they need succour. The owners of the island or oasis may then have to attract their attention in order to do business with (i.e. rescue) them. Locke, as we saw, argued that such business should not be done at a ruinous price, and that there is even a duty to be charitable. History shows, however, that private owners tend to be unable to sell water at a ruinous price, or to ban access to a desert island. Owners may have a monopoly on a *specific resource*, but if abused that simply opens up opportunities for other entrepreneurs with *other resources*. For example, water pipelines may be laid across the desert, other oases might be opened, or swifter means of crossing wastelands might be devised. Only when ownership of private property *in general* is banned is entrepreneurial entry into markets impossible. Property then is owned or controlled by government. And

30

indeed economic history does not demonstrate the widespread existence of private charity when entrepreneurial alternatives are proscribed.

Locke would not have been surprised by the history of the State's inhumanity to man in recent decades. He did, after all, write his *First Treatise* to justify opposition to Charles II, to the doctrine of the Divine Right of Kings, and so to support the overthrow of James II in the Glorious Revolution of 1688 (when James' sister Mary and her husband William assumed the throne). The *Second Treatise of Government* had as its task the role of establishing Natural Law (with its corollary of Natural Rights) as the legitimising factor for displacement, on occasion, of the civil authority. Locke, unlike Hobbes, did not believe that if man lived in a 'state of nature' the result would *necessarily* be 'solitary, poor, nasty, brutish and short'. Man could, after all, live according to the Natural Law, albeit that might require vigilant justice. Nor did he believe, as did Hobbes, that a tyrannical ruler is therefore better than no ruler at all. Indeed, in entering into a compact with a ruler to make one body politic men may 'still be in the state of nature' (*Two Treatises*, ii. 14). Aside from defence from foreign aggression, why then do men enter into a social contract with a governance structure? When do individuals voluntarily relinquish their rights to interpret and execute Natural Law, and hand over to the civil authorities the right to posit and enforce civil laws? Locke's answer (*Two Treatises*, ii. 222) is that:

> [t]he reason why men enter into society, is the preservation of their property; and the end why they chuse and authorise a legislative, is, that there may be laws made, and rules set as guards and fences to the properties of all the members of the society, to limit the power, and moderate the dominion of every part and member of the society.

2.4 Hutcheson and Hume

We have come a long way from the ruling caste of Plato's *Laws*. But we have not moved far from Aristotle's view that the ultimate goal of man is happiness. This latter perspective is joined at the hip with Pufendorf's interpretation of property as a 'tacit Compact' for the 'prevention of Quarrels'. That, in turn, is linked to Locke's emphasis on the right of resistance to governments that fail to protect, or that impinge upon, private property. This fusion is nowhere made clearer than in the writings of the Scottish Enlightenment, not least in the two books by Adam Smith, *The Theory of Moral Sentiments* and *An Inquiry into the Nature and Causes of the Wealth of Nations* (respectively 1759 and 1776, hereafter *TMS* and *WN*).

Smith was a student of Francis Hutcheson (1694-1746) in Glasgow University. Hutcheson it was (not Bentham) who wrote: 'that Action is best, which procures the greatest Happiness for the greatest Numbers' (1725, p. 125). Indeed Hutcheson was attacked by the established state Church of Scotland for teaching his students that the promotion of the happiness of others was the standard of moral goodness. And he was also reproached by the local Presbytery for contending that good and evil could be identified without knowledge of God. West (1976, pp. 42-43) notes that Hutcheson was a 'sparkling' teacher who strongly influenced Smith with a respect for 'natural liberty and justice'.[12]

Hutcheson argued that to call God's laws good, whether they are known from 'Reason' or 'Revelation', was 'an insignificant Tautology' (1725, pp. 180-81). It was more meaningful, he argued (p. 135), to under-stand that all men have an innate 'Moral Sense' the foundation of which is 'Benevolence' towards others. Secondly (p. 136), in others, it is the presence of 'Benevolence which commands our Approbation'. While, to the contrary (p. 120), if it is absent in others we may even perceive this 'as positively evil and hateful'.[13] Nevertheless, and thirdly, when we get to specifics Reason does have a role. When we ask: '"What Actions do really *evidence kind Affections*, or do really *tend to the greatest publick Good*?" [the answer is provided by] the particular *Laws of Nature*, or even of *Civil Laws*: This is the ...Field...of *Reasoning*...' (Hutcheson, 1728, p. 174. Emphases in original.)

But this raises a fourth question: what motivates individuals to act? The answer Hutcheson (1728, p. 24) gives is '*Desire* of the happiness of others', not as a means to an end, but as an end in itself.

This may seem a circular set of arguments. After all, it began with the question as to whether certain actions or affections would arouse general Approbation and why? The answer was positive, given the presence in each of us of a Moral Sense. But there is more. Hutcheson acknowledges the importance of actions motivated by self-interest. But casual observation and introspection shows us that many other actions are motivated also by selfishness at the expense of others. And while actions taken to benefit others do occur, their prevalence on an individual basis can vary from that of an Al Capone to a Mother Theresa. Clearly the desire to improve the happiness of others varies greatly in intensity. Hutcheson spends the bulk of his 1728 book indicating that there are several desires, passions and affections to which man is subject. Similarly the Moral Sense is but one of several senses, including beauty, honour and imagination. All desires should be 'managed', including the desire for the happiness of others. Our passions and affections should be 'governed'. Although 'Virtue itself' is originally implanted in us by God, it is (1725, p. 178) 'afterwards strengthn'd and confrm'd by our own Cultivation'. An act of *will* is required if benevolence is to be achieved.[14] (Aristotle used the weaker word 'habit', at least in English translations.) Hutcheson argues (1728, p. 118, original emphases) that, if we each exercise that will, then we are in harmony with both God and our fellow men:

> ...how admirably our Affections are contrived for good in the *whole*. Many of them indeed do not pursue the *private Good* of the Agent; nay, many of them...seem to tend to his detriment, by concerning him violently in the Fortunes of *others*, in their *Adversity*, as well as their Prosperity. But they all aim at *good*, either private or publick: and by them each particular Agent is made, in a great measure, subservient to the *good of the whole*. Mankind are thus insensibly link'd together and make one great *System*...He who *voluntarily* continues in this Union, and delights in employing his Power for his *Kind*, makes himself happy: He who does not...makes himself wretched; nor yet can he break the *Bonds of Nature*...we are formed with a View to a general good *End*; and may in our own Nature discern a universal Mind watchful for the whole.

Notwithstanding this argument, Hutcheson (1725, p. 186) is well aware that 'general Benevolence alone, is not a Motive strong enough...to bear Labour and Toil...which we are averse to from Self-love'. Indeed since self-love is coupled with the interests of family, close friends, reciprocal gratitude to others, and matters of honour, it is 'really as necessary to the Good of the Whole, as Benevolence'. Both Benevolence and self-love act 'cohesively' on the disparate parts of society. Without these additional interests, of course, self-love could too readily 'concur with Malice' and be opposed to Benevolence with a centrifugal effect rather than a cohesive one. From these reflections Hutcheson (pp. 186-87) develops his theory of property.

Unless one can retain the fruits of one's own labours, the motives of self-love and its associated sub-motives are removed. No other motive to be industrious other than general benevolence remains. Worse, the industrious is then a 'Prey to the Slothful'. This is the ground of private property, of the right to store up surpluses beyond current requirements, and of the rights to trade, barter and donate. The right to commerce in turn results in the right to contract and to promise. The great advantages which trade brings to all depend then on protection of property, and on the presence of an arbitrator to facilitate the settling of contractual disputes which routinely arise between traders in a world where self-love and partiality exist.

Hutcheson then deduces his theory of government (pp. 187-88). Happiness results from benevolence. But benevolence depends upon the exercise of a free will. Meantime man is motivated by two principles, love and self-love. These principles are sometimes complementary and synergistic, and at other times they are antagonistic, and this damages the cohesion of the whole. Which of the two motives predominates and whether they are synchronised is impossible to predict. Governments, to protect property and facilitate exchange, should therefore restrict themselves and exercise prudence rather than ideology:

> The Right Men have to constitute Civil Government and to subject their alienable Rights to the Disposal of their Governours, under such Limitations as their Prudence suggests. And as far as the People have subjected their Rights, so far their Governours have an external Right at least, to dispose of them, as their Prudence shall direct, for attaining the Ends of their Institution; and no further.

Hutcheson did not appeal to the Divinity to make his case. Rather he believed his conclusions pointed towards the Creator. In his 1725 book (pp. 196-97) he concludes by arguing that our innate moral sense and desire for the happiness of others indicates God's nature. Had the Deity not had benevolent intentions, rationally he would not have created us as we are. Our Moral Sense is itself 'one of the strongest Evidences of Goodness in the Author of Nature'. Yet we are also created with self-love and hence have a freedom of will to choose what combination of self-interest and Benevolence we pursue. Our choice is assisted and correctly channelled the more we reflect on the nature of God. In this way the calm passions are cultivated and desires appropriately directed. Contemplation of the Divine, deliberately done to cultivate virtue, is not always easy, and to some might be impossible. Hutcheson recommends it but understands the problems. Perhaps that is why we can view his argument (1728, p. 200n) for the important role of public worship 'on set Days, in which a stop is put to Commerce, and the busy part of Mankind instructed in the Duties of *Piety* and *Humanity*', as being much more than a conciliatory gesture to his local Presbytery.

It is probable that David Hume (1711-76) would also have had a chilly reception had he met with the Elders of the Kirk.[15] He was something of an agnostic in terms of conventional religion. Yet Hume was a gentle man who would shy away from causing hurt or offence.[16] It was not only in the area of natural religion that Hume displayed his scepticism. Rommen (1998, p. 100) indicted him for the '"destruction" of the *idea* of the natural law...in the Anglo-Saxon world' (emphasis added). Yet Hume famously claimed a close similarity between his own views on property and justice and those of Grotius.[17] Can we resolve such an apparent paradox? Certainly Hume rejected the notion that standards of justice are innate. In that sense there is no Natural Law if that is taken to mean some sort of creation *ex nihilo*. Nor is there a Natural Law that is the deliberate contrivance of human Reason. Rather:

> [the] distinction between justice and injustice [has] two...foundations, *viz....interest,* when men observe that it is impossible to live in society without restraining themselves by certain rules; and...*morality*...[when] men receive a pleasure from the view of such actions as tend to the peace of society, and an uneasiness from such as are contrary to it. It is the voluntary convention and artifice of men which makes the first interest take place; and therefore those laws of justice are so far to be considered as *artificial*...the sense of morality in the observance of these rules follows *naturally*, and of itself; though it is certain that it is also augmented by a new *artifice,* and that the public instructions of politicians, and the private education of parents, contribute to the giving us a sense of honour and duty, in the strict regulation of our actions with regard to the properties of others.
>
> Hume, Treatise, Vol. 2, 1911, pp. 234-35.
(Emphases in original.)

Hume's priority here lies in explaining how complex and interdependent societies grow and evolve.[18] He notes that man has 'numberless wants and necessities with which [Nature] has loaded him, and... slender means... afford[ed] to the relieving [of] these necessities'. Community living provides ways of ameliorating these problems. Man's productivity can be increased by teamwork, or by specialisation and hence exchange. Also 'mutual succour' and security is facilitated. But what draws man into a community in the first place? Hume (*Treatise,* Vol. 2, p. 190f) sees the origins of society in the attraction between the sexes. The family, in turn, realising the advantages of community, passes this knowledge to the next generation. However, selfishness becomes ever more of a problem to stability the more complex society becomes, particularly when relationships become more distant and impersonal. The solution is the convention of 'abstinence from the possessions of others'. This convention is an artefact, not derived from nature. Hume's example (p. 195) is that of two men who pull the oars of a boat. By experience and observation it is gradually discovered that transgressing the convention of acting in the common interest is costly to, and against the individual interests of, all. Only after the artificial convention that everyone should have 'stability in his possessions' is established, is it possible to talk of justice. 'The origin of justice explains that of property. The same artifice gives rise to both.' Hume argues (p. 199, original emphases) that had there been no *'scarcity'*, had man not been characterised by *'selfishness'* and *'limited generosity'* there would have been no need for justice.

Was Hume, therefore, a 'destroyer' of Natural Law? Certainly he denied that justice was innate, or that it was derived from reason. Nevertheless, what he attempted to show was that justice was necessary as a prerequisite in modern society. That its ultimate source was convention, discovery, trial-and-error and successful behavioural evolution was intellectually important to Hume, but not so critical as his conclusion that justice was indispensable given scarcity and selfishness. In fact Hume, in his typically gracious way, stated (p. 190, original emphases):

> To avoid giving offence, I must here observe, that when I deny justice to be a natural virtue, I make use of the word...only as opposed to *artificial*. In another sense...as no principle of the human mind is more natural than a sense of virtue, so no virtue is more natural than justice. Mankind is...inventive...and where invention is obvious and absolutely necessary, it may as properly be said to be natural as anything that proceeds...from original principles. Though the rules of justice be *artificial*, they are not *arbitrary*. Nor is the expression improper to call them *Laws of Nature*; if by natural we understand...what is inseparable from the species.

Man, therefore, tends to select justice, rather than injustice, as a behavioural rule, and does so as an inevitable consequence of pragmatic and empirical discovery. This explanation does not exclude a belief that Natural Law emanates from God. It no more does that than does the theory of biological evolution exclude the truth of Genesis that God is Creator. Hume's evolutionary approach to the discovery of justice analogously does not contradict the truth of Exodus that God inscribed the Decalogue on Tablets of Stone.

But how did property ownership originate? Hume did not agree with Locke, who argued that mixing one's labour with anything gives one 'the property of the whole' (*vide*, p. 209, n. 1). Rather he again emphasised custom and convention. After the slow, historical business of the gradual discovery that stability of possession is of social value, there then remained the question of who owns what? Hume's first order answer was not very satisfactory. Since he could not explain the *status quo*, he simply accepted it. Whether possessions have been obtained through violence, or happenstance, use or trade, it is those we are familiar with that 'we are always the most unwilling to part with; but we can easily live without possessions which we never have enjoyed, and are not accustomed to'. Initial property rights are therefore delimited by asserting *'that everyone continue to enjoy what he is at present possessed of'*. (*Treatise*, pp. 207-8. Emphasis in original.) His second order answer as to 'who owns what' is more satisfactory. People may have a relative sufficiency of certain types of good, while simultaneously being in relative want of others. 'Transference by consent' is 'the natural remedy for this inconvenience' (*Treatise*, p. 222). But consent alone, he argues, is not enough. Self-interest motivates consensual exchange, but it also incentivises poor performance. So for voluntary and mutually beneficial exchange to take place we need not only stability of possession and transfer by consent, but also the performance of promises. Without that condition, self-interest may be coupled with guile leading to what modern economics calls the transaction cost of opportunism. To avoid opportunistic behaviour, which discourages trade, the convention of promise-keeping arises. Hume (p. 224) explains this development as due to the discovery that it is in each individual's interest 'to execute...engagements...[or they will] never expect to be trusted anymore if [they] refuse to perform what [they] promised'. These three fundamental rules of justice are equated (p. 265) with Laws of Nature: namely stability of possession, consensual transfer and the keeping of promises. None was deliberately invented. It was self-interest that led to each being increasingly discovered, observed and then enforced. Society otherwise could not exist. In this conclusion, Hume was at one with Grotius (and indeed Pufendorf and Locke). The rules are antecedent to, and explain the existence of, government.

Government emerges because our primary natural instincts lead us to either indulgence in 'unlimited freedom' or 'to seek dominion over others' (Hume, *Essays*, p. 480). The natural rules of justice must be enforced, or expanded according to the circumstances of time and place, by legislators enacting and upholding the relevant positive laws. Two factors are important to Hume. First, the establishment of government for this purpose is not in any way contractually based (as Locke suggested). Rather 'a small degree of experience and observation suffices to teach us, that society cannot possibly be maintained without the authority of the magistrates', and that is the sole source of moral obligation to government. In *Essay XII* (pp. 465-87) Hume detaches himself from the debate over the Divine Right of Kings versus the democratic social contract that so exercised Locke. Governments come into being in many ways, often by force. But no matter how they originate, a government's sole call on our allegiance is that without it *'society could not otherwise subsist'* (p. 481. Original emphasis.) As with original possession, so with governmental powers, Hume pragmatically accepts the *status quo per se* as sufficient explanation.

As with ownership, so too with government, he gives a more satisfactory second order cause. Hume was concerned to show that the law is there to constrain man's myopic selfishness. For the same reason, governments, which are but groups of selfish men, should be limited. To help overcome their selfishness while still harnessing the motives of self-interest, the laws men pass must be impartial and predictable. The rules of law should not be 'derived from any utility or advantage which either the *particular* person or the public may reap from...*particular* goods'. (*Treatise*, Vol. 2, p. 206. Original emphases.) As Plato's Athenian put it (see above): 'States which have [partial] laws ...are but parties.' And Hume agreed (pp. 254-55), referring to the constitution of governments, that:

> ...if men were to [appoint legislators according to] the view of a particular *interest*, either public or private, they would involve themselves in endless confusion, and would render all government, in a great measure, ineffectual. The private interest of everyone is different; and though the public interest in itself be always one and the same, yet it becomes the source of great dissensions, by reason of the different opinions of particular persons concerning it. The same [self-interested, stability of possession argument], therefore, which causes us to submit to magistracy, makes us renounce [self-interest] in the choice of our magistrates...were we to follow the same advantage, in assigning particular possessions to particular persons, we should disappoint our end, and perpetuate the confusion which that rule is intended to prevent. We must, therefore, proceed by general rules, and regulate ourselves by general interests, in modifying the law of nature concerning the stability of possession.

However necessary government is to social stability, property, justice and promise enforcement, it also comprises self-interested men. In *Essay VI* (*Essays*, pp. 42-46), Hume therefore argued that in any form of government there should be checks and controls, since every man, motivated by self-interest, in politics *'must be supposed a knave'* (p. 42. Original emphasis.) Limited government is difficult to achieve. As Hume noted (p. 43): 'men are generally more honest in their private than in their public capacity. [In the former] Honour is a great check...But where...men act together, this check [is largely] removed; since a man is sure to be approved of by his own party, for what promotes [its] common interest; and he soon learns to despise the clamours of adversaries'.

So Hume, like Ferguson, advocated limited government. Like Ferguson he saw that to achieve happiness, the tensions between self-interest and benevolence require resolution by developing the moral sense and controlling the passions. Government has a role to play in protecting property and safeguarding contractual rights, but individual self-control is the priority. The tensions individuals feel as they struggle to develop their moral sense and control their more violent passions are described in four essays Hume wrote on alternative philosophies of life: on the Epicurean (elegance and pleasure); on the Stoic (action and virtue); on the Sceptic; and, finally on the Platonist (contemplation and philosophical devotion). Perhaps it is this last, *Essay VIII*, that comes closest to reflecting the approach of Hume himself.[19] He concludes it (*Essays*, p. 158) thus:

> The most perfect happiness…must arise from the contemplation of the most perfect object. But what more perfect than beauty or virtue? And where is beauty to be found equal to that of the universe? Or virtue, which can be compared to the benevolence and justice of the Deity? If aught can diminish the pleasure of this contemplation, it must be either the narrowness of our faculties…or the shortness of our lives…But it is our comfort, that, if we employ worthily the faculties here assigned to us, they will be enlarged in another state of existence, so as to render us more suitable worshippers of our maker: and that the task, which can never be finished in one time, will be the business of eternity.

2.5 The Scottish Enlightenment: the End of Natural Law?

Traditional defenders of the Natural Law such as Rommen believed that the Scottish Enlightenment dealt a severe blow to its doctrines. Jurisprudence to such traditionalists means understanding the essence of law, the source of its obligatory requirements, and why there is an intrinsic difference between right and wrong. In stark contrast with Aristotle, Rommen (1998, p. 109) claimed '[e]xperience teaches us nothing about all this'. Yet observation and rational deduction were at the heart of the Scots' methodology. Rommen (p. 108) condemned the scientific empiricism of Hume because it lacked 'a sense of the normative'. Indeed that attack could be and was extended back to Grotius and Pufendorf. To link justice to property could be regarded as purely utilitarian and expedient in origin. The Natural Law of the Scottish Enlightenment described 'what is' (most egregiously with Hume) and how it evolved through Smith's stages of economic development so that society could survive and prosper. It did not, apparently, arise from the immutable dictates of God himself saying what 'ought to be'.

By this view the Scots had dismissed metaphysics as a means of understanding the Natural Law. Moreover, contrary to earlier philosophers, they no longer assigned reason a role in determining right from wrong. As Hume put it (*Treatise*, Vol. 2, p. 127): 'Reason is, and ought only to be, the slave of the passions…' Our passions, as we read in the Scots works, boil down to self-interest and feelings of pleasure and pain. We have a 'moral sense'. But that is not a *reason* for judging right from wrong; it is only a *sentiment* of approval. Or as Hume expanded it, building on Smith's 'impartial spectator': 'virtue [is] *whatever mental action or quality gives to a spectator the pleasing sentiment of approbation*; and vice the contrary' (*An Enquiry Concerning Morals*, 1777, Appendix I, p. 289 [original emphasis]). Such a sentiment of approval, according to Rommen (p. 99), is not generated by an intellectually apprehended conformity of the action with objective metaphysical principles. In the first place, a sceptical agnostic does not acknowledge such principles. Secondly, awareness of an action prompts *ex post* subjective judgements of the gratification or utility the action has generated. These assessments, by their very nature, will be accidental, variable and arbitrary. The *ex ante* use of reason to uncover immutable truths coeval with mankind is precluded. The concept of Aquinas, that truth and goodness are intrinsically linked together, therefore has no place in the Scottish Enlightenment.

This is pretty damning criticism. And indeed Adam Smith's disavowal of some *prima facie* reasons for a natural obligation to keep one's word illustrates the apparent difficulties (see *LJ*, pp. 92-93). Grotius had claimed that the duty of promise-keeping arises from the will of the promise-maker. Smith disagreed. He argued that promises are sometimes made with no intention of their being kept. Nonetheless such promises would still be held to be legally binding by most jurisdictions. Pufendorf 's view was that the duty of holding to one's promise stems from the obligation of truthfulness. Smith rejected this explanation also. First, most legal systems attribute a higher degree of criminality to breach of contract or promise than they do to lying (although liars may well be held to be 'low and despicable'). Second, truthfulness can only apply to the past or present. A promise relates to the future where truthfulness 'can have no effect, as knowledge does not extend to it'. What then is the source of the obligation to perform and fulfil a promised undertaking? It is:

the dissapointment occasion'd by the breach [which] depends on two causes...the solemnity...with which the promise is made [and] the importance of the thing promised. [The obligation arises] intirely from the expectation and dependance which was excited in him to whom the contract was made.

So here we have a typical example of how the Scots used pragmatic, *ex post* utility to explain the existence of the universally accepted sanctity of contract. Not only that, but Smith explicitly rejected the use of Aquinas-like 'goodness' or immutable 'truth' to justify the obligation that a promise be kept. But the alleged tension between the Scottish Enlightenment and Natural Law is more apparent than real. A metaphysical underpinning (or at least a biblical one) for Smith's interpretation of promise-keeping can be readily introduced. For example, consider the restitution sanctioned for the 'dissapointment' in expectations occasioned by a theft in Exodus 22:1. The penalty varies with the future as well as the current value of the item stolen. An animal has breeding potential and so an apprehended thief must pay back more than one animal per beast stolen. Further, an animal-owner has a greater future 'dependance' on a trained, task-performing ox, which can also provide beef and skin for leather, than on a sheep which provides only mutton and wool. The restitution rate is therefore higher for the ox. Theft *qua* theft is certainly indictable, but it is the 'harm done' that breaches the Christian command of 'loving one's neighbour'.

The problem of the Scottish Enlightenment, if problem there is, for writers such as Rommen lies in what Hayek (1967, pp. 96f) called 'the misleading division of all phenomena into those which are "natural" and those which are "artificial"'. If 'natural' is confined to institutions, laws and practices emanating from God or nature, then all other practices or behaviour patterns are the ('artificial') result of human action and design. Alternatively, if 'artificial' is restricted to 'legal positivism' where laws and institutions are the product of deliberate invention and design, then those unintended behavioural patterns, conventions and regularities arising from human action are 'natural'. It was one of the great achievements of the Scottish Enlightenment to clarify this distinction. Hume's illustration of the two oarsmen was expressed more formally by Adam Ferguson (1767, p. 119): 'nations stumble upon establishments, which are indeed the result of human action, but not the execution of any human design'. Hayek (1973, p. 36) called such evolutionary legal and economic systems 'spontaneous orders'. Institutions such as property rights, the market mechanism, the common laws of contract, tort and delict have developed historically. In a process of social evolution, large populations of men, workers and traders have 'selected', in preference to the alternatives, an order that best satisfies their wants and needs. They have chosen what Herbert Spencer (1884, p. 6) called a system of 'voluntary cooperation under contract' rather than 'compulsory cooperation under status'.

And this was the great accomplishment of the Scottish Enlightenment. Contrary to Rommen's view it did not result in a rejection of Natural Law. Rather it upheld the Aristotelian view of property while rejecting the Platonic notion of the Benevolent Guardian. The Common Law and the Law of Nations were understood to be the spontaneous expressions or expansions of the Natural Law. Positive Law was built on this, not on the musings or reasoning of the Platonic Guardian, or of the Monarch imbued with a Divine Right. Further, since none of us knows in advance what type of social order will best meet our own wishes, and since none of us knows the tastes, preferences and abilities of others, either today or tomorrow, then it is a major error to suppose we, or anyone else can, design *ex ante* an optimal social order. (Although we can discover and grope towards explaining and understanding our discoveries to that end.) The belief that we can design such an order was the mistake made not only in Ancient Greece, by Plato, but also in Ancient Israel. We read (I Sam. 8: 3-19) how the Israelites rejected both God and His Law (I Sam. 12: 14-5). The Israelites had had the security from 'calamities and distresses' (I Sam. 10:19) that God's Covenant Law had provided, but this had rarely satisfied them. Of course, a godly king could have continued to apply and enforce God's law. However, this was not the essential wish of the Israelites. Rather, it was to have a king who would rule them, as did contemporary Canaanite kings, 'like all the other nations'. Samuel warned the people what adopting such a social 'contract by status' would imply in terms of centralisation of government, heavier taxation and loss of individual freedom, but to no avail. Twentieth century history also provides similar illustrations of governments, leaders and those who supported them who believed that, if only society could be engineered in pre-planned ways, a more satisfactory security from 'calamities and distresses' could be achieved.

Adam Smith disparaged the 'man of system' who:

...is apt to be very wise in his own conceit...so enamored with the supposed beauty of his own ideal plan of government, that he cannot suffer the smallest deviation from any part of it. He goes on to establish it completely...without any regard either to the great interests or to the strong prejudices which may oppose it: he seems to imagine that he can arrange the different members of a great society with as much ease as the hand arranges the different pieces upon the chess-board; he does not consider that the pieces have no other principle of motion besides that which the hand imposes upon them; but...*in the great chessboard of human society, every single piece has a principle of motion of its own, altogether different from that which the legislature might choose to impress upon it.*

TMS, pp. 380-81. (Emphasis added.)

It is the 'man of system' who rejects the Natural Law, not the writers of the Scottish Enlightenment. Indeed what Smith is arguing for here is the supremacy of the individual over the social engineer, the citizen over the Platonic 'ruling caste'. The life of the individual (including the groups with which he is voluntarily or contractually associated—for example, the family, the religious community and the corporation) is too complex to be assessed or directed by an outside agency. Natural Law supporters such as Rommen would accept this. But they would then add that any such discussion omits the essential (Aquinas-like) elements of the 'good' and of 'oughtness' (see Rommen, p. 142). This is not so. Just as Aristotle saw happiness as an ultimate goal, so too did Ferguson. The latter explained how happiness depends on benevolence, which in turn relies on free will and on determining where the Golden Mean lies between love and self-love. It is discovered through the exercise of free choice, perhaps at first empirically, but then by instruction, habit or cultivation. Indeed free choice, the supremacy of the individual conscience disciplined and controlled by the Impartial Spectator, is neither more nor less than a characterisation of 'oughtness'. (In chapter 3 we explore the role of the Spectator and the meaning of love in greater detail.) This Scottish Enlightenment 'oughtness' can be embraced in the single word 'subsidiarity'.

The 1931 Papal Encyclical *Quadragesimo Anno* described subsidiarity. It implied that all decisions that can be taken, or activities that can be done at lower levels of society, should be taken or done at lower levels. It is wrong for the state to arrogate to itself actions that the corporation, family or individual can do.[20] Rommen argued strongly for this normative 'ought'. As a child of his time he explicitly condemned National Socialism, Fascism and Communism (p. 217). Yet he failed, in his condemnation of the Scots, to understand their explanation, using Aristotelian 'habit' and Hayekian 'discovery', as to how this key, normative element of Natural Law was inseparable from empirical freedom of choice. This failure was not unique to Rommen. More recent writers, *vide* Piedra (2004), have been equally condemnatory.[21] Moreover, notwithstanding the doctrine of subsidiarity, several official church pronouncements (Protestant and Catholic) in the late nineteenth and early twentieth centuries negatively appraised the market system as first comprehensively explained in the Scottish Enlightenment.

Unfortunately these critiques, in their turn, resulted in strong anti-Christian reactions from early to mid-twentieth century market economists. Chapter 3 elaborates on this and describes how progress has been made towards a resolution.

3

Rationalism and Caritas

The concrete effects of envisaging the problem in terms of any sort of individual rights or obligations to [others] are positively evil... It implies...a social order...definitely contrary to fundamental moral ideals...the kind of legislation which results from the clamour of idealistic preachers—and from the public attitude which such preaching... tends to generate or aggravate—is especially bad. All this is the natural consequence of exhortation without knowledge and understanding—of well-meaning people attempting to meddle with the workings of extremely complicated and sensitive machinery which they do not understand.

Frank H. Knight, 1947*

Many churchmen in the early twentieth century had little time for the market system as outlined by the philosophers of the Scottish Enlightenment. We have already noted Rommen's view that the discovery and evolution of a spontaneous order was incompatible with Natural Law. On the other hand economists such as Ludwig von Mises had little truck with churchmen. Similarly, Frank Knight, a contemporary of Mises, had a pen that dripped with a scorn when writing of Christianity. What brought this about? Why did these economists react so virulently to Christianity? Knight and Mises had similar free-market economic views. They both held that an exchange economy, based on private property and contractual law, generates material benefits that cannot be matched by other forms of social organisation. To the extent that they had a higher value than utilitarianism, it was not God, but rather the belief that freedom of choice and action was a *sine qua non*. They were also united in their disapproval of official church statements arguing for intervention by governments in the market place. This disapproval manifested itself in a serious criticism of Christianity *per se*. The contention of this Chapter is that Knight and Mises were misguided in their judgement. Neither Christianity, nor caritas, is recognisable from their descriptions. Their disagreement with church policies and with the political actions of many in the Christian laity may sometimes have been appropriate, but their premises were wrong.

---

* Knight, F.H., *Freedom and Reform*, 1947, pp. 147-48.

45

They both claimed that Christianity, in its early history and in its modern occasional political role, was incompatible with market economics. Competition to satisfy partners in voluntary exchange, by investment and the achievement of property and wealth, received little or no sanction from a religion that preached 'no thought for the morrow' and commanded 'love of one's neighbour'. Prompted by their disagreement with the anti-capitalist policies promoted by some contemporary church leaders, they adopted faulty interpretations of early church history and caricatured Christian doctrine, in particular the implications of divine love, caritas. Later writers from both Catholic and Protestant traditions argue there is no incompatibility. Indeed Adam Smith's concepts of self-command, Propriety and the Impartial Spectator help us better to comprehend caritas. In turn this deepens understanding of the linkages between economic and institutional evolution under Natural Law.

We first examine the views of Knight and Mises. They believed (perhaps correctly) that the economic policies put forward by some church leaders were wrong and based on poor economics. They considered (perhaps incorrectly) that these same leaders were accurate interpreters of Christian doctrine. We then survey the alternative philosophies of the Christian writers Brian Griffiths and Michael Novak, published closer to the end of the century. They also rejected the kind of socio-economic policies advanced by many churches in the earlier half of the twentieth century, but neither accepted the highly restrictive interpretations of Christianity put forward by Mises and Knight. One crucial difference between the two sets of authors lies in their perceptions of the meaning of caritas (i.e. divine love). The chapter concludes by arguing that caritas properly understood has been analysed with approval by philosophers as far apart in time and theology as Smith and Hayek. The negative interpretation given by Mises and Knight to caritas may repel the unbeliever from examining the pith of Christianity. Alternatively, a believer with no background in economics, who uncritically accepts their arguments, may forfeit insights into how 'codes of conduct' in both moral and economic life may have evolved at the instigation of the Creator.

3.1 Knight

Frank Knight (1885-1972), writing in Chicago, was concerned with the damage that could be imposed on the enterprise economy by policy-makers paying heed to the formal teachings of the Church. In a 1923 article entitled 'The Ethics of Competition' (reprinted in a book of the same name:

henceforth *EC*) Knight got into his anti-Christian stride. He asked if the emulation motive, the contest motive, was ethically good or base? It adds zest to life. It promotes efficiency and it adds net utilitarian benefits. It provides consumers with comparisons of who can best satisfy their wants. It ranks producers according to how they organise society's resources in ways that best satisfy consumers. But has it an ethical dimension? Knight writes (p. 74):

> ...we appear to search in vain for any really ethical basis of approval for competition...It fails to harmonise with either the Pagan ideal of society as a community of friends or the Christian ideal of spiritual fellowship. Its only justification is that it is an effective way of getting things done; but any candid answer to the question, 'what things,' compels the admission that they leave much to be desired.

To Knight, Christianity is not even neutral on the issue. Although the spirit of contest is natural both in play and the rest of life, 'it is hard to think of sport or sportsmanship in connection with New Testament personalities' [*EC*, p. 134]. (Knight conveniently ignores numerous Pauline metaphors of fighting the fight and running the race.) On p. 73 he emphasised that Christ talked rather of how the last shall be first, and the chief would be servant of all (Matt. 19:30 and 20:26). His main assertion was that Christianity assesses value according to motive, not the quality or quantity of the outcome. Virtue then consists in conscientiousness, doing what one believes to be right, rather than in some objective goodness. Spirituality is the yardstick, not beauty or quantity.

Nearly two decades later (in 1939) Knight revisited the subject in 'Ethics and Economic Reform' (reprinted in *Freedom and Reform* [henceforth *FR*]). He wrote of a 'basic contradiction' between Christianity and its 'absolutist, negativistic, personal idealism' on the one hand, and the 'positive, activistic, relativistic and practical norms of utilitarian mutualism and sportsmanship which actually prevail' in everyday life. To the former, good is determined by motive; to the latter, 'it is "results" which count' and '"good intentions" are contemptible' (*FR*, p. 56). Another example of Christianity's alleged lack of relevance is its repudiation of power as a virtue; rather it is seen as a temptation. Knight sees another real life contradiction in the 'opposition between personal loyalty...and loyalty to abstract principle, especially to truth'. (For example, in Luke 9:60 Christ refuses to allow a man first to bury his father.)

Given that society is best organised on the basis of voluntary and mutually beneficial contractual exchange, Knight argued that policy should aim at removing frictions to the operation of the system, or at reinforcing natural tendencies working towards its success. Coercion should be absent, except where lack of trust, integrity and contractual compliance exist, requiring in turn mechanisms for contract enforcement. Laws in such societies are obeyed because they are 'believed to be right', not out of subjective 'sheer self-interest' (*FR*, p. 59). Knight then argued that Christian teachings 'give little or no direct guidance for the change and improvement of social organization [and]...even indirectly there is also little to be found in Christianity in the way of moral principles or ideals which can serve for the ethical guidance of deliberate political action'. Christianity 'is exclusively an emotional and personal morality' while 'social problems require intellectual analysis in impersonal terms'. The values of Christianity and the ethics of a market economy are different in kind. They are not even complementary. There is worse; he contends they are in opposition.

To support these charges Knight had further to elaborate on his interpretation of Christianity. He is inevitably brief, limited and selective. Such restrictions were in evidence in 1941 in his article 'Religion and Ethics in Modern Civilization' (reprinted in *FR*). There (p. 125 and p. 125*n*) he explicitly resorted to the following arguments: Christ's teaching in the New Testament took social conditions as a 'given'; obedience to rulers and to recognised masters was expected; not only were the early Christians expected to render to Caesar, they were instructed to obey the scribes and Pharisees; the dominant theme of the Sermon on the Mount is an attitude of 'supreme indifference' to worldly things; in any event if the kingdom and righteousness is diligently sought 'all these things will be added unto you' (Matt. 6: 33). Knight takes the view (*FR*, pp. 198-99) that the Sermons on the Mount and the Plain state simply that faith and love *à outrance* are sufficient to solve all earthly problems until the imminent Parousia—the second coming of Christ. If love fails, then the Kingdom in the next world will provide adequate compensation.

If there is no guidance in Christianity as to specifics, does the essence of the religion possess some inner driving force that might indirectly act as guide to social change or conscious behaviour? Knight (*FR*, p. 126) contended that the essence of Christianity is caritas, coupled with the second half of the great commandment (love your neighbour as yourself). He claimed (p. 128) that caritas in the New Testament was limited to the circle of early believers awaiting Christ's return (that is, it was explicitly fraternal, even escapist, not universal or generalisable). Explicitly 'passing over' any attempt to elaborate on alternative meanings, he argued that 'love', for example, for children, tells us nothing about 'how to raise them properly' (p. 130). Moreover, Knight queried, how can one possibly love other people's children as one's own without destroying the family and moving over to Platonic communism—contrary to 'the accepted teachings of Christianity'?

There followed other illustrations of the problems of the Golden Rule (p. 131): universal love is unworkable because too diffuse, unless constrained by personal relationship or functional connection; the beloved does not necessarily want what we would want in his place; whom to love and how cannot be answered exclusively in terms of the desires of the beloved. However these seem to be self-imposed problems for Knight, because to make his case he has constructed a straw man. This is his own misinterpretation of the last words of the Commandment 'love your neighbour *as yourself*' (Mark 12:31). He is aware of this, of course, and ironically says that what most of us want from others is to be left alone to mind our own business. If this is the desire of the beloved and of the lover there seems little problem other than to ask how should we treat each other when we are compelled to interact? Knight urged 'friendliness' and 'special sympathy, compassion and material helpfulness on 'appropriate' occasions'. He went on (p. 133):

> Each person ought to want, and very largely does want, to stand on his own feet, to play his own hand, in accord with the rules of the game...it is clear that much of what is commonly said about 'helpfulness' and 'service', etc., is 'mush', or worse...love, as concession to the other's wishes, often conflict[s] with respect for the person...with intelligent desire for his well-being [and/or] the higher values of civilised life.

Knight clearly believes this is what 'we ought to wish for others', since it is 'what they ought to wish for themselves' (with due 'regard for their actual opinions and feelings, of course'). And that, according to Knight, is 'hardly suggested by the wording of the Gospels'. But is that so?

If Knight is wrong then his denial of Christianity's relevance is grounded only in his misinterpretation of caritas, and so on an incorrect definition of the religion. He concedes (*FR*, p. 133*n*) that the Epistles come closer than do the Gospels to his own 'predispositions'. Even there, he argued, somewhat disingenuously, the obligation to work, *on pain of starvation* (II Thess. 3:10), stops short of requiring efficiency or productivity. But he could have called on Gospel support for his 'predispositions' had he himself not already rejected the option. The Parable of the Talents (Matt. 25:

14-30), after all, depends for its point on the aptness of productivity. The man who failed even passively to invest his talent stood condemned. Those who actively multiplied them were praised. The Parable of the Workers in the Vineyard (Matt. 20:1-16) expounds on issues of relative productivity, property rights, and the sanctity of contractual agreements. Of course, had Knight used these examples he would then have had to abandon his objective of denigrating the Gospel as giving no direct guide for ethical behaviour in economic matters. (The Vineyard Parable could have offered Knight the economist a fascinating expository challenge in his search for indirect guidance. While only the vineyard owner's right to offer to hire at whatever rate he chose was defended explicitly in the Parable, it is interesting that the hourly rate went up as the day progressed. Was it because a flat daily rate minimised negotiation costs when hiring casual labour in the village square? Were conditions such that the grapes had to be harvested that day? Were the Palestinian rains imminent? Was the marginal product of labour increasing in value as sunset approached? The Parables, after all, were based on common, easily understood, everyday occurrences.)

Knight, however, did not proceed down that route. Rather, as we saw above, he viewed Christian love as interfering 'mush' detracting from the self-respect of the so-called beloved. He reached that stage in the development of his thought from the starting point of his view of love in the early history of Christianity. Primitive Christian love, à outrance, took no thought for the morrow, and preached non-resistant passivity to circumstance. Whereas, says Knight (FR, p. 205): 'In modern society, personal relations rest on the ideals of mutual respect and friendliness, and especially on the "bourgeois virtues" of competence, foresight, and reliability, which are not conspicuous (to say the least) in New Testament teaching.' And (pp. 205-6): 'If men and life are to be made better, it will surely be accomplished by cultivating these ideals and attitudes, and not by trying to teach everybody to love everybody else in the world with undiscriminating fervour.'

What is this 'mush' love practiced with 'undiscriminating fervour', which so concerned him? Many Church and political leaders were putting forward social and economic policy proposals with which he profoundly disagreed. Writing in 1941 (p. 212), he warned that these policies were motivated by ill-informed concern for the disadvantaged, resulting in counter-productive policies and, worse, the evils of group-blame. '[D]issatisfaction with modern civilization' was so 'widespread and acute' that it 'threatens to engulf that civilization and all its achievements in a "holocaust" [*sic*] of destructive conflict'. '[K]nowledge and understanding with a view to action are no part of primitive Christianity.' And logically he claims this must be so since knowledge is a means to power. Wealth is condemned in the Gospels, and so by extension all forms of power, including organisation and 'intelligence itself'. On p. 213 he notes:

> Our natural impulses [as opposed to the use of intelligent analysis]... (perhaps especially!) where our intentions are good, run toward finding somebody... to *blame* for anything that seems to be wrong, and to proceed by way of... "liquidation". This may not seem to be a natural consequence of Christianity, but... [it] is very largely the case... (emphasis in original)

And then goes on:

> ...no other action [appearing to be]...a more natural or proper expression of love...is likely to be more effective, or much less disastrous. Let anyone reflect as to how far love will carry us toward a solution of the problem of money, the business cycle and unemployment! ...[D]epression profits practically no one...it cannot be due to exploitation; but it is the main source...of the whole culture crisis, including the war...it is all this chiefly because of the kind of remedies which are proposed and tried...

What are these remedies? He tells of the 'reformers' who wish to alleviate poverty on moral and religious grounds. As concrete examples Knight (*FR*, p. 148), but with no citations, uses the papal encyclical *Quadragesimo Anno* and the 1936 *Report on Christianity and the Economic Order* of the Oxford Conference of World Protestantism, largely authored by William Temple, the Archbishop of Canterbury. The reformers proposed remedies which sounded caring but which would reduce total wealth. The remedies, put forward on the basis of Christian principles or love of the downtrodden, would, he argued, lead to either Christian Marxism, liquidation of the oppressors, or merely to apparently innocuous preaching at the wealthy. But even the latter is 'vicious' since it distracts attention from rational analysis, and it encourages the attribution of group-blame. In particular, calls were made for higher than ruling market wages. These calls, Knight argued, if heeded would result in less employment, especially of those already in the weakest positions. That in turn would segregate them, permanently making them wards of society, or cause a reorganisation of society itself into an all-inclusive bureaucratic despotism. Knight, of course, was largely correct in his critique. Both economic history and analysis support him. He concludes (p. 152) by suggesting that when the 'Gospel of love' comes to mean 'active love for the lowly and downtrodden' in true Hegelian fashion, it 'tends to become both a gospel of hate toward the "privileged classes" and a conspiracy to seize and use powers to effect a social revolution in which these blamed groups will be "liquidated"'. Hence he foresaw Christianity joining hands with revolutionary Marxism and with socialism.

Knight genuinely sought an ethical underpinning for the system of voluntary and mutually beneficial exchange. If the hierarchical authorities of centralised churches attempted to restrict private property rights and the individual liberty of consensual exchange, then their advice was to be rejected as both economically inept and ethically inappropriate. But it was not only the Pope's encyclical and the Archbishop's *Report* that Knight found troubling. The 'reformers' were far greater in number than the two church leaders. Much of the church in both Europe and America seemed to be walking down this path, and it was doing so hand-in-hand with some leaders of the economics profession as well as other political opinion formers. This was the period identified by Robert Fogel (2000, pp. 22-25) as the Third Great Awakening, with its offshoot, the Social Gospel. In America a reaction was occurring in some quarters to the Scottish Enlightenment belief that voluntary exchange between free men was a desirable *process* in its own right. The Social Gospellers wanted not market economists of Knight's kind; but rather 'a new breed of social scientists was required' which would define a desirable end-state. This 'new breed' would detail policies to fulfil 'the obligation of the state to improve the economic condition of the poor by favoring labor and redistributing income'. This movement was, at least initially and in Knight's America, seen as emanating largely from Christianity.

Fogel notes (p. 24) that: 'During the nineteenth century and into the early twentieth, colleges and universities were religious institutions and focal points for revivals [and so for shifts in policy paradigms]'. The founding father of the American Economic Association (AEA), Richard T. Ely, exemplified this. Robert H. Nelson (2001, p. 8) writes: 'For Ely in the Social Gospel phase of his life...the chief motivating force in the world, even in labour and business, must be "love" of fellow human beings rather than the "self-interest" that most economists had long favored'. And when the AEA was founded in 1885, with fifty attendees, twenty of whom were, or had been, practising clergy, a call was made for the churches, the state and science to promote social reform (Fogel, p. 125). This type of thinking was anathema to Knight. Rather, argues Nelson (p. 11), he saw:

...great danger in the tendency of most social scientists to believe that human behavior is rationally explicable in terms of behavioral laws...This belief would serve merely to [support those who] sought...to bring human actions under [scientific] control...the end of human freedom was likely to be among the consequences.

Knight feared the consequences of putting Adam Smith's 'men of system' in positions of power.

3.2 Von Mises

Mises, writing originally in Vienna, was also perturbed by the links that existed between latter-day Christianity, socialism and social engineering. He wrote his book *Socialism* in German in 1922. In the section 'Primitive Christianity and Society', he asked (p. 372) whether Christianity 'has ever shown a bias in favour of this or that form of social organisation'? He argued, like Knight, that the earliest teachings of Jesus were to take no thought for the morrow. This was then consistent with the behaviour of the early converts in their communual sharing of consumption goods. But '[s]uch a way of living is untenable in the long run.' It is saving, not the transfer of all goods into a common consumption pot, that is necessary for investment, whether gross or net. So the behaviour could only be explained, Mises argued, by the expectation that the future Kingdom of God would require no manmade preparation, and furthermore was imminent. Therefore (p. 376) 'nothing binds Christianity to a definite social order' and that is why, throughout the centuries, it has been possible for it to be adoptable by all races and strata of society'. The Church then becomes 'a volitionless tool in the hands of time and fashion' (p. 381).

Knight and Mises interpreted Primitive Christianity in the same way. They both discussed it while ignoring the context of the Old Testament; and they were both highly selective in the use they made of New Testament writings. There is also something perturbing in the lack of logic in Mises' conclusion. He posed a general historical question relating to Christianity and provided a still-to-be-proven general historical answer— but he did so on the basis of his questionable description of a specific period. Mises' interpretation was influenced by the views of Tolstoy[1] after his conversion to anarchic Christianity. These reinforced his belief that the religion had no relevance to a modern socio-economic order (*vide* p. 379). However, it could damage a free economy. One source of potential harm Mises was particularly concerned with was the European political movement Christian Socialism. Originally a nineteenth-century reaction by some Christians to *laissez faire* individualism, it manifested itself in the UK in co-operative movements aimed at co-partnership and profit-sharing in industry; in France, the philosopher Saint-Simon and his followers argued for the abolition of inheritance rights to facilitate the transfer of capital to society as a whole; while in Germany a formal political party, the Christian Social Workers Party, was established by, among others, a preacher in the Prussian State Court. Mises wrote (p. 380) that the:

> ...Gospels are not socialistic and not communistic. They are...indifferent to all social questions on the one hand, full of resentment against all property and all owners on the other. So it is that Christian doctrine, *once separated from the context in which Christ preached it—expectations of the imminent Kingdom of God— can be extremely destructive.* Never and nowhere can a system of social ethics embracing social cooperation be built up on a doctrine which prohibits any concern for sustenance and work, while it expresses fierce resentment against the rich, preaches hatred of the family, and advocates voluntary castration.

(Emphasis added.)

Mises was a more colourful writer than Knight. But both interpreted Christianity in much the same way. 'Social cooperation' certainly cannot be achieved through Christianity if defined as Mises described it. But we have already seen that there is a concern for 'sustenance and work' in Christianity unless one deliberately ignores the teaching of the Parables and the Epistles, quite apart from the Law. The instructions given by Christ on being aloof from one's family and on self-mutilation (Luke 9:60 and Matt. 5:30) provided Mises with an opportunity for mischievous hyperbole. But the messages are metaphorical. They refer to proper prioritisation of the use of time in the one case, and to the need to appreciate that, unlike positive law, God's law condemns not only the act, but also the intent to do evil. In reality, having had his little bit of verbal fun, Mises was far more concerned with (as he saw it) mainstream Christianity's 'fierce resentment' of all property and the rich. The potential damage that could arise from the other-worldliness of Tolstoyan Christianity was slight. (Only a few are attracted by life in a monastic cell, and if they remain there they impact little on others.) The capture of Christianity by socialism was a totally different matter.

Mises was writing at the time of the Third Great Awakening. In America the Social Gospel was in the ascendant. In more secular Europe, the Church certainly condemned *atheistic* socialism. As Mises pointed out, failure to do so 'would strike at [the Church's] very roots; but [the Church] has no hesitation in approaching socialist ideals provided this menace is resumed (*sic*)'. In the world Mises lived in he noted (p. 386) that the 'Prussian Church stands at the head of Prussian State Socialism and the Roman Catholic Church everywhere pursues its special Christian social ideal'. But why did the Church, on occasion, pursue socialist doctrine with its antipathy to private property (and so the Natural Law) with such enthusiasm? Knight's explanation lay in the presence of woolly thinking coupled to 'mushy' caring, both leading to a misguided belief that socialistic control of markets would improve the human lot. He believed that the outcome would be a diminution of personal freedom, and thus an increase in state power. The reasons Mises provided were similar, but the sequence was reversed. The Church authorities, according to Mises, wished to recapture the secular power they possessed prior to the Renaissance when they had 'ruled unchallenged' (p. 384). In this way the church would regain its control over the individual, not least in socialist form. But (pp. 385-86):

> ...[t]he Church knows it cannot win...[a]s long as rationalism and the spiritual freedom of the individual are maintained in economic life, the Church will never succeed in fettering thought and shepherding the intellect in the desired direction...Therefore it cannot rest content to live as a free Church in a free state; it must seek to dominate that state...Now independent production does not tolerate any spiritual over-lordship...dominion over the mind can only be obtained through the control of production...[this] was first made clear to [the churches] when the socialist idea [independently] made itself felt... It then dawned upon the Churches that theocracy is only possible in a socialist community.

The logical consequences were that private property became suspect and returns on property, regarded as 'unearned income', were often deemed morally improper (pp. 392-93). Income inequality came to be viewed as ethically undesirable. Aquinas' claim that 'some are poor because others are rich' (p. 394) was, according to Mises, interpreted as an axiomatic zero-sum game. Finally, the profit motive and acquisitiveness came to be condemned on both ethical and aesthetic grounds (pp. 394-96), a condemnation with which theologians such as Aquinas would also allegedly have acquiesced.[2]

The progression of Mises arguments is actually not easy to follow. Like Knight he saw primitive Christianity as 'mushy', impractical and communistic. He saw institutional Christianity, once the imminence of the Parousia had been discounted, in mediaeval times, as powerful and successful. And he argued (p. 394) that the 'spiritual inheritance of classic antiquity could not shake its dominion'. Yet on the other hand, we already know that the Natural Law was an important part of the accepted Christian heritage in late mediaeval times. And in particular we know that Aquinas' views on private property were akin to, indeed derived from the classical arguments of Aristotle. According to Mises the Renaissance and the return to the classical were acceptable to the church leadership but not to the 'people'. The revulsion of the 'people' to the institutions of the Church saved Christianity, and led to the faith as we know it today, essentially one dependent on an individual relationship with God. Mises does not tell us what sort of Christianity was 'saved'. Was it 'primitive' Christianity, Christianity 'as we know it today' or the Christianity of the institutionally successful mediaeval church? Whatever the answer, Mises tells us the Church (presumably the leadership) knows 'it cannot win' the battle against Renaissance and Enlightenment ideas (which according to Mises were at least originally acceptable to the princes of the Church). It cannot win because of the rationalism and individual spiritual freedoms that have been unleashed. But what cannot the Church win? Apparently it is 'dominion over the mind' and 'control of production'. Church leaders apparently want a return to a pre-Reformation theocracy. The power thereby provided, according to Mises, is only possible under socialism. Private property is therefore rejected, and Mises somewhat dubiously called on the authority of Aquinas for support.

He did ask (p. 381): 'Might not the Church reconcile itself with the social principle of free co-operation by the division of labour? Might not the very principle of Christian love be interpreted to this end?' He answered with a negative. Feudalism had gone. Further transformation of the Church or of Christianity, he argued, is unlikely. Socialism is diametrically opposed to free market capitalism. And he pessimistically notes (p. 387 of the 1936 English translation of *Socialism*) that the Catholic Church (in 1931) was still wedded to statism:

> If the Roman Church is to find any way out of the crisis into which nationalism has brought it, then it must be thoroughly transformed. It may be that this…will lead to its unconditional acceptance of the indispensability of private ownership in the means of production. At present it is still far from this, as witness the recent encyclical issued by Pius XI in 1931, *Quadragesimo Anno*.

Like Knight (*vide supra*) he gave no supporting citations for this condemnation of the encyclical. In fact, as the final sections of this chapter demonstrate, by the later twentieth century the Church *had* begun to accomplish this reconciliation between caritas and mutually beneficial, voluntary exchange behaviour. And we have already noted in chapter 2 that this same encyclical devoted much effort to expanding on the concept of subsidiarity, and hence the importance of private property.

How did Mises perceive the outcome? He did not suggest immediately that caring, 'mushy' or otherwise, emerges. Rather, the desire for power becomes coupled with 'resentment' (p. 394) towards inequalities. This argument enabled him to make a colourful detour. The alleviation of resentment through socialist means, with the approval of religion, not only fails, but is venal. In contrast to the 'grandeur of capitalist society' where there is equality before the law, vastly improved material and cultural living standards, freedom of thought and opinion, racial and gender equivalence, and international harmony, 'Christianity has acquiesced in slavery and polygamy, has practically canonized war, has, in the name of the Lord, burnt heretics and devastated countries' (pp. 397-98).

In 1949, and living now in New York, he published *Human Action* (henceforth *HA*). In that work Mises completed his inversion of Knight's hypothetical progression ('mushy' love leads to woolly thinking, socialism and hence loss of freedom). Having argued in *Socialism* that the church wished to reclaim power and hence remove individual freedom, in *HA* Mises claimed (more impartially than he did in *Socialism*) that 'Christian social reformers' were intent on supplanting the profit motive with the motive of helping others. There he also argued (again with more logical coherence than in *Socialism*) that the pursuit of a 'soft-headed' doctrine of care would feed back, in Knightian fashion, into a forfeiture of freedom and, importantly, would also fail to achieve its own stated social goals. In the section of *HA*, 'Righteousness as the Ultimate Standard of the Individual's Actions' (pp. 724-30), he explained the views of these 'reformers'. They argue that: 'What is needed is not a reform of government...but the moral purification of man...a turning away from... selfishness. Then it will be possible to reconcile private ownership...with justice, righteousness and fairness' (p. 724). Here we have something that may even be close to the Third Way talked of by politicians in Europe and America in the 1990s. Indeed, a little earlier (p. 716), Mises refers to a 'Third System', neither fully capitalist, nor wholly socialist. There 'conscience will be supreme and not the urge for profit...there will be no need for government interference with the market' (p. 724). But Mises notes (quite correctly) that there is a basic and unavoidable internal inconsistency in such a system. There would be an implicit need somehow to ban 'selfishness, acquisitiveness [and] profit-seeking' in order to replace them with 'other impulses' such as 'altruism, fear of God [and] charity' (p. 725).

Moreover, he argues (again correctly) that the proponents of this Third Way fail to understand that 'the requirements of society's productive effort and the pursuit of the individual's own concerns are not in conflict' (p. 725). A market economy does not require detailed government orders since in 'indulging in his "acquisitiveness" each actor contributes his share to the best possible arrangement of production activities' (p. 726). These are valid counters to the ill-thought-out Third Way of the 'reformers'.

Who are these Christian social reformers whose economic under-standing Mises finds wanting? He is unusually reticent in identifying them. He describes them as ascribing 'primacy to…conscience, to charity and brotherly love' (p. 727). He argues that they are not only soft-hearted but also soft-headed. If they practiced their beliefs they would have to assess who was most worthy to receive the presumed benefits of their conscience-directed acts. If a seller asked for a below-market price, which buyers should benefit and which be excluded from consuming? If a buyer offered an above-market price, which sellers should benefit from his generosity and which be refused? If entrepreneurs can no longer use price and profit to inform and incentivise themselves into directing resources towards the uses most valued by society, the outcome will be less satisfactory whether decisions are taken on the basis of brotherly love or—very probably—by eventual appeal to *diktat*.

The reformers appear to be those who advocate the concepts of a just price and a just wage. (It is possible, therefore, see chapter 7 below, that Mises had Jacques Maritain in mind as one such reformer. But Maritain is nowhere mentioned in *HA*.) The 'just price' was prominent in the thirteenth century at the time of Aquinas. It was 'essential in the social teachings of the doctors of the church and…the reformers want to raise [it today to] the ultimate standard of economic conduct' (p. 727). Mises partly, but only partly, misses the mark here. In 1949, and indeed throughout history, there have been those who believed the concept of a 'just price' could be defined without recourse to market valuations. (Very often 'justice' would be linked to cost of production, in particular labour cost.) This appears to have been the aim of the reformers, but Mises was perhaps wrong to link them with the Scholastics. Historical research since 1949 (to which Mises *ipso facto* did not have access) shows that the Scholastic philosophers of the Middle Ages were divided among themselves as to how define the just price. Reviews of that research are available in work by Rothbard (1976) and Friedman (1987). Many believed the just price to be the market price that would be willingly paid by buyers and willingly accepted by sellers. In other words, although the Scholastics, including Aquinas, did not have access to the modern economic concept of marginal utility, many of them nonetheless arrived at conclusions that would not be inconsistent with sound economic reasoning. They regarded just prices as those arrived at willingly and subjectively by market participants assessing values; not as monetary figures arrived at objectively by either third party *diktat*, or unpredictably by appeal to brotherly love.

Mises selectively criticised the Scholastics in *Socialism*. In *HA* he attacked their notion of the 'just price' as received at the time of his writing, and ascribed the associated implications to the Christian social reformers of the 1940s. (These could well have included the Social Gospellers who so upset Knight. Recall Mises was now working in America.) His critiques were valid but we now know they were inappropriate in the context of an attack on the theology of the Middle Ages. Mises' 'reformers', however, saw the (misinterpreted) Middle Ages as a 'bliss experience' where 'at least the elite lived up to the principles of the Gospels' and people 'had not defied the commandments [nor] coveted unjust profits'. The reformers believed, said Mises, that: 'What is needed is to bring back those good old days'. In *HA*, therefore, Mises' line of argument was approaching that of Knight. If care, or 'justice', supplants the profit motive, this leads to a diminution of individual liberty (and material well-being). In *Socialism* he saw the formal Church as bent on power, with a policy of social reform as its means to that end. Both he and Knight, however, had been strongly influenced by their own questionable interpretations of very early Christianity. By the middle of the twentieth century reactions to the aggressive anti-Christian stance of Knight and Mises had begun to appear. The next section demonstrates this from two alternative perspectives. Later, in chapter 4, we see also how the Social Gospel movement itself came to be superseded.

3.3 *Griffiths and Novak*

Two Christian academics (one British and Protestant, the other American and Roman Catholic) provided theological frameworks for the better understanding of market economics. The first, Brian (now Lord) Griffiths, wrote *Morality and the Market Place* in 1982. The second, Michael Novak, published *The Spirit of Democratic Capitalism* in the same year. Griffiths, in 1982 (p. 77), emphasised the need to interpret the Gospels and the behaviour of the Primitive Church in the light of the entire Bible. Indeed, he claimed, the social ethic of Christianity is largely derived from the Old

Testament. So he dispenses with the critiques of both Knight and Mises, restricted to the early church, *ab initio*. He identifies five factors (pp. 78-91) underlying his belief that Christianity does not undermine, but is rather supportive of, and complementary to, a market economy.

First, the creation and the fall indicate that Man is a steward on behalf of the Creator, with a mandate to create wealth and to exercise dominion over natural resources as trustee (Gen. 1:26-7). The fall introduced the ultimate economic problem, scarcity, and so the dilemma of choice, while the underlying act of choosing is further complicated by the presence of preferences, including covetousness and idleness. Second, the political economy of Old Testament Israel explicitly underpins the right personally to possess the means of production and distribution. The Commandments banning theft and covetousness emphasise the sanctity of private property. Property, scarcity and different tastes then lead to exchange, which has to be carried out honestly (Lev. 19:35-7). Neither *caveat emptor* nor *caveat vendor* was endorsed as a trading principle. Directly God-given factor inputs were subject to the Jubilee provisions. Land (and labour) was to be returned to its original ownership. But capital, which takes time to build or to think of, was not subject to the Jubilee. It could either be held, passed to heirs, or sold outright, in perpetuity (Lev. 25:30). Taxation and income redistribution, for the help of the poor, as well as rules on altruistic giving, including gleaning rights (e.g. Lev. 19:9), are well described, and detailed with some sophistication. Taxation was never progressive, it was either proportionate (the tithe) where the rich paid more than the poor, or levied at a flat rate (the poll tax). The right of the poor to glean from the fields of others involved their commitment and effort. Gleaning was a tough chore.

Griffiths thirdly moves on to economic allusions in the Gospels. He discusses the coming of the Kingdom and the teachings of Jesus (pp. 85-88). God, through the Holy Spirit, has the ability to be present in each of our lives. As subjects of that King, his laws must be obeyed. The laws involve matters of attitude, and include appropriate self-denial and sacrifice, and crucially they emphasise an avoidance of hedonistic materialism. '[T]he teaching of Jesus...is not a condemnation of wealth as such but a much needed perspective on the material world in an age of materialism, (p. 88). The teaching promotes caritas properly understood. It nowhere involves a rebuttal of Old Testament economics. Private property, voluntary exchange, managerial shrewdness and the work ethic are each, in the Parables and teachings of Jesus, not condoned, they are advocated. Nowhere does Christ 'ever suggest that the material world is evil and that wealth itself is bad'. Griffiths points out that Jesus would not and did not deny Old Testament teaching on economic issues. He took 'ownership of private property for granted'. Moreover, shrewdness in its exploitation was expected, *pace* the Parable of the Unjust Steward (Luke 16:1-12). Christ praised astuteness and single-mindedness. But what of the life of the early church on which Knight and Mises laid such stress in their critiques? This is Griffiths' fourth element. He rejects as untypical the 'communistic' practices of the Jerusalem church identified in Acts (2:44-5; and 4:32-5). These events occurred just after that particular congregation had had the supernatural experience of Pentecost. The gift of the Holy Spirit prompted many to share their possessions and to live a common life. Griffiths (p. 89) emphasises two features. The communal sharing that took place was 'spontaneous and not master-minded' or centrally planned. And second, 'it was voluntary not compelled'. In short, the book of Acts is recording a unique way of life, which took place at a unique point of time, after a unique spiritual event, and unlike state socialism it was neither mandatory nor universal, even in that congregation of believers. Griffiths notes (p. 90): 'There is no suggestion even in the passage[s] quoted...that as Christians we should strive' to imitate that particular way of life. Indeed, to do so would be 'disastrous'. Mises and Knight would concur, if not with the interpretation, at least with the conclusion.

Griffiths expands on this in his fifth element of Biblical Christianity: eschatology. History not only has a Creation but also an end. Ultimately the 'personal return' of Christ will establish his Kingdom. There will be (Rev. 21:1) 'a new heaven and a new earth'. To the Christian, history is a process with a known endpoint. Christ's return and reign will see (p. 91) 'the establishment of a just society...and the restitution of all things'. Mises and Knight, of course, argued that the Primitive Christians held this return to be imminent. That was why the Early Church behaved in the economically irresponsible manner described. [3] Griffiths, we noted, disagreed with this interpretation. He saw the behaviour of the Jerusalem church as an emotional response to an actual event in the recent past (Pentecost), rather than prompted by an ill-founded expectation of an event in the immediate future (the Parousia). It was an aberration. It was quickly demonstrated to the Church that the communual sharing was both impractical and fostered dishonesty (Acts 5:1-10). Ananias sold his house (which Peter emphasised was his to sell) and then claimed to hand over all of the money received (which Peter underlined was his to keep). Peter rebuked both Ananias and his equally dishonest wife for their deceit and hypocrisy, not for failing to share. Nowhere else in the New Testament did Christians hold all that they had in common. Clearly such behaviour was not an illustration of the caritas principle that characterises Christianity.

Griffiths, a man of the Book, started with Genesis and proceeded through to Revelation in his arguments. Michael Novak,[4] a man of the Church, was less confident that that was the way to proceed. He argued that Biblical revelation must be seen in the context of intellectual and social history. This permits us to arrive at 'religious doctrines which have [led] to those institutional practices which have made economic development, political liberty, and a moral-cultural commitment to progress on earth emerge in history as a realistic force'. To support his argument he lists and expands on six such doctrines (1991, pp. 335-36) and contrasts them, often by analogy, with social and economic institutions. First, the Trinity illustrates 'pluralism-in-unity' throughout creation, including social systems. Socialism may aim at community, but its arrangements are often made at the expense of individuality. By contrast, in what Novak calls 'democratic capitalism' each individual can participate in a whole range of organisations, from commercial corporations to national governments, from churches to schools, from families to neighbourhoods. This 'is by no means the Kingdom of God' (p. 338), but plurality and unity coexist. The individual and the state are in a constructive tension not possible in either socialism or anarchy.

Second, the Incarnation, God becoming man, teaches humility and realism. Christ, as man, had to accept the limits of the world as it is. He taught us to seek perfectibility, but warned it is unattainable. We, in turn, must strive to construct institutions consistent with man as he is, not for man as he should be. Incentive structures should be put in place and aligned with the reality of man's selfish motives and weaknesses. A market or enterprise economy achieves this. The result will not be Utopia but only an optimum subject to constraints. It will be 'a political economy for sinners' (p. 343). The alternatives, a command economy or reliance on mutual goodwill, are perversely inconsistent with reality and doomed to fail. Only the market system provides the information necessary (prices) and the incentives (profits) to permit non-coercive, social cooperation in larger and complex economies.

Third there is the doctrine of competition. As Knight pointed out, most individuals are indeed competitive. They wish to better themselves. The challenge, says Novak, is to channel the desire for self-improvement to creative not destructive ends. Nowhere in Scripture is equality of outcome argued for. Inequality of result is to be expected and the competitive process will and should be tough. Paul, writing to a church whose members would be familiar with the Isthmian Games, used metaphors from racing and boxing to stress the rigour of the Christian life (I Cor. 9:24-7). 'Run to win', was the Pauline injunction; hardly in line with Knight's assertion that that Christianity condemned the competitive spirit. Novak (p. 347) says: '[T]o live in a slack age of low standards is a curse upon self-realisation. To live among bright, alert, striving rivals is a great gift to one's own development.' Democratic capitalism provides such a benevolent environment, because it is tough and competitive. Certainly the prizes tend to be measured in material terms. But competition for money is 'innocent in itself', and indeed is 'socially binding', since the 'winners' are chosen by those they serve, not those they compete against. Suppliers compete with suppliers, purchasers with purchasers, but buyers and sellers willingly and beneficially co-operate. The winner in competition is the trading partner who best satisfies the conditions required of the proposed exchange. Nevertheless, success places responsibilities upon those who become rich. Although money obtained through voluntary exchange reflects the approval of others who have benefited, God goes one step further. All men have obligations as stewards of Creation. Given the fourth doctrine listed by Novak—original sin—these obligations are difficult to discharge for both rich and poor. Evil and selfishness are inherent in man. He argues (p. 343) that the 'single greatest temptation for Christians is to imagine that the salvation won by Jesus has altered the human condition'. The fulfilment of our obligations, i.e., the twin commands from the Sermon on the Mount, is particularly difficult if we are wealthy. As Griffiths put it, scarcity, choice, covetousness and a preference for idleness over work are forever endemic. And, Novak continues, sin is rampant under democratic capitalism, as it is in any human society, although its expression may be different. The objective of democratic capitalism is not to repress sin, but to 'fragment and to check power'. Novak argues (p. 350) that the modern world's tendencies toward an unattractive and evil Dionysian hedonism would be more readily checked by a totalitarian or socialist regime (if it so cared), but then many other freedoms would also be suppressed. The net moral impact may then be negative.

In his fifth doctrine (p. 351), the separation of realms, Novak cited the well-known principle of rendering unto Caesar the things that are Caesar's. '[The] political system of democratic capitalism cannot... be a Christian system.' His argument, basically resting on the pluralism of humanity, is certainly valid when used to support the separation of realms in governance. A multi-faith population group cannot have, to paraphrase Novak, a 'free polity' that 'is also a Christian polity'. Novak (p. 14) defines 'democratic capitalism' as a market economy, coupled with appropriate cultural institutions moved by ideals of liberty and justice, all subject to 'a polity' similar to the American system of representative democracy.[5] Separation of realms at that order of governance is appropriate, indeed ordained. Novak, of course, is attempting to defend the whole concept of democratic capitalism from a Christian perspective. It is intriguing, however, that it is the politics, not the economics with which he feels least comfortable in terms of his apologetics. Griffiths did not stress the separation of the realms. He restricted himself to only the lower order features of a market-based economy. Certainly he argued for limited governance, but its form was of less concern to him than it was to Novak. The economies of the Scriptures ranged from kingdoms, to theocracies, oligarchies and imperial colonies. Novak's 'democratic capitalism' embraces an enterprise economy. Griffiths discussed that type of economy, but the form of political governance was immaterial to him, provided only that the governance system did not inhibit the market's operation.[6]

Neither Novak nor Griffiths, however, was optimistic that any organisation, whether a 'little platoon', a corporation or a government, could be Christian. Griffiths (1982, p. 99) stated that even 'a Biblically constituted Church is no guarantee that it will be a community of life, growth and love'. While Novak (1991, p. 352) was even more dogmatic: 'No intelligent human order—not even within a church bureaucracy—can be run according to the counsels of Christianity.' What is required is 'Christian commitment' (Griffiths) or 'moral behaviour that seems counter-natural'[7] (Novak). Both were discussing caritas.

Caritas, Novak's sixth and final listed doctrine (p. 353), is Latin for divine love. It embodies compassion or sacrificial love and is the 'theological symbol...closest to the personality of God'. 'Love your neighbour as yourself' is a command in both Testaments. Aquinas defined it as 'willing the good of the other as other'. Novak notes that 'good' itself must be interpreted without being influenced by either the predispositions of the lover or the loved. Frank Knight illustrated the problem here by asking whether one could (or should) love other people's children as one's own. His question was rhetorical. But Novak (p. 352) noted a similar difficulty: 'Often it is easier to love the poor and the oppressed than to love one's next door neighbour.' If so, is not the alleged lover then engaging merely in some 'mushy' self-indulgence? In fact, Novak (p. 352) argues, Christianity demands 'a high level of charity that is not of this world'. So of what earthly use is caritas? Novak expands and explains this, the sixth of his Christian doctrines, with a helpful and delightful analogy: human marriage (p. 355).

Caritas Properly Understood

In Latin there are four 'loves': *amor, dilectio, amicitia* and *caritas*. Courtship between man and woman begins with *amor*, instinctive physical attraction. (Other examples include the reaction of a newspaper reader to a photograph of a starving peasant half way round the globe, or the instinctive love for one's parent.) As time passes this gives way to *dilectio* or predilection. There is a conscious level of choice involved. And it is a delight, for example, when children choose to have their parents as friends. The giving of affection is a level more complex than *amor*. Courtship between spouses develops further into *amicitia*. The predilection is reciprocated. '[T]wo independent persons each begin to love the other as other'. The affection is transformed into friendship. Finally caritas appears:

> ...in the recognition that the good which one loves in one's friend, and the good one's friend loves in oneself, is God...[and] the recognition arises that of all things known to human experience, the love of friends for one another is not only the most like God, but in fact the way by which humans participate in the life of God.

> Novak, 1991, p. 355

There is progression in spiritual depth from instinctive attraction or concern to affection, to friendship, to charity. There is another aspect. Adam Smith pointed out that love varies at different distances. While the call of God takes priority over that of our nearest and dearest, this does not imply that our immediate human obligations should be given a lower priority than our more distant human interests. Smith put it as follows:

> ...[t]he care of the universal happiness of all rational and sensible beings, is the business of God, and not of man. To man is allotted a much humbler department, but one much more suitable to the weaknesses of his powers, and to the narrowness of his comprehension—the care of his own happiness, of that of his family, his friends, his country: that he is occupied in contemplating the more sublime, can never be an excuse for his neglecting the more humble department...or the smallest active duty.

> *TMS*, p. 386

The concepts of progression and distance or intensity help explain the problems Knight had with loving the children of others as our own. The instinctive desire to love them is, understandably, absent. The relevant love for the children of others is not *amor* but, depending on their social proximity to us, some degree, miniscule or great, of either *dilectio* or *amicitia*. Similarly, the anonymous peasant, whose only claim to our attention is a media picture, arouses only instinctive concern or *amor*.

C.S. Lewis (with Greek, not Latin terminology) used a similar approach in 1963. He added an extra dimension to both progression through time and varying intensity or distance levels across time. Lewis' gloss is that the four loves merge, can even become one another, while retaining their individuality. Novak would surely agree.[8] Yet the three natural loves can each deceive, distort and pervert. They can each be dangerous if the sweetening grace of charity, the divine love that must be the sum and goal of all, is missing. For example, there can be times when responding to instinctive love or predilections can damage reciprocal friendship. Love must be assessed in terms of priorities and of net effects. Caritas provides this. Mises was bewildered by Luke 14:26 where Christ commanded his followers to hate their families. Lewis points out that this is not the hatred either of rejection or the desire to harm. Rather it is a directive that any instinctive, unilateral or reciprocal love for parents must be secondary to, or subsumed within, divine love. To put it positively, it is divine love that must be demonstrated. With a spouse, sex can express all four loves simultaneously (Lewis, 1963, p. 113). Rape, to the contrary, may demonstrate instinct, even predilection. But it merits the hatred of rejection. So love progresses, varies in intensity or distance, and has a four-fold manifestation of unity in diversity. But only one of the four loves, caritas, is truly divine, untainted by Original Sin.

Only caritas can resolve the tensions and order the priorities of the other loves. To explain further, as a first step, consider how Adam Smith demonstrated the tension between prudence and benevolence, both of which can be subsumed within any of the four loves. Smith (*TMS*, p. 437) drew on the Aristotelian Golden Mean to assist in his explanation. Just as courage is a virtue falling between the vices of rashness and cowardice, so he argued that a compromise[9] has to be drawn between the three subsets of virtue: prudence, justice and benevolence. Prudence gives self-love its due recognition. We may hear about famine in foreign parts, but it is going beyond the bounds of prudence to starve oneself on that account. Smith notes (p. 72): 'As to love our neighbour as we love ourselves is the great law of Christianity, so it is the great precept of nature to love ourselves only as we love our neighbour, or, what is the same thing, as our neighbour is capable of loving us.' We are duty bound to love, even express anguish, but prudence dictates that some ranking of importance or practicality be made when we define our neighbour and how we deal with him. Love correctly varies with distance. The second sub-virtue, justice, involves legal rules, externally imposed, securing freedom and outlawing coercion. Both these sub-virtues, says Smith, are necessary but not sufficient for full virtue. Another discretionary and voluntary characteristic is required, namely benevolence. Prudence may be the strongest human behavioural motive, but benevolence is the highest. Smith writes (pp. 71-72): 'to feel much for others, and little for ourselves…to restrain our selfish, and to indulge our benevolent, affections constitutes the perfection of human nature; *and can alone* produce among mankind that harmony of sentiments and passions in which consists their whole grace and propriety' (emphasis added).

But we know that, as a mode of social organisation, mutual benevolence is impractical because of information constraints and weak incentives (predilection and mutual affection) as organisation size and complexity increases. As the old saw has it, charity must begin at home. Totalitarian societies overcome the information problem by ignoring the wants of those ruled; and they resolve the incentive problem by arrogating to the centre the motivations of the rulers. But a large and intricate market economy resolves the two problems through the decentralised price (information) and profit (incentive) system. Smith (*WN*, pp. 26-27), in the best known of all his arguments, indicated 'it is not from the benevolence of the butcher, the brewer, or the baker that we expect our dinner, but from their regard to their own self-interest'. If we can comprehend these tensions that Smith identifies with benevolence, we can begin to understand how Novak (p. 357) concluded that Christianity is compatible with the voluntary exchange economy:

> A system of political economy imitates the demands of *caritas* by reaching out, creating, inventing, producing, and distributing, raising the material base of the common good. It is based on realism. It respects individuals as individuals…An economic system which makes individuals dependent is no more an example of *caritas* than is a lover whose love encourages dependency.

But can we take a second step? Can we go beyond not only the religious rejectionists, Knight and Mises, but also beyond Griffiths and Novak who argue only that there is compatibility between an exchange economy and caritas? If voluntary and beneficial exchange reduces the tensions between, and correctly prioritises, the four loves, is this part of the Law of Nature? To take the discussion further, we show how Smith and Hayek argued (with more than a two-century gap between), that aspirations both to caritas and to the market order have spontaneously evolved from our religious origins as created human beings. They are part of Natural Law.

3.4 Caritas, Social Evolution and Natural Law

Hayek asked (1988, pp. 135-36) how and why we have evolved from humans living in tribal, self-sufficient societies to dwelling in the inter-connected economy? How can market traditions which:

> ...people do not like or understand, whose effects they usually do not appreciate and can neither see nor foresee, and which they are still ardently combating, continue to have been passed on from generation to generation? [The answer is provided by the] evolution of moral orders through group selection: groups that behave in these ways simply survive and increase. *But this cannot be the whole story.*

(Emphasis added)

If it was not understood why the 'beneficial effect [of] creating an as-yet unimaginable extended order of cooperation', a market, arose from certain 'rules of conduct' or laws, how did market economies originate? And more importantly, how did they survive given that instinct does not encourage deferred gratification (the essence of capitalism), and that the 'conceit of reason' often suggests that what is designed (a planned society) must be superior to the product of spontaneous order?

Hayek argues that custom and tradition cannot be appealed to as explanations. They would both fail as upholders of 'rules of conduct' over any period of time, particularly when the institution within which the behaviour takes place is itself misunderstood or unpopular. Rather, particular patterns of behaviour are more likely to be followed when the rules are supported by religious beliefs or magical superstitions. These beliefs themselves grow or are revealed to help man interpret his environment. Their preservation may be helped by threat of punishment if transgressed. But such codes, says Hayek (1988, pp. 136-37), must have a chance to 'produce their beneficial effects...on a progressive scale before selection by evolution can become effective'. Myths or religion can provide the 'generation to generation' transmission motivation, 'especially where rules of conduct conflicting with instinct are concerned'. '[L]ike it or not, we owe the persistence of certain practices, and the civilisation that resulted from them, in part to support from beliefs which are not true—or verifiable or testable' (pp. 136-37). Even atheists, says Hayek, 'ought to admit that the premature loss of what we have regarded as nonfactual beliefs would have deprived mankind of a powerful support in the long development of the extended order that we now enjoy, and that even now the loss of these beliefs, whether true or false, creates great difficulties'. And furthermore, as if to provide a two-way test, if religious discipline has helped the successful evolution of private property-based, market economies, Hayek notes that *the only religions that have survived are those which support property and the family* (emphasis in original).

Although he shies away from using the term Natural Law, Hayek's discussion here is nothing more nor less a than a *précis* of the discussion on the subject in chapter 2 above. However, he did not ask the question: how did the religious standards and rules themselves evolve? Hayek (perhaps because of his agnosticism) is weakest on this point. Certainly the inter-generational transmission mechanism was present in Christianity (*cf* Deut. 6:7-9); so too was Hayek's requirement of long-term success in a situation that is counter-intuitive. But there are still gaps in his discussion. Adam Smith, even if regarded merely as a deist, can help us better understand how our religious rules, our consciences, are formed.[10]

Smith explained the adoption of moral standards by which people judge, first, themselves, and second, others. People go from having no standards as children to commonly shared ones as adults. This occurs because each of us desires a 'mutual sympathy' of sentiments with others. He goes on (*TMS*, p. 54): ' Nothing pleases us more than to observe in other men a fellow-feeling with all the emotions of our own breast; nor are we ever so much shocked as by the appearance of the contrary.' Otteson (2000) calls this a desire for a 'concord of emotion'. That 'concord' is in its turn an engine of social cohesion and solidarity over time and across groups. To increase the likelihood of attainment we may, for example, join small groups of similarly inclined people, Burkean 'little platoons'. Also, to increase the probability, we each modify our behaviour to mutually acceptable levels. This 'self-command' is a repetitive process of reciprocal mutual adjustment. The resulting moral discipline would appeal to neither a Freud nor a Keynes.[11] An unintended and unconscious system of standards or proper behaviour thus evolves. To determine what is proper (to achieve mutual sympathy) we learn to adopt the standpoint of the 'Impartial Spectator' to assess our own behaviour and that of others. And it is that judgement that is *the* moral standard. We none of us like pre- or ill-informed judgements of ourselves. We prefer impartial assessments by others, and reciprocally do so for them. Hence we also modify our behaviour in the hope that others will judge us more favourably. Rules handed down become internalised, revised and fine-tuned.

What is the ultimate sanction for the standards of the Impartial Spectator? Are they justified simply because they have evolved? Are they merely the product of enlightened self-love? Not at all. 'Man naturally desires, not only to be loved, but to be lovely' (*TMS*, p. 209). People not only want praise and approbation, but they want it for just cause. If it is unmerited, self-respect destroys the value of the approbation of others. The origin of the process is 'nature'. Nature planted the seeds of the process 'in the human breast…intend[ing] the happiness and perfection of the species'. And (p. 195) 'every part of nature, when attentively surveyed, equally demonstrates the providential care of its Author; and we may admire the wisdom and goodness of God even in the weakness and folly of men'. Our standard of propriety, argued Smith, then involves the relevant mix or tension between the sub-virtues: prudence, justice and benevolence. It was argued above that caritas could, *inter alia,* resolve the tensions, particularly between the discretionary virtues of prudence and benevolence. Smith awarded the role of striking that balance (encouraging self-command) to the Impartial Spectator. Or to put it differently, the Impartial Spectator's function can be seen as being subsumed within caritas. But we have still failed fully to define caritas. That task is impossible, of course. The search to understand God never ends. Nevertheless, understanding the Impartial Spectator helps us comprehend our Creator. Further, Smith argued, the social organisation of which the Impartial Spectator would approve, 'virtue in propriety', is near to identical, except for a lack of 'sympathy', with that which would be advocated by libertarians like Mises, and perhaps Knight, whose stress is on utility. Smith writes (*TMS*, p. 484):

> That system which places virtue in utility, coincides…with that [of] propriety. [In the former] all those qualities of the mind which are agreeable or advantageous, either to the person himself or to others, are approved of as virtuous [provided each] is confined to a certain degree of moderation…[V]irtue consists…in the proper degree of all the affections. The only difference [between that system] and that which I have been endeavouring to establish [virtue in propriety] is, that it makes utility, and not sympathy, or the correspondent affection of the spectator, the natural and original measure of this proper degree.

Because Smith's wording here is temperate it would be easy falsely to deduce that he saw little moral difference between a society driven only by the goal of utility and one that sought 'virtue in propriety'. He denied this explicitly in a chapter in *TMS* (pp. 499-502) discussing, *inter alia*, Pufendorf's Natural Law arguments on self-love, property and quarrel avoidance. Certainly the effect of self-love is utility, a well-ordered society. But we, *as observers*, do not approve of such a society because of *our own self-love*. Rather the *approbation we have is due to the sympathy we feel for others* should a change for the better (or worse) occur in their welfare. Similarly Smith was at pains to reject the notion that *reason* was the basis for a moral sense (pp. 503-06) of approbation. A system that maximises happiness or minimises pain can apparently be discovered or deduced by reason. But pleasure and pain are distinguishable not by reason but by 'sense and feeling'.

So to summarise, Knight and Mises poured scorn on the socialist economic policies of Christian leaders of their day. To support their positions they bitterly criticised Christianity itself. Indeed they injected a large part of their work with arguments suggesting that caritas, the essence of Christianity, was what underpinned the 'mushy' and damaging economic policies advocated by the Church of their day. Such policies, they claimed, would not advance what Smith called 'the virtue of utility'. Several decades were to pass before Griffiths and Novak demonstrated that Christianity was compatible with a non-socialist approach to economics. Or, as Smith might have put it, while the 'virtue of utility' is indeed apparently coincidental with that of 'propriety', it falls short in moral terms since it is devoid of 'sympathy'. It lacks the 'sense and feeling' that are the prerequisites for assessing whether such a system of utility has succeeded in providing happiness.

By mid-twentieth century, however, many had deduced that the socialist policies condemned by Knight and Mises were Christian *per se*. Others, Christian and non-Christian, must have been confused by the Knightian and Misesian interpretations of caritas. Griffiths and Novak provided a theological underpinning that is consistent with the economic views of Mises and Knight, and they did so without accepting Knight's or Mises' misinterpretations of caritas. Caritas, loving your neighbour as yourself (and the self-command which that requires), can be partially understood using the evolutionary concept of Smith's Impartial Spectator. Harm and hurt might have been lessened had these two, somewhat virulent critics, contrasted their religious interpretations with the writings of Smith and of Hayek (in his own youth, a colleague of Mises). The fact is they did not. Their antagonism to Christianity may have had deeper roots than simply intellectual dissent from the Christian leaders of their day. James Buchanan noted in his Foreword to *FR* (p. xi) that:

> Frank Knight did not preach a gospel (despite the old University of Chicago saying that 'there is no God, but Frank Knight is his prophet'). There was, to him, no gospel to be preached...He taught that 'truth' was whatever emerged from the free discussion of reasonable men who approached the dialogue without prejudice and as good sports. The question as to the possible existence of something external to such a discussion-agreement process was not within his range of interest for the simple reason that it could never be answered.

Fair enough. But where then is the 'moral sense' of the Natural Law *sans* reason and *sans* self-love? Were the 'dialogues' and approaches of Knight and Mises to Christianity really those of 'reasonable' men 'without prejudice'? Perhaps not.

The next chapter examines the social and political policies prompted by the religious establishments of the late nineteenth and early twentieth centuries. These policies reached their zenith in the corporatist and welfare states. Knight and Mises clearly abhorred that outcome. Many Christians, rightly or wrongly, did not. They approved of, as many still do, the communal solidarity, cohesion and social guarantees provided by agencies of modern governments. Is this approval a misinterpretation of caritas? Novak (p. 356) hints that it might be. But although it is clear where he stands, he is much gentler and more balanced than Mises or Knight when he notes that:

> The problem for a system of economy is how to unleash human creativity and productivity while coping realistically with human sinfulness. To love humans as they are...while seeking a way to transform (their) sinfulness into creative action for the commonweal. Some argue that the best way to do this is to appeal to social solidarity and high moral ideals...Others that the common good is better served through allowing each individual to work as each judges best and to keep the rewards of such labour...[the profit motive, coupled with voluntary contracting and mutually beneficial exchange] will simulate greater economic activism [and so] the common prosperity.

Chapter 4 looks more closely at the social and economic history underlying this dilemma. It was not only the teachings of the Social Gospellers that caused revulsion towards Natural Law. The French Enlightenment, a vehemently anti-Christian affair, elevated human reason, the 'men of system', above the sympathy stressed by the Scots. The idea of the state as god, a *Volksgemeinschaft*, where individuals have no rights, only duties to the greater culture, took root in Germany. The outcome of these influences everywhere has been increasing levels of state-provided welfare and poverty relief. It will be argued that the results have been perverse and include unintended consequences. Not least, levels of social solidarity may have been achieved at the cost of forfeiting responsible and self-fulfilling levels of subsidiarity.

4

Caritas and Social Welfare

Nobody but a beggar chuses to depend chiefly upon the benevolence of his fellow-citizens.

Adam Smith, 1776*

No benevolent man ever lost altogether the fruits of his benevolence. If he does not always gather them from the persons from whom he ought to have gathered them, he seldom fails to gather them, and with a tenfold increase, from other people. Kindness is the parent of kindness; and if to be beloved by our brethren be the great object of our ambition, the surest way of obtaining it is by our conduct to shew that we really love them.

Adam Smith, 1790†

The advantage of economic growth is... that it increases the range of human choice...it gives man greater control...and thereby increases his freedom.

W. Arthur Lewis, 1955‡

A market economy does more for 'the common prosperity' than any other system. The fruits of that prosperity carry with them certain duties. Locke and Pufendorf emphasised the obligations of property owners to those in need. Ferguson and Smith stressed the virtues of benevolence and the moral sense. How should caritas be understood in this area, often known in the modern world as 'welfare'? Christ (Matt. 25:31-46) exhorted us to feed the hungry, clothe the naked and tend the sick. He was not speaking to the central Roman authorities, or to the local Jewish rulers, but to his own disciples. And he did so 'in private' (Matt. 24:3). Pope Leo XIII, in his encyclical *Rerum Novarum* (1891), noted that the giving of alms is a duty of Christian charity, 'not enforced by human law'. In the same context, he defended private property and individual freedom, stressing the primacy of the family over the state, and so condemned:

---

* Smith, A., *The Wealth of Nations*, 1776, p. 27.

† Smith, A., *The Theory of Moral Sentiments*, 1790, p. 369.

‡ Lewis, W.A., *The Theory of Economic Growth*, Homewood, Ill., 1955, pp. 420-21.

...Socialists [who] by endeavouring to transfer [by taxation] the possessions of individuals to the community at large, strike at the interests of every wage earner, since they would deprive him of the liberty of disposing of his wages.

Yet when we look at the world around us it appears that the bulk of all social welfare activities are either funded by, or provided by, state agencies, and often both. This chapter examines the origins of state welfare developments in Germany, Britain and the United States. Germany was the first to launch a modern welfare state, although Britain had a history of official poor relief going back to the first Elizabeth. One factor common to each of these countries is that national welfare systems were introduced at times of economic stagnation or decline. Another common element was a shift in religious and philosophical thinking, away from the individualism and benevolence of the Natural Law and towards more collectivist economic and social doctrines. These doctrines owed more to the French *philosophes* and their successors than they did to the other Enlightenment writers so far discussed.

Finally, the chapter notes several perversities. Poverty relief on an increasing scale has noticeably failed to eliminate the problems of poverty. Yet by other yardsticks such relief is often unnecessary. Many recipients have ample income or wealth over their lifetimes to cope with life's vicissitudes, whether they draw on current resources, buy insurance or borrow. Worse, when provided, dependency not independence can result, often accompanied by the inducement to engage in hedonistic, selfish and individualistic behaviour at the expense of others. Responsibilities towards 'little platoons' are shunned in order to access immediate personal gains. There certainly is inequality in society, but the inequality is not one of finance, or of political rights, it is one of spiritual capital. Evening out the stock of spiritual assets across society, an exercise in caritas, requires not only prompting those who are willing and able to share their wealth (an increasing pool of people, as we discuss below) but also persuading people to be receptive to 'getting and using' spiritual assets. This is a much tougher proposition. After all, it is not immediately obvious, especially with intangible, spiritual assets, that the costs of accumulating such capital, the self-discipline of deferring immediate gratification, are less than the benefits of a richer quality of life in the future. And if we are told, beforehand, that we are also expected somehow to share these future benefits with others, we may well require still further convincing. This requires teaching and learning, or in religious language, preaching that convicts, and arguments that convince and persuade.

4.1 Germany's Volksgemeinschaft

Bismarck was the first European statesman to devise and introduce a comprehensive system of social security offering workers insurance against sickness, accident and old age. Introduced in the years 1883-9, the Bismarck reforms have been described by Friedman (2005, p. 294) as a 'response to economic stagnation'. They were used to purchase social peace and to draw the teeth of Bismarck's political opposition. However, his collectivist welfare proposals did not appear on his desk ready for enactment on the first day of an economic downturn. They were developed after a lengthy period of political and street unrest and were heavily influenced by prominent socialist thinkers. Two important examples were Johann Rodbertus (1805-75) and Ferdinand Lassalle (1825-64), who acted also as a consultant to Bismarck.

Rodbertus was socialist in economics and conservative in politics. He believed the misery he observed in the working classes was permanent. His 'iron law of wages' postulated that the worker could never earn more than sufficient to cover his subsistence requirements. Should there be any economic growth the increment would accrue to the owners of capital. The share going to workers would then fall which in its turn would lead to recurring economic crises as consumption would fail to match output. The state, therefore, should step in to alleviate the hardships of the working classes by ensuring that the proportion of increasing national wealth going to capitalists was matched by a rise in that going to workers. Nevertheless existing laws of property ownership should remain unchanged. He assumed that existing state institutions could achieve this gradualist shift to the curing of the 'underconsumption problem'. He did not perceive that property owners or capitalists could, themselves, increase their demands, and so consumption. Nor did he foresee that if workers then continued to experience increasing absolute incomes they in turn would become savers, property owners and capitalists in their own right. (And, of course, this is what has happened historically. Today, most capital is owned by workers—whether directly, or indirectly through financial institutions such as pension funds and unit trusts.)

Lassalle's analysis of the 'iron law of wages' was similar. The historic growth of private property, he argued, contrary to the principles of Natural Law, was only apparently linked to the evolution of individual freedoms. He advocated gradual socialisation of the economy so that self-employment (with capital provided by the state) would replace the wage system. The reality would then be 'that this...reduction of the sphere of private property [would be] based on...the positive development of human liberty'. No arguments or justification for this dismissal of the so-called apparent by the so-called real was provided by Lassalle.[1] Nevertheless, Bismarck, in 1863, invited him formally to express his views on 'working class conditions and problems'. Lassalle, who by then had founded the first German socialist party—the General Union of German Workers—provided written proposals to and had several face-to-face meetings with Bismarck. Engels (in 1891) blamed this relationship with the Chancellor (and hence its outcome: the welfare reforms) for the subsequent close alliance of the workers' movement with the monarchy and with German nationalism.[2]

Writers who normally held diametrically opposed views to those of Engels came to similar conclusions. Hayek (1944, p. 170) wrote:

> The 'German idea of the state,' as formulated by... Lassalle, and Rodbertus, is that the state is neither founded nor formed by individuals, nor an aggregate of individuals, nor is its purpose to serve any interest of individuals. It is a *Volksgemeinschaft* in which the individual has no rights but only duties. Claims of the individual [to the contrary] are always an outcome of the commercial spirit.

Hayek (p. 168) saw Lasalle and Rodbertus as among the 'most important ancestors' of National Socialism. What brought their ideas to power was the 'absence of a strong bourgeosie' with commercial values. It was not the socialist element of Marxism that was opposed in Germany from Bismarck to Hitler, rather it was its 'liberal elements', namely its 'internationalism' and 'democracy'. Mises' (1922, pp. 457-58) interpretation of this period of history was similar. Private property in Germany, he argued, had not passed to the stage where it had come to be recognised as the legitimate possession of an owner who had acquired it through consensual transfer and commercial exchange. The land-owning classes still held property on a feudal basis that 'can be traced back to seizure by violence'. He goes on:

> The Junker is not concerned with the maintenance of private property as disposal over the means of production, but rather with maintaining it as title to a special sort of income. Therefore State Socialism has easily won him over. It is to secure him a privileged income.

The world's first welfare state thus was established partly to purchase social peace in order to preserve group privilege. The underlying humanitarian motives of Rodbertus and Lassalle were to provide for class- or group-based assistance. They were not prompted by any desire to expand individual freedom, choice or social mobility. Bismarck, in fact, prior to his association with Lassalle, even made the strange and presumptuous request (in 1847) that the Church keep the *misera plebs* modest and content with their earthly lot (cited in Mises, p. 458). It should rather serve the interests of the privileged classes, directing the eyes of the poor towards heavenly things. Bismarck's attitude merits well-deserved rejection by Christians. Unfortunately, it can also be used by those antagonistic to the religion to illustrate the uselessness of Christianity as a means of facilitating or supporting social change. Or, for those who are less antagonistic, it is an attitude that can impel a desire somehow to change the religion's focus. Instead of supporting the currently affluent, as Bismarck suggested, why not actively assist the group or classes that are currently disadvantaged? That approach was how the Social Gospel developments in America preceded the beginnings of the welfare state during the New Deal of the 1930s.

4.2 America's 'Great Awakenings'

Roosevelt passed the Social Security Act in 1935, thereby establishing not only the old-age pension system (which today still has the name Social Security), but also unemployment and disability insurance. As with the German welfare state, the Act was introduced at a time of and 'in response to economic stagnation' (Friedman, 2005, p. 214). Like Bismarck's reforms, the American legislation did not appear on legislators' desks in an intellectual or moral vacuum. Robert Fogel's book *The Fourth Great Awakening* (2000) provides the context. He argues (pp. 17-43) that there has always been a strong thread of egalitarianism running through American history. Thrusts to achieve that objective have been provided over time by four identifiable religious revivals. Each of these changed mind-sets that in turn initiated major political reforms. The First Awakening, 1730-60, was identified with the preaching of George Whitefield and Jonathan Edwards. In it, the prevailing Calvinist view that salvation was predestined was challenged. Personal decision-taking and self-reliance were encouraged, while an ethic of personal benevolence was commended. By 1760-90 the political phase appeared in the form of criticism of the colonial authorities. A desire for political equality and self-determination then manifested itself in the American Revolution. For Fogel, the Second Awakening, from 1800-40, saw the preaching of a doctrine that sin could be struggled against not only internally, but also externally; a state of grace could be fought for; and man, if his life was virtuous and benevolent, would be rewarded by God. The corresponding political phase from 1840-70 saw the growth of abolitionism, attacks on corrupt city government and the emergence of suffragettes.

Both of these movements stressed benevolence and sympathy, both emphasised the importance of subsidiarity and individual freedom. Fogel's Third Awakening, from 1890-1930, was a different matter. Here society itself was what should be transformed. It began with a theological battle between 'fundamentalists' and 'modernists'. Those in the scriptural 'inerrancy' camp lost out to the 'liberals'. The latter argued that the Kingdom of God could be brought to earth and man could be perfected—provided the precepts of a Social Gospel were followed. Sin, poverty and oppression were not the results of personal failure but rather of society's imperfections. Social reform, therefore, was a necessary, prior condition for the personal salvation of those in the grip of poverty (p. 12). 'Social Gospellers worked diligently within their denominations to create sympathy for the plight of wage-earners and to point up (sic) the avarice of the leaders of big business' (p. 124). The similarity between the Social Gospellers and Rodbertus and Lassalle, if not in theology or in economics, is evident. Groups or classes, not individuals, were to be the objects of their sympathy. And workers, in both cases, were deemed worthy of particular succour, not those who offered work.

The leaders of the Social Gospel 'worked vigorously to mobilize universities to support egalitarian legislative programmes' (p. 125). As remarked in chapter 3, this impacted on the founding of the American Economic Association. Amongst the recommendations adopted at its inaugural meeting were calls for churches, the state and science to co-operate to promote social reform. As this Awakening moved into its political phase the 'champions' of the Social Gospel began to come over-whelmingly from outside the church. Most university teachers were convinced. Their students graduated in their 'tens of thousands'. As '[j]our-nalists, essayists, historians, social scientists, novelists, and drama-tists...[they became] entrenched in the new mass media...' (pp. 24-25). It was during this phase, from 1930-70, that the United States experienced, first, the establishment of the welfare state, and then its further expansion, particularly in the 1960s, with the introduction of Medicare (for the elderly) and Medicaid (for the poor).

In religious terms, Fogel claims a reaction has occurred. The Fourth Great Awakening began in 1960 and continues. He calls it (p. 25) the period of 'enthusiastic' religion. It is widespread in both the Protestant and Roman Catholic churches and is typified by a 'return to sensuous religion [a] reassertion of [an] experiential content of [the] Bible [as well as a] reassertion of [the] concept of personal sin' (p. 28). Moreover, according to Fogel, its political impact, from 1990 on, has broadened to reach a wider coalition including more members of mainline churches, Jews and blacks (p. 26). The political outworking has been 'attack on materialistic corruption; [the] rise of pro-life, pro-family, and media reform movements; [the] campaign for more values-oriented school curricul[a]; [the] expansion of tax revolt; [and the] attack on [welfare] entitlements' (p. 28).

Fogel argues that one common thread runs through each of these American eras: namely some form of normative egalitarianism. The first three Awakenings respectively resulted in forms of political, racial/gender and economic equality. But the third case was different. There, as with most welfare states, equality of economic *outcome* was of more importance to its political advocates than was equality of *opportunity*. Policies designed to address outcome rather than opportunity are not the same. One big difference is their impact on individual freedom. Attempts to achieve outcome equalities generally require the erection of barriers to free choice. Opportunity equality, however, demands the removal of obstacles to freedom. By 2000, when Fogel's book was published, America was independent, the franchise was colour- and gender-blind blind, and economic growth had rid the country of many overt problems of poverty. Moreover, people were enjoying the benefits not only of not being poor, but also of being rich. Fogel noted that leisure time for the average person trebled in the century to 1995 (p. 184). But the Third Awakening had not succeeded in removing the moral problems that it was believed economic advancement and rising incomes would cure. The issues of concern to the Social Gospellers remain. Indeed Fogel argues, they may be greater than they were. Drug addiction, crime, violence, abuse of women, teenage pregnancies and broken homes, were all symptoms of a cultural and moral malaise, apparently brought about by poverty in an environment of urbanisation and industrialisation. Their continuance, despite the presence of the welfare state, has encouraged not only the adherents of the Fourth Awakening but also others in the belief that curing social ills must be undertaken at the level of the individual, not of society. Personal salvation rather than government provision has again come to the fore.

4.3 Britain: from Poor Laws to Welfare State

Gertrude Himmelfarb, in her book *The Idea of Poverty* (1985), placed less of a stress on swings in religious interpretation than did Fogel. Nevertheless, she discovered in England similar oscillations in the approach of the state to the overt problems of the poor, who had been supported by government since the Elizabethan poor laws. She quotes (p. 5) Benjamin Franklin who after a visit in 1766 commented:

> There is no country in the world where so many provisions are established for them; so many hospitals...so many almshouses for the aged, together with a solemn law made by the rich to subject their estates to a heavy tax for the support of the poor...you offered a premium for the encouragement of idleness... it has had its effect in the increase of poverty.

In a later book (2004, especially chapters 5 and 6) Himmelfarb discusses at more length the impact of religion in Britain. The philanthropy and benevolence noted by Franklin preceded or coincided with America's First and Second Great Awakenings. Nor, indeed, is this surprising. Several of the chief actors in both countries were the same men preaching the same message (e.g. the Wesley brothers and George Whitefield). Although John Wesley 'deplored' and 'decried' the religious beliefs of Francis Hutcheson and David Hume (pp. 120 and 126), he approved their ideas of a moral sense and conscience 'that made men relish the happiness of others'. While the Scots were writing, the Methodists were putting the doctrines of self-reliance and personal benevolence into practice. By the nineteenth century the prominent evangelicals William Wilberforce and Ashley Cooper (the seventh Earl of Shaftesbury) were leading respectively the anti-slavery cause and the free education movement, the Ragged Schools, for the destitute.

The political debate in Britain over the centuries was not about whether the poor should be aided, but rather how (1985, p. 6) that 'moral commitment...could best be discharged'. Government sponsored relief of poverty seemed to create as many problems as it purported to solve. Franklin's dilemma has never been resolved: if the price of being poor falls more poverty will be consumed. Himmelfarb (p. 67) quotes Edmund Burke who, in 1795, argued against any *government* involvement in poor relief. Burke argued: 'Charity to the poor is a direct and obligatory duty upon all Christians, next in order to the payment of debts, full as strong, and by nature made infinitely more delightful to us.' Further (p. 69), to Burke, the only poor were those who could not work. The decrepit aged, the infirm and sick, and orphan infants were the only proper objects of pity and hence charity. To pity the able-bodied simply taught them to seek resources where none were to be found, in something other 'than their own industry, and frugality, and sobriety'.

Despite the high levels of philanthropy, government in Britain never went so far as to suggest the sick, orphans and aged become recipients of private charity alone. Nor did it suggest excluding the able-bodied from the mandate of the poor laws. Burke, writing not only on principle, was also attempting to discredit the Speenhamland system, which would have brought all labourers within the province of the poor laws. In 1795 the justices of the peace in Speenhamland in Berkshire determined that 'every poor and industrious man' would receive a parish subsidy to bring his earnings to a predetermined level (linked to the bread price). These 'rates in aid of wages' spread to other parts of the country as well. The contemporary critiques of that system (which endured for several decades) included the charges that it: necessitated a rise in the poor rates levied on the more prosperous; decreased wages paid—which were then supplemented; led to a decline of the self-employed yeomanry—who had to pay the rates but received no subsidy since they had no employed labourers; displaced yeoman and further increased their unemployment; reduced productivity—pauper labour being less efficient than independent labour; lowered productivity in turn led to higher food prices; resulted in an increase in population—since relief encouraged the poor to marry younger; resulted in lower wages—due to increased labour supply; and so on in a vicious cycle so that the 'poor laws pauperised the poor' (p. 155).

In 1834 the Poor Law Amendment Act was passed. One aim was to re-establish proper contractual relations in the labour market. A wage should reflect both supply and demand: that is both what the employer believed the job was worth, as well as the budget from which the worker had to meet his obligations. Another was to distinguish between the 'pauper' and the 'poor' (p. 163). To establish this distinction the condition of the able-bodied pauper had to be such that it was less 'desirable, agreeable, [and] favourable' than the 'lowest class' of independent labourer. 'Need' was no longer the qualifying criterion (Speenhamland had used price of bread and size of family) but rather (p. 164) the consideration that 'relief [was] in all cases less agreeable than wages'. A main method of enforcing this was the expansion of the workhouse system—in other words liberty deprivation. Outdoor relief was abolished. The poor, for policy purposes (as opposed to the paupers—the workhouse inhabitants), disappeared. This story encapsulates Franklin's dilemma, and it is the basis for the debate that continues today. In America, it is exemplified by the transition from the Third to the Fourth Great Awakenings. In Britain there is angst when distinctions are made between notions of respectable and non-respectable poverty. Terms such as 'welfare scroungers' are bandied around as frequently as the words 'I know my rights' (i.e. entitlements). Policy, likewise, has oscillated from 'universal' to 'means-tested' benefits; from permanent to time-limited benefits; from supplementary and needs-based benefits to flat-rate grants. Meanwhile, writers such as Charles Murray (1996, p. 23), for both Britain and America, have talked of 'an underclass [that] does not refer to a degree of poverty, but to a type of poverty'. And again we are seeing consumers of poverty relief who nevertheless remain poor.

The British welfare state proper was inaugurated with the Old Age Pensions Act of 1908 and the (health and unemployment) National Insurance Act of 1911. As with America and Germany, Friedman (2005, p. 243) notes that the Acts were passed in response to a period of economic stagnation. And as with America and Germany, there had also been a period of time beforehand during which the existence of a problem came to be recognised. Himmelfarb argues that for policy purposes the poor in Britain were 'rediscovered' in the 1880s (p. 529) when studies claimed to show how badly off were the labouring or 'deserving' classes. And as 'deserving', this implied they merited assistance. Clement Atlee, as a young MP in 1920, cited one of these studies, a report of 17 volumes by Charles Booth, that 'dispelled forever the complacent assumption that the bulk of the people were able to keep themselves [sic] in tolerable comfort'. In fact, says Himmelfarb (p. 531), it 'had confirmed just that assumption'. Booth claimed that under one third of the people were below the line of poverty. The flip side of that figure is that over two thirds of the people, including a large majority of the working classes, were above it, and 'in comfort'. But it was the employed population who were the chief beneficiaries (p. 531). Lloyd George, when gathering support for the 1911 Act, promised 'nine pence for four pence'. The Act's operations were to be funded by a four pence contribution from the employee, three from the employer and two from government.

Paupers had been the beneficiaries of the poor laws and of private philanthropy. But how had the employed 'poor' emerged from the nineteenth-century era of self-reliance and self-help? David Green tells us (1993, p. 30) that prior to the Acts 'by far the most important organised method by which [these] people met the needs of their fellows was mutual aid'. In particular, the friendly societies were the main forms of social welfare provision during the nineteenth and early twentieth centuries. By 1801 there were 7,200 such societies in the UK with 648,000 members (adult males) out of a total population of nine million.[3] By 1911, when compulsory social insurance was introduced for 12 million persons, nine million were already covered by the friendly societies or other insurance bodies—and this at a time when membership had been increasing at 140,000 per annum for over a decade (Green, pp. 31-45). In 1911 the Societies went into an inevitable decline from which they never recovered. The final blow to the Societies, and to organised self-help, was the 1946-48 establishment of the universal welfare state.[4] Green lamented (p. 53) that while the state now compelled membership of its social insurance scheme for all, it could not make a man a careful, thrifty or a good citizen. What it did do was destroy voluntarism, mutual aid and self-help.[5] And, as its *eminence grise*, Lord Beveridge, warned, it would fail to generate an environment in which innovation would flourish, either in the financing or the provision of insured benefits.[6] Organisational rigidity, provision for the collective, not care of the individual with personal and unique needs, has been the consequence.

So in Germany, America and Britain the welfare state was introduced at times of—and hence in apparent response to—economic stagnation. In each case, however, that may have been more of a catalyst than a cause. In each case the notion that the collective good of society was of greater importance than the sum of individual welfares had become a dominant view. In Germany there was *kultur*. In America (and also, to a lesser extent, in Britain as it moved towards the post-war welfare state) there was the influence of the Social Gospel as broadly defined by Fogel; while in nineteenth-century Britain, as it moved towards the Lloyd George reforms, there was the very profound impact of writers such as Booth, and in turn their influence on the growing movement of Fabian Socialists. (Atlee has been mentioned above. Booth was related by marriage to the Webbs.) But there was one other common factor underlying this shift from societies where personal benevolence and individual choice were emphasised towards societies where state-arranged income transfers and other elements of socio-economic design were pre-eminent. To this point we have stressed only the development of Natural Law, the mutual reinforcement between it and evangelical philanthropy, and the subsequent appearance of the Social Gospel, whether in secular, nationalist or religious guise. One lacuna remains in the discussion: the impact of the French Enlightenment on the role of the state in society.

4.4 The Influence of the French Enlightenment

The Scottish Enlightenment stressed the principle of subsidiarity. It emphasised that love and concern for others could and should vary by distance and degree. The values of the Impartial Spectator are passed through the generations as children grow to adulthood within the family. The moral sense of the individual, the role of the Creator and of Natural Law were prominent. To the contrary, Diderot, in the early French Enlightenment, did not see Natural Law as a First Cause institution. Rather, he argued, it was the product of the reason of the General Will. The group, not God, was the First Cause. The Enlightened Despot, guided by reason, not the individual steered by his moral sense, was exalted. By the time of Comte, after the culmination of the French Enlightenment, *solidaire* had become a religion in its own right. And private philanthropy, or certainly church-based charity, was almost entirely eliminated by the anti-clericalism of the Revolution.

It was not always so. French, British and American intellectuals once had much in common. John Locke was drawn on by Jefferson when drafting the Declaration of Independence.[7] Montesquieu's *The Spirit of Laws*, published in English in 1750, laid out the theory of the separation of powers (executive, judicial and legislative). That separation, he asserted, was necessary to enable a state to promote liberty. Modelled on Britain, the concept inspired the structure of the American Constitution. Montesquieu also investigated the distinction between codified and customary law. His view that Natural Law antedated society might have proven acceptable. However, his associated belief that the laws of church and state were therefore both subsequent to, and also inferior to, Natural Law proved more controversial. His work was placed on the Vatican's *Index Librorum Prohibitorum* in 1751. In France itself Rousseau (at one point a friend of Hume) was more influential than Montesquieu. He adapted the latter's assertion that Natural Law antedated society. From there he could argue that primitive man, the savage, had been virtuous in isolation. The savage was motivated, 'prior to reason', by self-preservation and compassion. When men then entered into more complex societies, however, they did so through a 'social contract' with society as a whole. At that point it was to the sovereign law of the General Will, not the Natural Law, that man should look in order to preserve his rights to be alive and to receive compassion. And it was on this issue, the implications of the General Will, that the French and Scots began to diverge. For the Scots the questions as to whether there were one or two Natural Laws (before and after the Fall), when and how Natural Law was discovered, whether it was revealed or designed, had already been resolved. There was one such Law, it had been discovered, with the help of experience, reason and revelation. Furthermore, according to that Law, self-preservation and compassion were two of the senses to be cultivated and harnessed by man as a social and economic creature subject to the trainable mores of the Spectator, his own conscience.

But what did the General Will entail? Denis Diderot provided the answer in *Droit Naturel*, an article in the *Encyclopédie raisonée*.[8] He instructed his readers to (cited in Himmelfarb, 2004, p. 168):

> ...meditate carefully on the above, you will remain convinced: 1) that the man who listens only to his individual will is the enemy of the human race; 2) that the general will in each individual is a pure act of understanding that reasons in the silence of the passions about what man can demand of his fellow man and what his fellow man can rightfully demand of him; 3) that this consideration of the general will of the species and of the common desire is the rule of conduct relating one individual to another in the same society...

As Himmelfarb explained, the 'theory of the general will was a surrogate for the enlightened despot. It had the same moral and political authority as the despot because it, too, was grounded in reason, a reason that was the source of all legitimate authority.' Diderot had claimed that man must reason about 'all things', and that only an 'insane or wicked' individual would refuse to accept the outcome of reason. But who assesses what is right or wrong? Only the human race could express the General Will, since individual wills are suspect. And the General Will is always good and never can be wrong. Of course, in practical terms it is improbable that society could be based on reason determining or discovering laws approved by the General Will. Communities are simply comprised of too many individuals with differing interests, preferences and priorities. The division of knowledge and its ever-changing nature is too great for it to be assembled meaningfully at one time and place. A Platonic Guardian, a single sovereign or an enlightened despot would be preferable from a utilitarian perspective. That would imply over-riding individual liberty by Smith's 'man of system'. But the *philosophes* were not disturbed by this implication. Indeed some attempted to influence European monarchs, and were beneficiaries of their patronage. Voltaire spent two years in Berlin and Potsdam, at the court of Frederick the Great; while Diderot, after completion of the *Encyclopédie*, spent several months in St Petersburg advising the Czarina Catherine on economic and other matters. Himmelfarb (p. 164) notes, however, that at the end Diderot did begin to doubt whether any sovereign could ever combine all of the qualities 'in a single person' necessary to access reason as understood by the General

Will. But (p. 165), 'it was a failure of character and will, not of liberty, that gave [them] pause'.

So how should the despot operate? Baron Holbach, a German and utilitarian, made several hundred contributions to the *Encyclopédie* (translated into French) including the entry on the 'Legislator'. There he stated that a lawmaker must always 'propose to change private and property interests to community interests'. If he did that, resulting 'legislation is more or less perfect'. Holbach attacked Christianity as contrary to reason and nature (in his book *Christianity Unveiled*, 1761). Later, in his *System of Nature*, 1770, a strictly utilitarian tome, he argued that man is but a machine, devoid of free will. And in what Himmelfarb (p. 170) called an obvious dig at the Scots, Holbach also claimed that what the moral philosophers termed 'sympathy' was only an act of imagination. Most people, he claimed, were unmoved by distress in others, and either turned aside, or worse, attempted maliciously to add to the misery of others.[9] It was not only the sense of sympathy that most people lacked. The *philosophes* argued that the idea of reason itself, a concept, unlike sympathy, that they did exalt, was also unavailable to the common people. Reason was an attribute of the elite. Himmelfarb reminds us (pp. 171-74) that Voltaire had a disdain for *la canaille*, the rabble, while Diderot wrote that 'the common people are incredibly stupid'. And again in *Droit Naturel*:

> ...whoever does not wish to reason, renouncing his nature as a human being, must be treated as an unnatural being.

Where Francis Hutcheson had talked of the 'greatest Happiness for the greatest Numbers' he meant it in a simple, although not a simplistic sense. That is, it merely involves aggregating the happiness of individual men. When Rousseau, to the contrary, spoke of the 'greatest happiness of all', he explicitly indicated that it 'is of little importance...who gets a greater share of happiness...[since] For the sake of reason...we must have pity for our species still more than [we have] for our neighbour'. The 'common good of men' to the French was something very different from the sum of the goods of individual men. What was this 'common good' of all? The beginnings of the *Volksgemeinschaft* and of *kultur* can be seen from some of the *Encyclopédie* articles. Himmelfarb (pp. 175-76) again quotes Holbach's Legislator entry. He demands that the Legislator educate children as a way of:

> ...attaching the people to the country, of inspiring them with community spirit, humanity, benevolence, public virtues, private virtues, love of honesty, passions

useful to the state, and finally of giving them and of conserving for them the kind of character, of genius that is suitable for the country.

While Rousseau, in his entry on Political Economy, was no less sure that the collective was of superior importance to the family. He was almost Plato-like in his attitude: 'the state remains, and the family dissolves'. The public authority had to teach children 'the laws of the state and the maxims of the general will'. Only in this way would they learn:

> ...to cherish one another mutually as brothers, to will nothing contrary to the will of society, to substitute the actions of men and citizens for the vain babbling of sophists, and to become one day the defenders and fathers of the country of which they will have been so long the children.

There would then be a 'reign of virtue' whereby all 'particular wills' would have to comply with the 'general will'.

So there we have it. The French Enlightenment elevated human reason above individual benevolence. It placed the collective will, the totality of humanity, above the individual and his freedom to choose whether and how to dispose of that which was his. Concern for others was approved of; but it was to be an equivalent concern for *all* others, not the sympathy that varied with distance and so increased with the proximity of individual knowledge, relationship, empathy, affection and understanding. The individual and his natural rights were of little consequence. In any event most individuals were too stupid to comprehend the meaning of the reason that determined the General Will. Voltaire must have been delighted to pass on to his fellows a letter from Frederick the Great in 1773. There Frederick pledged that '[no] monarch will henceforth begin a war before he has obtained the plenary indulgence of the philosophers. These gentlemen will govern Europe.' We know now they did not. The relationships they had with monarchs became sour. Then the French Revolution intervened. In France the poor became more impoverished. In Britain and America, the Scottish emphasis on the individual and the Moral Sense, complemented in practice by the evangelicals' stress on private philanthropy, alleviated many of the social problems of the indigent in the late eighteenth and early nineteenth centuries. But in France, the 'most obvious legacy of the Enlightenment was anti-clericalism' (Himmelfarb, p. 182). Church-based schools and charities were abolished in the Revolution. A vacuum resulted. It was not filled by private charity, but by workhouses and price and wage controls, ineffectively designed and applied, 'leaving the poor…worse off' at the end of the Revolution than they were at its beginning. In the meantime Voltaire's remains were reburied in the Panthéon. And in the process of de-Christianisation, the cathedral of Notre Dame was 'consecrated' to Reason.

Edmund Burke in his *Reflections on the Revolution in France* (1790) was appalled by what was happening. He discussed the constitution proposed in the assembly of September 1789. For purposes of representation and in order to discover 'society's general will' France was to be sub-divided into otherwise homogeneous, mass segments on the basis of territory, population and contribution (1790, p. 279). The assembly hoped to reconstruct France 'with no better apparatus than the metaphysics of an undergraduate, and the...arithmetic of an excise-man' (p. 292). But it is useless, Burke argued, to pretend that all French citizens are exactly alike, or to treat them as if they were the subjects of a military conquest. Rather the proposed system would ensure that (p. 291):

> electors and elected...will be...without any civil connections, or any of that natural discipline which is the soul of a true republic. Magistrates and collectors of revenue are now no longer acquainted with their districts, bishops with their dioceses, or curates with their parishes... In better and wiser days...[the Romans] were careful to make the elements of a methodical subordination and settlement to be coeval; *and even to lay the foundations of civil discipline in the military.*
>
> (Emphasis added.)

Burke, quoting Tacitus, noted that even a well-designed army could become aimless and directionless. A well-designed structure with tribunes and centurions, and with a single military objective, was not enough. A multitude of individual soldiers had differing aims. How could unity of action be achieved from such a diversity of purpose? Smaller platoons with which individual legionaries could identify and be loyal had to be nurtured if an army was to be successful. If this was true in an army with limited military goals, it was even more so in civil society with its diversity of objectives. But the importance of families, churches and a variety of private clubs and philanthropic institutions (little platoons), so evident in America and Britain during the Scottish Enlightenment, was anathema to the *philosophes*. Men varied according to tastes, education, lifestyle, career, places of residence and birth. Accordingly, Burke (p. 293) wrote with approval that the legislators of Rome:

> ...thought themselves obliged to dispose their citizens into such...situations...as their peculiar habits might qualify them to fill, and to allot to them such appropriated privileges... as their specific occasions required [and] might

protect [them] in the conflict caused by the diversity of interests, that must exist...in all complex society.

The French, rather, were attempting to destroy this orderly diversity in society and to replace it with engineered social homogeneity. Burke prophesied that if France again experienced a monarchy, the monarch would no longer be curbed by 'the indirect restraints which mitigate despotism' (p. 294)—a forecast amply fulfilled when Napoleon declared himself Emperor.

Burke deplored the Revolution's rejection of Natural Law. He agreed with the concept of a social contract, but any such contract, he argued, was deeper and more eternal than a simple secular deal. It was part of the Natural Law itself. He noted (p. 193): 'Each contract of each particular state is but a clause in the great primeval contract of eternal society...linking the visible and invisible world.' He went on: 'The municipal corporations of [the] universal kingdom are not morally *at liberty at their pleasure, and on their speculations* of a contingent improvement' to stage a Revolution. (Emphasis added.) Natural Law, the 'great primeval contract', cannot be broken. Francis Canavan in his Foreword to the *Reflections* notes that Burke did not deny that a Revolution was sometimes 'necessary'. But he insisted (p. xxviii) 'it could not be justified but by reasons that were so obvious and compelling that they themselves were part of the moral order'—in other words, to restore the principles of Natural Law, not to overthrow them. God, after all, as the originator of Natural Law, is (p. 194):

> ...the institutor, and author and protector of civil society; without which...man could not by any possibility arrive at the perfection of which his nature is capable, nor even make a remote and faint approach to it...He who gave our nature to be perfected by our virtue, willed also the necessary means of its perfection.

Burke, the believer in Natural Law and supporter of the evolutionary improvement of diverse human beings, argued for subsidiarity within civil society. Civil society, in its diversity, provided the social cohesion required by its individual members. The state was there to protect that society, not to improve upon it at the whim or pleasure of an elite.

Burke's concerns notwithstanding, the French Enlightenment continued to develop after the social upheavals of the Revolution. Christians were not completely eliminated, but their influence was quickly diluted or displaced. One, Henri de Saint-Simon, an officer in Washington's army, returned home and became perhaps the earliest Christian Socialist. He believed scientists would replace priests in guiding and designing an optimal social order. His work was over-shadowed by that of Auguste Comte, his disciple and secretary from 1818 to 1824. Comte also believed that an ideal society's pattern of reforms and intellectual direction should be furnished by a specialist group of scientists that he termed sociologists. Comte's 'Positivism' rejected Christianity. He created a new religion of *Humanité* which glorified man and worked for his betterment in the here-and-now. Comte argued that man proceeds through three historical stages of 'improvement'. His conception of cause and effect, and of order, is initially determined by a theological phase. This is superseded by an attempt to discover 'order' through reason. Finally, there is a 'positive' stage, where science (and in particular sociology) brings man to a kind of perfection through a religion of Comte's own design.

Comte's religion, for which he even designed a ritual and priestly hierarchy, was a logical culmination to the French Enlightenment. It would define and impose the General Will. It would arrogate to itself the role of the supreme legislator, and individuals would be bound to obey. Universalism and collectivism would then follow, as night follows day. Such a religion, explicitly directed at designing and then ordering society, is far removed from, indeed it is the antithesis of, the concept of freedom of worship understood in liberal societies. Indeed Rousseau had anticipated Comte on this issue (*vide* Himmelfarb, p. 184). He too had advocated a civil religion requiring a 'profession of faith' in the 'social sentiments [required] to be a good citizen'. Those who did not accede would be expelled, not for impiety, but because they were 'anti-social being[s] incapable of truly loving the laws and justice, and of sacrificing, at need, [their] life to [their] duty'. The French Revolution had the words 'Liberty, Equality, Fraternity' as a clarion call. The members of the French Enlightenment, unlike the Scots, downplayed, indeed rejected the first of these concepts.

Comte's ideas spread and attracted some surprising followers. John Stuart Mill was for some time a convert. Gertude Himmelfarb in a detailed study (1990) of Mill's work and correspondence sheds significant light on the Comte-Mill relationship. Mill described in his writings (condensed here, but quoted from various sources in Himmelfarb, pp. 88-89) how *Humanité*:

> ...carries the thoughts and feelings out of self, and fixes them on an unselfish object loved and pursued for its own sake... [It would cultivate to the highest degree the] sentiments of fraternity with all our fellow beings, past, present and to come...[It would make the] happiness and dignity of this collective body [the standard for all actions]. [Indeed the purpose of *Humanité*, as of any religion, is

to make the welfare of all of humanity an] obligatory limit to every selfish aim, an end for the direct promotion of which no sacrifice can be too great.

Here we have Comte's concept of solidarity-by-compulsion approvingly described by Mill. To Comte the collective good of humanity was a goal to which all selfish, egotistical interests held by individuals should be subordinated. Mises wrote disparagingly (HA, p. 151) that this is simply the 'universalism and collectivism' of 'contemporary advocates of socialism, planning, and social control'. The 'priests' of Comte's creed, Mises continued, made an idol of qualities they ascribed to themselves, and which conventional believers attribute to God: namely 'omnipotence, omniscience, infinite goodness, and so on'. Earlier, in 1877, Lord Acton (1985, p. 84) had deplored Comte and his priests, whose job it was, he said, to manufacture political ideas for an end 'which no man shall be permitted to dispute'.

The French Enlightenment's exaltation of reason, of the collective will as determined by an elite, had culminated in the Comtian religion of *humanité*. Mill the libertarian eventually broke with Comte.[10] But by the time he did, the solidarity-by-compulsion that Comte had preached had already begun to take root. Hayek (1944, pp. 167-68) tells us how he influenced German thinking through to Rodbertus and Lassalle, advisers to Bismarck prior to the founding of the German welfare state. In Britain it was the German example, rather than Comte's direct influence, that mattered. Certainly Mill paid attention. But Christian Socialists (as distinct from the evangelicals) such as Charles Kingsley and F.D. Maurice paid little heed. Ronald Preston (1986, p. 184) notes rather that they were open to the ideas of Comte's original employer, the Christian Socialist, Saint-Simon. Their political priorities were more related to industrial organisation, ownership and conditions of work than they were to matters of welfare. It was a Liberal government, specifically two of its leaders, Churchill and Lloyd George, that pushed the 1911 welfare legislation through parliament. And they did so, not as a result of reading Comte, but because they were impressed by 'the successful experiences of Germany in social organisation'.[11] The French themselves did not introduce social insurance until 1930, and detailed rules for that system were not set out until after the peace of 1945. This relative lateness was perhaps less an unwillingness to go down the Comtian route, and more a consequence of the frequent political discontinuities suffered by France in the nineteenth and twentieth centuries. The United States was the last to introduce a welfare state. Reinhold Niebuhr, the protestant theologian and founder in 1932 of the Fellowship of Socialist Christians, certainly approved of the principles of the New Deal. But he noted, with implicit regret, that the Social Gospel movement that so influenced Roosevelt's policies seemed 'to be a programme of action only', 'cut adrift from all God-centred religion'.[12]

Solidarity-by-compulsion as favoured by the 'general will' is a long way from caritas. Looking back, in 1991, John Paul II lamented in *Centisimus Annus* (para. 351) how solidarity, without subsidiarity, can 'degenerate into a Welfare State'. More explicitly, he noted how:

> In recent years the range of intervention has vastly expanded, to the point of creating a new type of State, the so-called 'Welfare State'. This has happened in some countries to respond better to many needs and demands by remedying forms of poverty and deprivation unworthy of the human person. However, excesses and abuses, especially in recent years, have provoked very harsh criticisms of the Welfare State, dubbed the 'Social Assistance State'. Malfunctions of the Social Assistance state are the result of an inadequate understanding of the tasks proper to the State...by intervening directly and depriving society of its responsibility, the Social Assistance state leads to a loss of human energies and an inordinate increase in public agencies, which are dominated more by bureaucratic ways of thinking...and which are accompanied by an enormous increase in spending.

4.5 Paradoxes and Perversions

What are the 'malfunctions' of the Social Assistance state? Empirical criticism of welfare funded through 'a heavy tax for the support of the poor' stretches at least as far back as Franklin's critique of Britain's poor laws in 1766. If there is a premium to be paid for idleness, he said, there will be 'an increase of poverty'. More recently, the work of Charles Murray (1984 and 1996) has attributed the emergence of what he calls the 'underclass' in Britain and America to large-scale increases in welfare expenditures. Murray's argument (1984, pp. 26-30) is that prior to the early 1960s poverty (at least among the able-bodied) was perceived to be present only in 'pockets' of time or space. Economic growth would reduce or eliminate these pockets and only small and temporary assistance would ever be required. By the 1960s a new paradigm had appeared and had gained political acceptance. Poverty was 'structural'. It was embedded in the nature of the economy and its demographics. Large-scale income redistribution and social engineering would be required. Self-help was inadequate if 'the system was to blame'. Money was consequently transferred in large amounts. Between 1950 and 1980 American federal social welfare expenditures expanded twenty-fold in real terms, while the population only doubled (p. 14).

Murray records that by almost all yardsticks this massive welfare programme was a failure. For example, at a time of improving technology for rehabilitating disabled persons, numbers of beneficiary claimants could be expected to drop. Yet (p. 47) from a figure of below 700,000 in 1960, long-term beneficiary claimants rose to close to 4.5 million in 1975. Other indicators made for equally 'odd' reading. Unemployment among the young, particularly the black young, increased. Among the poor illegitimacy rose, crime increased, job market drop-out and school drop-out rates both went up, as did drug usage, crime and casual violence (Murray, 1996, p. 24). So not only were measures of poverty increasing, but among the poor many undesirable traits, formerly marking only a small proportion of poorer people, were becoming widely spread as distinguishing characteristics. The 'underclass' was emerging and growing. Murray's conclusion is that the problem is organisational rather than one of resource shortage. The question is (1996, p. 50) how 'to make up for the lack of community that rewards responsibility and stigmatises irresponsibility'?

Now we already know that organisations require information to function effectively. We also know that if the price mechanism is absent, only small organisations or ones with limited objectives are able to generate and process the information necessary. Furthermore, members of organisations require incentives. If we rule out profit and the fruits of power as motives, we are left with only benevolence and fraternal concern. And these, as again we know, are incentives that diminish with distance or organisational size. Here lies the answer to Murray's question. A welfare state based on Comtian solidarity-by-compulsion is *ipso facto* information deficient. And it relies on two inappropriate 'drivers': the 'general will' and an inevitably emasculated sense of benevolence. The welfare state is too large for the social cohesion, mutual knowledge and concern of Burke's 'little platoons' to emerge. Furthermore, the environment surrounding the recipient of welfare and charity is also inappropriate. When he or she receives aid or assistance in the setting of a 'little platoon' (e.g. from an employer, a friendly society, a religious grouping, the family, or other community organisation) the concept of scarcity will be apparent, both to the helper and the helped. The notion that there is a cost, that others are sacrificing parts of their private property, will be present. Wasteful consumption and provision will be minimised. The person helped will be encouraged to assume an appropriate level of self-responsibility. The incentives of individuals and those of the group will tend to be aligned. To the contrary, in the welfare state of solidarity-by-compulsion both helper and helped will perceive the assistance to be a Pufendorf-style 'public good'. Provision and consumption will have no apparent cost. Assistance is mandated for all (who meet the relevant criteria, say, of age, disability, income, number of dependants, etc.). Benefits are apparently non-rival and non-excludable and this encourages 'free-riding' rather than prudential self-help. Invidiously, the incentive to 'free-ride' also generates a motive to meet the mandatory criteria. By this argument, the size and growth of Murray's 'underclass' is a problem caused by organisational flaws, not resource constraints.

The sociologist Peter Saunders (2002) went a stage further. To him the problem is neither financial nor organisational but moral. He noted that in both Europe and America the welfare state is bureaucratic, rigid, high-cost and increasingly non-viable. But most households, Saunders demonstrated, do receive sufficient income across their lifetimes to finance their own purchase of housing, healthcare, unemployment and sickness insurance, and pension plan without recourse to net receipts of income or wealth from third parties. State welfare simply transfers resources by taxation and returns these same resources as 'benefits' to—by and large—the same individuals (albeit generally at a different stage of their lifecycles). In the process, however, the system jeopardises work incentives while increasing disincentives to effort. The virtues of self-reliance, family- and community-responsibility are crowded out. Instead of bringing out the best in people and helping those down on their luck, welfare policy appeals to our weaker natures by pandering to our desires to grab what we can get.

The American economist, Kurt Leube (2003), added a further gloss. He argued (p. 8) that rent-seeking bureaucrats and vote-seeking politicians encourage the Comtian approach.[13] Its adoption and promotion benefits their career prospects. And (p. 8) its promotion in turn results in '...new moral norms...within the...law without [us] feeling guilty or immoral'. As more and more responsibility is transferred from individual to state, the 'volume of redistribution' becomes a proxy for individual 'affection', and the latter as well as 'individual responsibility, quickly dr[ies] up' (pp. 9-10). Leube claims this process results in an increasing volume and range of demands. Health, welfare, 'social standing' and even 'happiness' (p. 10) become apparently legitimate expectations. Private initiatives and responsibilities are 'out-priced' by the apparently costless state-provided alternatives. Instead of a safety net, state-provided welfare is regarded as 'the helper of first choice', not the 'last resort'. But the welfare state can never meet its aims. Indeed, new demands appear 'usually at the pace of democratic elections' (p. 13) as politicians seek for an ever-increasing range of vote-attracting welfare benefits. If artificially inspired aspirations are not achieved in spite of all interventions, then even 'cultural frameworks must be adjusted' to remove conditions now 'unjust' (p. 13). Often '[t]his means the only way to put unequal persons into equal positions would be to treat them unequally'. In turn this leads to the assumption that if inequalities prevail somebody must be guilty. So (pp. 13-14) 'government is called to action to ease the inequalities by punishing the privileged' either through progressive taxation or through obstacles to achievement.

The paradox has emerged, says Leube, that 'that enjoyment of personal freedom requires collective institutions' (pp. 14-16). Little platoons are becoming redundant. The family, for example, is losing its functions to the state kindergarten, to the government retirement centre, and to other forms of collective provision for the weak. Divested of their personal responsibilities, individuals are free to pursue hedonistic lifestyles, shunning annoying obligations that would prevent individual emancipation and seeking instead an extreme and perverse form of subsidiarity. The presence of solidarity-by-compulsion has permitted individuals to maximise their exploitation of personal and individual subsidiarity beyond the optimum. The extravagant, the egotistic and the selfish are the true beneficiaries as they seek for 'an everlasting condition of happiness'. The elderly and the needy can be institutionalised at no (apparent) cost. They are impediments to pleasure. Spontaneous and even deviant life styles can be pursued. Freedom and independence are attained for the individual because of the collective provision of care. [14] The 'paradox' arises that individual liberty is enhanced, and duties and obligations reduced, the more economic liabilities are met by the collective. The individual can live a hedonistic, Dionysian life so long as the collective state assumes the responsibility. Of course, the paradox is resolved whenever one realises that the liabilities are borne by the collective and that some individuals, by law, have had their liberty reduced in order to finance through taxation the unconstrained behaviour of others. This is not Natural Law, but what Plato termed the law of the 'party'.

This is all a far cry from the solidarity inherent in caritas. The *Catechism of the Catholic Church* (1939-42) explains that the principle of solidarity is articulated, *inter alia*, in human and Christian 'friendship' and 'social charity'. Friendship is a socially localised concept, not something which can be imposed from a distance. 'Social charity' can be dictated through the welfare state. But the dangers of Comtian solidarity-by-compulsion then appear. The Christian principle of subsidiarity is breached. And Comte, as social engineer, wished to 'deaden the personal passions and propensities' (*vide* Himmelfarb, 1990, p. 89). To the contrary the Catechism states (1885 and 2209):

> The principle of subsidiarity is opposed to all forms of collectivism. It sets limits for state intervention. It aims at harmonising the relationships between individuals and society. Following the principle of subsidiarity, larger communities should take care not to usurp the family's prerogatives or interfere in its life. [Only] where families cannot fulfil their responsibilities, [should] other social bodies have the duty of helping them and of supporting [not displacing] the institution of the family.

The Christian virtue of sharing spiritual goods and assets, as well as temporal ones, should be carried out within all levels and sectors of society. The Catechism (1941-2) indicates that socio-economic problems can only be resolved with the help of '*all the forms* of solidarity' (emphasis added). In this way, caritas can generate, in the words of Pius XII, 'the social conditions capable of offering to everyone possible a life worthy of man and of a Christian'. Christ's position in Matt. 6:33, misunderstood by Knight and Mises as a disdain for the morrow, then becomes clear as a directive not to indulge in the anxiety of self-centred materialism, but rather to strive truly to practice caritas. A material outcome of adequate sufficiency will follow.

The tension between self-interest and benevolence is acute in the modern world with its high degree of division of labour, and its social and geographic mobility. In small self-contained subsistence groupings, self-interested actions damaging to the group can readily be apprehended. In large, economically interdependent groups, commercially dysfunctional self-interest is also quickly penalised. People refuse to trade with an actor who fails to comply with the Natural Law provisions of stability of property and exchange of title by consent. To the contrary, once outside of the commercial arena, self-interested and socially dysfunctional actions are not subject to such self-correcting mechanisms. Behavioural and moral codes can be ambiguous. Religious leaders have not always spoken with one voice. The Natural Law may be insufficiently codified, or social engineers and politicians, for reasons of rent and vote seeking, may have introduced positive laws inconsistent with the Law of Nature.[15] Hayek (1988, p. 135) was aware of this:

...mankind... [is] torn between two states of being. On the one hand are the kinds of attitudes and emotions appropriate to behaviour in the small groups wherein mankind lived for more than a hundred thousand years, wherein known fellows learnt to serve one another, and to pursue common aims. *Curiously, these archaic, more primitive attitudes and emotions are now supported by much of rationalism, and by the empiricism, hedonism and socialism associated with it.* On the other hand there is the more recent development in cultural evolution wherein we no longer serve known fellows or pursue common ends, but where institutions, moral systems, and traditions have evolved that have produced and now keep alive many times more people than [ever before existed], people who are engaged, largely peacefully though competitively, in pursuing thousands of different ends of their own choosing in collaboration with thousands of persons whom they will never know.

(Emphasis added.)

'Cultural evolution' has resulted in economic progress, in a victory over tribalism in terms of material wealth. It has generated individual freedom, competition, choice and interdependence in line with Natural Law. Solidarity and subsidiarity complement each other. But this has not proven to be so with changes in social welfare. Comtian solidarity has instead replaced tribal solidarity, 'wherein known fellows learnt to serve one another, and to pursue common aims', with tribal individualism. The simple sum of the individualistic tendencies, as determined or approved by the tribal chief, of uniformity, rationality and hedonism has replaced tribal solidarity in the large, modern, welfare state.

4.6 The Reaction: Redistribution of Spiritual Capital

Recall Fogel's historical analysis (2000). He identified four secular, political movements, driven by normative egalitarianism. The first two, political, and racial- and gender-based, measured success by the achievement of outcome equality. The third, economic, using the policies of the welfare state, has been less successful. This may have been because economic outcome equality, unlike opportunity equality, requires constraints on rather than increases in freedom. Or it may have been because the policies adopted, reducing the cost of misfortune, are inevitably perverse. It is, after all, a law of economics that if something becomes less costly to consume, then more of it will be consumed, and this includes 'misfortune'. A fourth type of egalitarianism is now emerging, partly as a reaction to this failure. Fogel's thesis is that there remains a maldistribution of assets in society, but the assets that require reallocation are not economic. The inequities that need to be addressed are non-material. They are spiritual. It is spiritual capital that is unevenly distributed across society, and this matters.

Fogel explains this as follows: after World War II people have become immensely better off. The working day has been dramatically reduced in length. The supply of labour has consequently fallen and wages have risen accordingly. Leisure has been democratised and 'we are approaching saturation in the consumption not only of necessities but also of goods...that were only dreams during the first third of the twentieth century' (p. 189). People are not only richer but their quality of life is substantially better. In 1995 two thirds of American consumption was directed at leisure spending. By contrast, in 1875, three quarters of consumption expenditure was accounted for by the basics of food, shelter and clothing. And neither income data nor leisure hours fully capture the improvements. People now have the time and resources to question the meaning of life, to pursue sporting, arts and educational activities, to share time with family members, and to enjoy a lifestyle open only to the rich as little as a century ago. But there is a catch. Successful pursuit of these activities requires more than health, money and time. A key input in this pursuit of 'self-realisation'[16] is a stock of spiritual assets. And it is spiritual capital that is not distributed equitably throughout society. Those 'most deprived' (p. 203) include the 'chronically poor, the alienated young, the defeated mid-lifers, the estranged elderly', and also those who pursue the goals of 'consumerism' and hedonism, both of which hinder self-actualisation.

What are these spiritual assets that are unevenly distributed? Fogel (pp. 205-7) lists them as including:

- a sense of purpose;
- a vision of opportunity;
- a sense of the mainstream of work and life;
- a strong family ethic;
- a sense of community;
- a capacity to engage with diverse groups;
- an ethic of benevolence;
- a work ethic;
- a sense of discipline;
- a capacity to focus and concentrate one's efforts;

99

- a capacity to resist the lure of hedonism;

- a thirst for knowledge;

- an appreciation of quality;

- a sense of self-esteem;

- a capacity for self-education.

Each is required in moderation. If held (or withheld) in an extreme form they could rather be liabilities. Generally each is acquired or assimilated early in life. Families, schools, churches and youth organisations all have a role in building up the asset stock. But how can these assets be distributed more evenly to today's deprived children and, for that matter, their parents? And what about today's deprived elderly, who may even be materially comfortable, but because of their age cohort may be poorly educated? They may be located in retirement homes, cut off from family and lacking the literary skills to pursue programmes of self-improvement. Loneliness, depression and alienation can result. How can people's asset base be increased? To help answer, consider one distinguishing factor between spiritual assets and normal goods. With normal goods, inequality in property holdings is often simply a precondition to mutually beneficial trade and exchange. Entrepreneurs spot two people holding stocks of goods, one of whom values part of the stock less and the other, also at the margin, values his stock more. The entrepreneur buys, or arranges to buy at a low price (but higher than the owner's valuation) from the former, and sells, or arranges a sale at a higher price to the latter (but at a price lower than his valuation). Both parties to the trade are consequently better off, and the entrepreneur makes a profit. In the jargon it is a 'positive sum' game. Alternatively, when consensual trade does not occur, and inequalities in endowments of property are present, these inequalities can be removed using the tax system of the welfare state. One party gains exactly what the other loses. It is a 'zero sum' game. Indeed, if the administrative costs of the system are also taken account of, it may be a 'negative sum' game.

But spiritual assets are not normal goods. They may be unevenly distributed, but they cannot be traded. Nor can they be taxed away and transferred to others. Rather, says Fogel, they are like a special class of Pufendorf-style 'public good'. They are indeed privately held and unevenly distributed, but if transferred the stock held by the transferor is undiminished, and there is no cost to the transferor in terms of stock given up. The quality of life of a transferee can be improved by acquisition. But the transfer process (say by counselling, teaching, providing companionship, etc.) can be accomplished with no diminution in the stock of the transferor. Spiritual assets are non-rival. Non-excludability and free-riding is also present. Once the total asset stock has risen, the total community becomes better off and spiritually richer. All then benefit from living in a world where trust and compassion are more widespread. And they can do so at no further cost to themselves.

Is it feasible for such redistribution activity to take place? Fogel believes conditions have never been more favourable. We know people in the twenty-first century have shorter working days. But they also have chosen to have much shorter working lives. Work starts later in life, formal retirement comes sooner, part-time work is more common, lifespans are longer, and so on. People spend more of their discretionary time outside of the workplace where they earn their income, what Fogel (p. 187) calls doing 'earnwork'. In 1880 earnwork time accounted for 80 per cent of an American male's discretionary lifetime hours (i.e. excluding eating, sleeping, illness, personal hygiene, work, chores, etc.). The balance of our lives, he termed (p. 188), in a bit of jargon, 'volwork'. Today volwork has grown from 20 to nearly 60 per cent of lifetime discretionary hours. This increased capability provides more opportunities for those well endowed with spiritual capital to change the skewed pattern of distribution. Fogel cites examples of organisations aiming to do just that. They include 'little platoons' as diverse as Promise Keepers (p. 212), the University of the Third Age (p. 211) and the Girl Scouts (p. 209).

But is Fogel, in his optimism, perhaps not confusing an 'is' with an 'ought'? His term 'volwork' sounds good. But, when pushed, even he had to define it (p. 188) as 'doing what we like', which is very different from serving voluntarily to redistribute spiritual assets. Fogel's book, and its accompanying economics, assumes that there will be both an effective supply of and an effective demand for the spiritual capital that is so unevenly distributed. There must be a wish both to 'give and share', as well as a desire to 'get and use'. Fogel believes correctly that the ability to give and share has never been greater. He complements that with an analysis of public good economics. But his optimism that 'giving and sharing' will occur on an appropriate scale must be tempered. There is the problem of the 'altruistic externality'. This is the mirror image of the free-riding problem. A transferor must give up time in exchange for the benefits of his altruism to others. True, his own asset base may thereby expand. It is also true that the whole community benefits as a consequence of his actions and he is a member of that community. But only a tiny portion of the benefits to the community at large accrue to him. Others free-ride. In technical language there are 'external benefits' resulting from his activity. In the cold calculus of economics, individuals act and give up time only so long as the extra benefits to them of carrying out the activity exceed the extra costs to them. But, by definition, the external benefits will not enter that selfish calculation. Thus an individual, as a transferor of spiritual assets, may well stop short in his activities before all of the possible benefits to the wider community have been realised. In aggregate, across the population, this deficiency could be large. The incentive, as opposed to the ability, to 'give and share' spiritual assets may be relatively low.

Second, is there an effective desire to 'get and use' spiritual capital even if and when it is shared? The concern is that the underprivileged will be marginalised, alienated, brutish and/or licentious. Smith (*WN*, p. 782) was worried that living and working in an industrial society characterised by an excess of specialisation can:

> [make a man] as stupid and ignorant as it is possible for a human creature to become. The torpor of his mind renders him [incapable] of conceiving any generous, noble, or tender sentiment and consequently of forming any just judgement concerning many even of the ordinary duties of private life...in every improved and civilised society this is the state into which the labouring poor, that is the great body of the people, must necessarily fall, unless the government takes some pains to prevent it.[17]

He might just as well have been referring to the hedonism, materialism and lack of 'tender sentiments' that occurs in consumerist societies. But such characteristics are not necessarily due to a *lack* of spiritual assets. Heedless pursuit of Dionysian pleasure never has been. On occasion the Impartial Spectator can be ignored at no apparent cost. A desire for decadence often overcomes Apollonian restraint. Choice and free will determines whether spiritual capital is *used*. There is always a temptation to yield to the apparent attractions of sin, and to shun the less attractive options of individual responsibility and self-control. The Parable of the Prodigal Son tells of a man who had both material wealth and spiritual capital. Only when he had squandered the former did he 'come to his senses' (Luke 15:17) and return to his father. Fogel's recommendation for greater equality in our holdings of spiritual capital is incomplete. Removal of the inequity is a necessary condition for improving our chances of self-realisation. But it is not a sufficient condition. There must be a desire to 'get' and a desire to 'use', as well as a wish to 'give and share' spiritual capital.

And here we have a dilemma, which Fogel ignored. It is what Roger Shinn (2000, pp. 478-79) calls the 'love-justice dialectic' of the theologian Reinhold Niebuhr. Love without justice degenerates into sentimentality. The transferor of spiritual assets, motivated by love, has also a legitimate expectation that the transferee will 'get and use' them. But failure to 'get and use' thwarts these legitimate expectations. The expectations have either not been perceived in any way as implying a duty by the transferee to comply, or the benefits of compliance are seen by him to be of little worth. If the transferor then seeks justice by compulsion, the conflicts endemic to human society emerge.[18] The transferee, like the Prodigal, like any party to a consensual trade, must have the freedom to reject the transfer. And the transferor, like the Prodigal's father, must have the patience to persist, and the ability to avoid bearing a grudge if his offer is at first rejected. Somehow the terms of trade must be made sufficiently attractive for the transfer to be effectively implemented. The issue becomes, in religious terms, one of evangelisation, whether formally, or by example. Frank Knight argued (*FR*, p. 140) that the question, from the viewpoint of Christianity, 'is that of how far it is possible to perfect human nature simply by preaching goodwill [and] by "converting" individuals'. The answer may well be: not very far. But that is not the point. Caritas embodies both the love of empathetic concern and also the love of persistence. (*Vide* 1 Jn. 3:17 and 1 Cor. 13: 4-8.) In the jargon of commerce: hang-in until the client is persuaded to close the deal.

Reconsider the gains to the trade. The standards and ultimate sanction of Smith's Impartial Spectator are not financial, nor are they the product of enlightened self-love. People not only want praise and approbation, but they want it for just cause. Self-respect destroys the value of the approval of others when we know it is unmerited. Nature planted the seeds of this desire 'in the human breast...intend[ing] the happiness and perfection of the species' (*TMS*, p. 194). And 'every part of nature, when attentively surveyed, equally demonstrates the providential care of its Author; and we may admire the wisdom and fullness of God even in the weakness and folly of men' (p. 195). The problem is not defining the gain to be achieved from fulfilling the Law of Nature. The problem is how to be alert enough to see that there is a gain to be had. Fogel's contribution has been to explain, and hence make us more alert, as to how and why we can all gain from 'giving and sharing' spiritual capital. Feelings of benevolence are engendered. And because of the public good qualities of spiritual capital, the giver also benefits from the externalities of living in a more wholesome society. Further, the smaller the grouping within which these transfers are made, the bigger the share of the externalities the giver himself can internalise.[19]

But a consummated trade requires two parties. The transferee must also be sufficiently alert to 'get and use' his opportunities to acquire and exploit the assets transferred. This can be extraordinarily difficult. In an article written in 1941, 'Religion and Ethics in Modern Civilisation' (FR, pp. 194-218), Knight claimed, like Fogel, that men want self-realisation and development, both at work and play. To achieve this (p. 206): 'In modern society, personal relations rest on the ideals of mutual respect and friendliness, and especially on the "bourgeois virtues" of competence, foresight and reliability.' And (p. 206), if these are to be acquired, and: '[i]f men and life are to be made better, it will surely be accomplished by cultivating these ideals and attitudes, and not by trying to teach everybody to love everybody else in the world with undiscriminating fervour'. Quite so. Knight never understood the meaning of caritas, but he had a very good idea of what should be preached, and what conversion implied. Cultivating the 'bourgeois virtues' is merely his choice of words for 'transferring spiritual assets': namely establishing the natural rights of stability of possession, consensual transfer of title and the moral senses of prudence and benevolence.

But this gets no closer to explaining how a transferee could be alerted to 'get and use' the assets. In the commercial context Knight once referred approvingly to advertising as 'industrial poetry'. Proper preaching might be referred to as 'moral poetry'. Advertising increases people's alertness to purchase opportunities. Preaching can increase people's alertness to 'get and use' transferred spiritual capital. But, of course, no advertising (or preaching) whatever its poetic content can be guaranteed to close a sale (or make a conversion). The advertising (or preaching) must not only be informative, it must also be persuasive. A successful sale requires not only alerting the purchaser, but also convicting the purchaser that it is worth his while to change his existing behaviour pattern.

Moral or spiritual poetry is required to alert people to 'get and use' spiritual assets. Knight (FR, p. 140) argued that 'converting' by 'preaching' was not enough. The words obviously stuck in his craw. But he made the good point that all human action involves uncertainty, it is 'explorative'. A behavioural change, for example to 'get and use' spiritual capital, is 'not simply fabricated by creative thought...[there must be] criticism of what is, and rational reflection on the possibilities of improvement' (p. 141). Voluntary and mutually beneficial trade and exchange, cooperation by contract, is to be preferred in a society of free men to the alternative, co-operation by status. In addition, cooperation by contract has also made us materially better off than our fellows in societies run under the model of cooperation by status. Co-operation by contract fulfils those parts of the Natural Law that rest on natural rights, private property, consensual exchange and self-interest. But benevolence towards others, the obligations we have towards others, the need to avoid quarrels, our moral sense and the directives of the Impartial Spectator all operate in tandem with our self-love to compel us to help those in material need. These obligations, in turn, can be more readily and better fulfilled in a prosperous and growing economy, rather than a stagnant one. Our primary duties are to those closest to us. As we grow richer, not only are we better able to care for those who are close-by, but also for those more distant. Both the scale and the propensity for altruism can increase. Moreover, personal caring, unlike centralised welfare provision, does not sacrifice solidarity at the expense of subsidiarity. Social cohesion is spontaneous, occurring in relatively low social orderings, such as families and faith groups. This encourages the voluntary assumption of the duties and responsibilities properly associated with solidarity.

The alternative view is that economic growth can fund ever more generous welfare benefits by transfer through taxation. This in turn will result in an ever more humane society. This is perhaps the received and dominant wisdom of our times. It tends to ignore intellectual history and political and economic behaviour. The French Enlightenment with its glorification of 'reason' and the 'general will' denigrated the common people and exalted centralised solidarity. The ruling elite purchased a form of social peace in Germany, and built a *volksgemeinschaft kultur*. In America and Britain people were puzzled by the way in which some of the measures they targeted with welfare budgets did not fall, but increased. And, equally perversely, the hedonism of some types of individualism was facilitated, individualism which simultaneously began to erode desirable forms of social cohesion.[20]

To care for the poor, the hungry, the homeless, those without clothes or shelter is a *sine qua non* of Christianity (see Matt. 5:34-6). So, too, is caring for the sick. This is the subject matter of the next chapter.

5

Competition in Healthcare

Healthcare precedes rights.
*Alain Enthoven, 1988**

Gold that buys health can never be ill spent.
John Webster and Thomas Dekker, 1605†

Markets and subsidiarity are fine, as long as they are in their place. One place where they should definitely not be is in the financing and provision of healthcare. This is the welfare orthodoxy in many economies throughout the world. This orthodoxy should be challenged. Healthcare is largely or predominantly a state-based activity. This is true whether one looks at the USA where the government programmes of Medicare (for the aged) and Medicaid (for the indigent) account for almost half of the country's health spend; or at continental Europe where social insurance is the norm; or at the tax-funded National Health Service in the UK accounting for around 90 per cent of the country's health outlays, and politically an untouchable sacred cow. Even among economists the orthodoxy that solidarity-by-compulsion is necessary in the area of healthcare funding and provision shows few signs of going away. There are strong reasons, however, why it should. One leg on which the orthodoxy stands is the notion that healthcare is 'different'. There are three arguments used in support of this claim. These are: first, it is (or can be) a matter of life or death; second, healthcare is often claimed to be a 'natural human right'; and third, as a variant of the second, it is often claimed for humanitarian reasons that healthcare should be equally accessible and equitably provided. The other leg on which the orthodoxy rests is that of high transactions costs, or 'market failures'. Supposedly, consumer wants are less than adequately catered for by the unfettered market. If there are unexpectedly high costs of exchange or transacting, the market may 'fail' to respond and government intervention can then be argued for to correct the 'failures'.

---

* Enthoven, A., *Theory and Practice of Managed Competition in Healthcare Finance*, New York, 1988, pp. 2-4.

† Webster, J. and Dekker, T., *Westward Ho!*, 1605.

This chapter looks in more detail at these two issues. There have been some breaches in conventional thinking. One study by Frech (1996) noted that competition in American healthcare has grown in recent years as regulation of private health insurance has been relaxed. Monopoly power among the health professions has correspondingly weakened. And the record has shown (p. 151) that:

> ... competition can reduce the cost of medical care, improve efficiency and allow for greater consumer choice. But [it] cannot provide medical care for poor people...

And there's the rub. Another step is required before the conventional orthodoxy can be properly challenged. If the alternative to non-competitive government funding and provision of healthcare is, in practice, competitive provision, then what about the poor? Lower costs, increased efficiency, greater choice for consumers is generally approved of. Rising productivity and innovation in most markets is usually seen as helpful to all, rich and poor alike. But is that so in healthcare? Richard Epstein (1997) has argued that case. He concluded that the poor, and much of the rest of society too, is worse off in a non-competitive environment. The chapter ends by recalling that since the alternative to markets (which may 'fail') is, in practice, government (which may also 'fail'), the real moral choice, when evaluating the current orthodoxy, is between two imperfect human institutions. One of these, the market, embraces subsidiarity, and everywhere and always spontaneously adjusts, and by means of voluntary exchange, provides (inadequate?) solidarity through cooperation. The other, government, provides solidarity (perhaps?) at the expense of subsidiarity. In the light of the discussion a way forward is then proposed.

5.1 Is Healthcare Different?

Is it possible to apply economics at all when examining healthcare? One tool in the economist's kit box is the allocation of available resources, the science of choice. This is an area where economics has a comparative advantage over other disciplines. Here the economist's role is to solve the problem of designing the system to maximise some selected index of 'good health status' and to do so within constraints. On occasion this can involve arriving at decisions that recommend no supply of care in times or places of scarcity. But some say one should never say 'no' to a request for healthcare. Then there is that other area of the economist's expertise: the study of trade and exchange. There the economist does not take decisions. Instead, he examines the consequences that follow from setting particular institutional rules. He explains how incentives affect individual behaviour, and how that behaviour affects others. The goals, towards which limited means are directed, are not pre-selected by the economist. Rather he explains how only individual behaviour by producers and consumers ultimately reveals the ends preferred. It is only *ex post* that the ends will be open for scrutiny. To Smith (1776, p. 25), 'general opulence' arises from spontaneous trading, not from 'human wisdom'. But some say healthcare should not be studied as if it were a commodity bought and sold like houses, baked beans or computers.

To paraphrase, Robinson Crusoe could use his stock of knowledge to optimise his prospects of survival and escape. Once Friday appeared, the story was altogether different. Then, in the absence of slavery, co-operative behaviour was necessary. That required agreement or voluntary trading. And, as we have seen in earlier chapters, the prerequisite of exchange is right of ownership. Alain Enthoven, however, argued (1988, pp. 2-4) that healthcare precedes such a right. It is a good or service that should be allocated Crusoe-fashion, i.e. we already know what it is that society wants, and governments have an obligation to provide that:

> It is part of being a decent, moral human being to want to help relieve... suffering. Access to a decent minimum level of medical care is *a precondition* to 'life, liberty and the pursuit of happiness'. Governments exist to secure these rights for all citizens.

(Emphasis added)

Health is a Matter of Life and Death

The idea that healthcare should be treated differently from other goods and services (and hence be provided prior to any exchange relationship) is based on the assumption that health is different. Only healthcare, it is argued, out of all the goods and services we otherwise happily trade, is, or can be, a matter of life and death. The argument should be dismissed. Both doctors and patients depend on the other for their continued existence, as do all traders. Neither is more important than the other, and neither is a slave to the other. They trade services. Doctors certainly deal in life and death, but so do patients, who may be plumbers, farmers, policemen, airplane pilots or any of the other thousands of occupations that contribute to our survival. The case for treating healthcare differently is no stronger (or weaker) than an argument for treating differently the civil engineer responsible for our bridges, the parachute manufacturer, the farmer raising

108

beef, or the teacher training minds. All are important to our livelihoods, just as their 'consumers' are to theirs.

Is Healthcare a Human Right?

Is healthcare a 'natural right'? What rights do we have? The United Nations in 1948 provided a six-page list which included social security (Article 24) and holidays with pay (Article 26). Jefferson was more diffident, limiting himself to three, life, liberty and the pursuit (not the achievement) of happiness. We know that he drew on John Locke who argued for a similar number, life, liberty and property (chapter 2 above). The three can be compressed into one: self-ownership. Locke certainly argued that men are willing to give up a certain amount of autonomy to obtain protection of that right. Government is subordinate to economic activity, preventing theft and monitoring judicially any property disputes. As Locke (1953, p. 368) put it, men 'unite for mutual preservation of their lives, liberties and estates, which I call by the general name, property'. But is healthcare, or social security, or a holiday with pay, a 'natural right'? A legal 'right' to something can be declared by anybody with the power to enact and enforce a law that embodies that right. A 'moral' right to something can be similarly established according to some accepted code of morals. Legal and moral rights to something are sometimes referred to as 'positive rights'. But a 'natural right' is restricted to self-ownership.

Does self-ownership, a 'natural right', extend to healthcare? Are positive rights included in the concept of natural rights as understood in Natural Law? The answer is 'no'. To Locke natural rights are generalisable (i.e. they are available to each of us all of the time) and they are non-contradictory (i.e. any listing is internally consistent).[1] Healthcare, then, by this definition, cannot be a natural right. If it is claimed that I do have such a right, then it is immediately implied that someone else has a duty to supply it, in which case my so-called right is not available to him. That is a contradiction. My so-called right cannot be generalised. Life, liberty and estates are the only rights that can be generalised and are non-contradictory. The only logically consistent, interpersonal right is the right to offer portions of one's property to someone else, and *vice versa*—in short, the right to enter into mutually beneficial trades, subject, of course, to the normal conditions of entitlement (one owns what one offers), consent (both parties voluntarily agree) and escape (either party can walk away unharmed if the terms of exchange are unacceptable). The apparent ethical problem with this argument, of course, is that the endowments of potential traders (what they

109

own as entitlements to offer in exchange) can vary tremendously. The rich (if they choose) can offer to buy more and better healthcare than the poor.

So healthcare is not a natural right. To assert otherwise either imposes on others the obligation to supply the care, or implies initial identical endowments with which to purchase the care. The contractual conditions of entitlement, consent and escape are not possible when such non-generalisable obligations exist. Enthoven, in the quote above, went much further. To him healthcare is a 'positive right' to be allocated in pre-Friday, Crusoe-fashion, determined in some Comtian solidarity-by-compulsion framework.[2] Enthoven is implicitly arguing for the obligatory alleviation of social and economic inequalities when he uses the word 'precondition'.

The Harvard philosopher John Rawls (1972) had a similar egalitarian objective. His reasoning, at first glance, seems to rest on natural rights and contractarian principles. Imagine, said Rawls, that neither you nor anyone else knows who will be rich or poor, well- or ill-endowed. All are ignorant of their future relative positions in the socio-economic order. How much inequality would then be voluntarily and mutually acceptable? What ranking in society would each accept as fair and just in a social contract? Rawls argued that the only contract that each of us would make with everyone else is a 'maximin' conservative one where all possible social orderings are screened and each of us (rationally) assumes that everyone else is doing a similar screening to make the best choice for him- or herself. Since we all know that everyone else is doing this, each of us will look only at the worst individual possibilities and so choose the best outcome for the ill-endowed just in case we are they (we will make the best of a bad job—a maximin outcome in Rawlsian jargon). A unanimously agreed societal contract is the result. Inequalities persist—not on the basis of producer merit or consumer wants but because they are tolerated on a maximin basis. Inequality is acceptable which makes the poor as well off as possible even if the non-poor are consequently much worse off. This notion of a right to government action to reduce inequalities is apparently based on a foundation of mutually beneficial contracting. 'Positive' rights, say to healthcare, can then apparently be equated with Lockean 'natural' rights.

Two years later another Harvard philosopher, Robert Nozick (1974), blew the whistle on the misleading implications of the Rawlsian viewpoint. He did not require his readers to imagine a situation where no one knew his own or anyone else's merits or wants. He did not ask his emasculated actors to make the best of a bad job. He did not force them into arriving at an imaginary unanimity. As in real life and with natural rights contracting, he presumed that individuals follow a maximax strategy. People will try to self-actualise and live life to the full. They will not simply strive for the second-best solution of attempting to avoid the outcomes consequential on a perverse interpretation of human nature. In essence Nozick assumes man is motivated by a benign self-interest, and not a malign indifference (or worse) to the condition of his fellow man. If so, and if all trades are voluntary, and subject to the entitlement and escape conditions, then any present-day inequalities are simply a consequence of successive choices and contracts in environments characterised by natural rights. By extension, to interfere with the current situation, say by obligating others to provide the positive right of healthcare to third parties, is to breach the natural rights of self-ownership and stability of property, currently and legitimately held through the contractually valid chain of entitlements.

So the conclusion that healthcare is not a 'natural right' can remain in principle. But while the Rawlsian analysis has its faults, so too does the Nozickian approach. Not least is the key assumption that all trades throughout history have been voluntary and complied with the entitlement, consent and escape conditions. We know that is untrue. However, with most goods and services we act, perhaps for good pragmatic reasons, as if it were so. The question, in practice, often remains one of prudent judgement, which in turn implies a comparison of institutions. In this instance, is healthcare sufficiently different to require its provision (Enthoven-style) as a 'precondition' to exercising the natural rights to trade and exchange in other areas? Should it be financed and provided through the state? Or would this so stifle information and incentives (prices and profits) that it would harmfully diminish the ability of people to express the intensity of their wishes for care, on the one hand, and simultaneously suppress the incentives for suppliers to provide, on the other?

The judgemental arguments for and against the use of state or market as institutions will be examined in the next section. But before this we look at some of the issues underlying equity and egalitarianism. These concerns inspired the writings of Rawls, and they also lay behind much of the debate surrounding health in the last several decades.

Optimal Resource Allocation Requires Inequality

In the UK National Health Service, as in ex-President Clinton's Health Security Plan (1993, p. 11), the stated goals are equal access for all, irrespective of income, to comprehensive provision of the best medical care available, according to 'needs'. The list sounds unobjectionable, even praiseworthy. However, it defies logic, natural rights analysis and economics. For instance, the fact that health-care technology is dynamic and advancing is ignored. As Hayek (1960, p. 297) pointed out (in this context):

> ...in every progressive field what is objectively possible to provide for all depends on what has already been provided for some...

The corollary is that to provide the same for all today would negate improvement in supply for all tomorrow. Even in a static situation, all that is required to justify inequality in healthcare provision is an application of elementary economics. Optimal resource allocation is the science of choice. Resources should be allocated until they yield equal benefits, but *for the marginal patient, not for the average patient*. It is marginal equality, not equality of either outcome or of input that matters. Assume that what 'matters' is that the health of the whole community is maximised, given a healthcare budget. Say the budget is $10 million and that there are two diseases to be treated (or any two competing customer sets, say geographic regions, or age groups). The diseases can be treated if funds are provided in $1 million increments. Assume lives can then be saved as follows:

Total spend $mn	Disease 'A' Lives Saved	Marginal Lives Saved	Disease 'B' Lives Saved	Marginal Lives Saved
1	1	1	5	5
2	3	2	30	25
3	40	40	50	20
4	75	35	60	10
5	105	30	69	9
6	130	25	75	6
7	150	20	80	5
8	165	15	84	4
9	175	10	87	3
10	180	5	89	2

There are at least three possible 'equalities' in this data set with a total spend of $10 million. These are:

1. An *equality of outcome* can be obtained by spending $4 million on 'A' and $6 million on 'B'. A total of 150 deaths would be averted.

112

2. An *equality of expenditure* could be achieved by spending $5 million on each disease, thus averting 174 deaths (105+69).

3. *Marginal benefits are equated* where 20 lives are saved in each disease category per marginal $ million spent. A total of 200 lives are saved at that point (150+50) by spending $7 million on 'A' and $3 million on 'B'.

The figures in the table are hypothetical, but are realistic. Disease 'B' is the costlier to treat in overall terms. Each disease category (or customer grouping) has a threshold of expenditures that must be incurred before much impact is achieved. Thereafter the total of averted deaths rises with increasing outlays. Because of the law of diminishing returns, in both cases that rate of increase slows down after a point. The numbers in the 'marginal' columns start to fall.[3] Further injections of resources are ever less successful in saving lives as fewer and fewer easy-to-treat cases remain, and ever more intractable cases require ever more resources for a cure to be effected.

So to conclude this section, healthcare should not be viewed as 'different'. It is a commodity that can be traded in the market place like every other commodity. It is unique in the sense that every good or service is unique. It is not uniquely linked (economically) to life or death; it is not a natural right; and if maximising the health status of all is a goal, then budgets should not be allocated equitably (whether in a static or in a dynamic situation) either by expenditures or by result. Of course, the concept of marginal equivalency is 'institution neutral'. It should be applied as a decision tool in any situation where output maximisation subject to budgetary limits is required. Whether the budget holder is operating in a state funded or a market-based institution would be irrelevant. So what are the pertinent issues regarding institutional choice?

5.2 'Market Failures' and Transaction Costs

The literature surrounding health economics focuses on four main questions. Is the aggregate national spend and its growth a cause for governmental concern? Second, should healthcare be regarded as a 'merit' good, and if so is it appropriately distributed? Third, is healthcare a 'public good' and if so what then is government's role? And finally, given the peculiarities of the commercial marketplace (primarily due to the dominance of insurance *vis à vis* out-of-pocket payment) when might transactions costs, or 'market failures', impede or prevent exchange?

National Expenditures on Healthcare

This first question can be quickly dealt with. The total spent on healthcare, whether expressed as a percentage of GDP, or money units per capita, is not in and of itself a matter for approval or otherwise. It is simplistic to regard some country's level of expenditure as 'too high' or 'too low'. What a country spends on healthcare is a matter for its individual citizens to decide, in relation to other desired goods and services, not for outsiders to pontificate on in relation to some national statistical averages. There is also a concern about the rate of growth in healthcare expenditures. In fact, worries about so-called rising healthcare costs can also often be pushed aside. Baumol (1995) describes healthcare as a 'handicraft industry' belonging to the 'non-progressive' sector of the economy (other examples include hairdressing or violin playing). Unlike the 'progressive' sector (for example the manufacture of automobiles), which is characterised by cumulative increases in labour productivity due to scale economies and technological change, sub-sectors like healthcare, where labour services are part of the end-product, are characterised by zero or slow-growing productivity. To prevent labour moving out of the non-progressive sectors in search of higher incomes in the progressive sectors, wage increases have to be similar in both. Given differential rates of productivity increases, unit costs in sub-sectors like healthcare inevitably increase. But this is a matter of fact, not an issue for concern that there is distortion in the economy.

Is Healthcare a 'Merit' Good?

The view that healthcare is a merit good implies it is a kind of 'positive' human right, as discussed earlier. A merit good is a somewhat pompous name for a good or service in respect of which government believes individuals should not be allowed free choice because of lack of information about its effects, whether good or bad. Thus there are restrictions on the sale of narcotic drugs in most societies (a presumed 'bad'), whereas fluoridation of tapped drinking water is encouraged (a presumed 'good'). It is difficult, however, to identify particular merit goods in healthcare that the market 'fails' to supply. Even if identified, they must be allocated. One way, as the Musgraves suggested (1989, p. 180), is to assign 'merit-weights' according to user characteristics, to achieve a desired objective in the most efficient manner. Somehow the 'value weights to be attributed to those objectives are given in advance'. This is merely a variant of the science of choice. If the weights are appropriately selected then it becomes possible to use the merit good argument as support for and as a means to apply a

114

system of positive rights. For example, in the table used earlier, different people's lives could be awarded different weights according to their income or wealth, or sufferers from disease 'A' could be given a higher weight relative to those who suffer from 'B'. This would change the numbers in the table and so also the optimal resource allocation decision.

One argument put forward in favour of a state-funded healthcare system, free of charge at the point of use, is that the weights used, like the table above, explicitly ignore income or wealth. A life is a life, irrespective of any other factor. This assumes, of course, that there is a major wedge between personal utility, or satisfaction, and wealth. Those who reject that assumption admit there is a distinction, but argue that by and large wealth is a convenient proxy for utility. Furthermore, they claim, if regulators attempt to make interpersonal comparisons of utility *not* based on income or wealth, the outcome is inevitably to invite vested interests to advance tendentious arguments for self-interested purposes. (The presence of vocal lobby groups for particular diseases or social categories shows that this is commonplace in most societies.) Individuals are then allocated to groups to minimise administrative costs and the whole process enters the domain of political wheeling and dealing. Epstein (1997, pp. 111-15) illustrated the perversity that results from not using wealth as a discriminatory device in healthcare resource allocation. The use of wealth involves markets and exchange. To ignore wealth and apply merit ratings is to apply the science of choice to attain given ends. The outcome, says Epstein, simply 'prejudices the rich and poor of the second generation for the benefit of the poor of the first generation'. For instance, one plausible Rawlsian (*vide* 1972, p. 285) definition of intergenerational fairness is that the present generation leaves its successors sufficient wealth so that persons deciding behind a veil of ignorance would be indifferent as to whether they were born today or tomorrow. A system of positive rights, based on treating healthcare as a merit good, tends not to do this. Epstein gives the stark numerical example of spending today's limited healthcare resources equally on rich and poor. Assume equal survival chances per unit of resource spent. Market allocation would have raised the survival chances of the rich and productive, but would have lowered the survival prospects of the poor. With equal spending, however, in the second generation there would be a decrease in total wealth, in resources available for healthcare and a rise in the numbers who need that care. Epstein emphasises that 'the argument here is not that we should ignore all claims for compassionate redistribution today'. It is rather that the consequences be understood, that legislation is inappropriate, and that 'we make accommodations at the field level'.

Is Healthcare a Public Good?

It is often argued that healthcare is a public good. If so it should also be regarded as a kind of 'positive' right. Consumption, it is claimed, is non-rival and non-excludable. Free-riding will occur. There will be so-called externalities. People will consume the benefits of healthcare, but because of free-riding these social benefits will exceed the private benefits firms can recoup in the market place. There cannot then be efficient private markets for public goods. Too few goods will be supplied. The market will be deemed to have 'failed', and government must either fund provision, or provide directly. The problem with this argument is that it is plain wrong. Healthcare is not a public good, and it provides little by way of externalities. Most incidents of ill health are suffered by identifiable individuals who can indeed be excluded and who, if not excluded, would be rivals for the consumption of finite healthcare resources, whether these resources are pills or dialysis machines. The costs of exclusion (or benefits of non-exclusion) are borne by or received by the individual (plus family and friends) and are reflected in the price he has to pay for care and the earnings (and therefore other goods or services) he has to forgo to obtain that care. The social and private benefits (and costs) are equal. There simply are no externalities.[4]

Altruistic Externalities

But why have people been misled on this issue? Healthcare is not a public good, but many still believe it should be collectively funded or provided. There still is a view that healthcare should be a 'positive' right. The reason comes back to concern for the poor. Even if that concern has been wrongly articulated when the 'public good' argument is advanced, there remains a belief that markets will 'fail' the poor. After all, market participation requires purchasing power. Without that prerequisite, suppliers will not appear in the market place. This brings us to yet another argument in favour of recognising some form of 'positive' rights to healthcare, and doing so at government level. The reason is that *charitable* markets (as opposed to the *healthcare* market) are alleged to 'fail' because of free-riding and 'altruistic externalities'.

When private charity is relied upon to ensure that the indigent have access to healthcare then there will be what Pauly *et al.* (1992, p. 11) have called 'altruistic consumption externalities'. This means that a wealthier individual may wish that the poor receive some minimum level of healthcare, but for public good reasons he has little incentive to pay for such provision since the benefits of his altruism would be enjoyed by many, not merely by himself (and the individual poor and sick recipients). The community at large would be a better place for all to live in if the visibility and presence of the indigent sick is reduced as a consequence of charitable healthcare funding or provision. Charity motivated by Smith's concept of 'sympathy' may thus 'fail' because of free-riders. Because the social benefits exceed the private benefits (externalities), less charity will be provided than would be required. It could then be argued that some minimum level of healthcare provision is one where the political process as opposed to the market process has a role to play. Even here, however, history cautions us. Green (1993b) has detailed how in the UK an entire financing mechanism for healthcare was lost due to government substituting a questionable alternative. Prior to the 1911 National Insurance Act, charities and the friendly societies had a history of growth in coverage, innovative control of costs, provision of patient autonomy and a decentralised ability to target resources to areas of need. Their growth was shackled in 1911, and after the passage of the 1948 National Health Service Act they essentially vanished. Epstein noted a similar 'disappearance from view' (p. xii) of charitable care in America after the advent of Medicare and Medicaid. Markets may 'fail', but the alternative is government, which can also 'fail'. Altruistic externalities are real. But as the previous chapter argued, it may be better to attempt to attenuate them by cultivating a greater sense of sympathy and social cohesion at lower orders of society. The alternative, Comtian solidarity-by-compulsion may destroy the diversity of private altruism, resulting in a centrally determined system of merit good weightings, influenced by the politically powerful, rather than by the economically productive.

Governments are required to overcome altruistic externalities (in simple language, a deficiency of charitable giving). But are there also 'failures' in the commercial (as opposed to the charitable) market for healthcare? It is here that the regulatory role of government in the healthcare market place can, for economic reasons, arguably be increased. What are the transactions costs which hamper or impede mutually beneficial trade? Once identified, what actions could government take to attenuate these costs, so permitting the capture of the benefits of any unconsummated exchanges? There are four areas normally identified. These are agency, monopoly, moral hazard and adverse selection.

The Agency Problem

On the demand side of the market there is an 'agency relationship' between doctor and patient. Informed and responsible consumers—necessary for a market to work effectively—are allegedly absent. We need physicians, pharmacists and so on to take decisions for us. By extension we need government to tell us who these 'experts' are. The counter-argument is that while the 'agency relationship' may be unavoidable *in extremis*, patients can nearly always get a 'second opinion'. Moreover, and increasingly, vertical integration is taking place between insurers and providers in so-called managed care organisations so as to overcome the problem of information asymmetry. As with other markets, the patient's safeguard against a supplier is the existence of other suppliers. If he can select an insurer who best meets his requirements (in terms of price and coverage—matters which he is better able to judge than a distant outsider), and if the insurer can, in turn, select a provider or providers with the optimal blend of skills and resources at the required cost to meet the needs of his client base, then the agency problem is resolved. The growth in many national markets of increasingly sophisticated contractual relationships between patients, funders and providers are examples of how an *ex post* study of trade reveals institutional entrepreneurship which an *ex ante* policy choice might have suppressed.

These innovations notwithstanding, it is often argued that there is 'supply-induced demand', i.e. doctors or hospitals operating in a market will either over-provide or over-price. An ill-informed patient will either be unaware that the treatment or the equipment used is unnecessarily expensive, or alternatively will be persuaded (inappropriately) that costly procedures are necessary. But to the extent that this is so, it must be a consequence either of moral hazard, due to third-party payment (in the case of over-provision), or the existence of some degree of monopoly (in the case of overpricing). Agency problems *per se* in a voluntary exchange environment are not an issue when patients can gain information in advance from family, friends, or professional intermediaries. Even in acute circumstances, the long-term relationship between a patient and a doctor, like any customer/supplier relationship built on trust generates the confidence that past satisfactory performance will be carried into the future. In fact, the controversy over 'supply-induced demand' due to asymmetric information is simply a sub-set of the general debate over advertising in any market where consumers are not fully and objectively informed. As Frech (1996, p. 85) claims, 'it is not at all unorthodox'. As in the advertising debate, the empirical evidence on inducement and the policy conclusions in the literature are mixed. But the institutional innovations of the last two to three decades, where expert purchasers of healthcare have appeared, suggests that, as in the advertising debate, early understanding of supply inducement was less than complete.

In a more *dirigiste* environment, such as a state healthcare system, the agency problems, however, tend to be enhanced not attenuated. 'Internal markets', whether of the variety tried in the UK in the 1990s or in their more recent manifestation in the mid-2000s, pay obeisance to patient choice. But the providers of information to patients (doctors) are not in the employ of patients, as they would be in a market system. They remain with the identical paymaster—government—as the providers of health care itself (who are merely the same or other doctors). Patient choice, easy and well-informed movement of custom and reward to alternative and competing suppliers is thus heavily constrained.

Monopoly

On the supply side of the healthcare market, there is indeed monopoly. But such monopoly has generally been government-induced. Identified producers do not compete for custom because professional codes of practice often given legal status by government-approved occupational licensing, prohibit rivalry between producers such as price competition, product variation or the advertising of such differences. The professions, in addition to regulating behaviour, often restrict entry to new students by laying down unnecessarily high standards or exerting pressure on government to do so. In the USA such pressures were reinforced for much of the twentieth century by racist sentiments (Wasley, 1992, pp. 47-75). Whatever the cause, the result is the same: supply goes down and price rises. Such a monopoly, of course, can be disciplined by regulation, but then there are the dangers of additional perversities or over-reactions.

For instance, in Britain the 'shortage' of doctors and nurses, from the 1950s to the 1980s, may have simply reflected the monopsony[5] hiring power of the National Health Service. When the NHS was established Aneurin Bevan, as he put it in his endearing way, stuffed the doctors' mouths with gold to ensure their co-operation. A human capital study covering three decades of the attractiveness of British doctors' salaries by Lindsay (1980, p. 59) showed an overpayment to doctors (in terms of rate of return on educational investment and earnings foregone relative to skilled manual workers) of 98 per cent in 1948. This fell over the next few decades to an underpayment of 32 per cent in 1978. As a consequence of the mono-psonistic 'squeeze' on salaries, many British medical personnel either emigrated on qualification or otherwise left the industry. A 'shortage' emerged. A reaction occurred, of course. At the time of writing UK doctors have incomes second only to those paid in the USA.

Moral Hazard

A third transaction cost is that of moral hazard. This is a well-known concept in the insurance industry in general. Moral hazard is the tendency for insurance itself to increase the likelihood of the insured event. People, if covered by insurance, take fewer precautions against the insured incident than they would have if uninsured. Because of insurance, supply and demand in the healthcare market often do not directly meet in a cash nexus. Suppliers have little incentive to conserve costs if paid a guaranteed fee by the insurer for the service provided. In America, under the Blue Cross/Blue Shield, patients traditionally received 'first-dollar' cover. They had no direct expenses and so had little incentive to refuse treatment (whatever the cost) or to avoid initiating it in the first instance. One symptom of moral hazard was apparent 'waste' due to duplication of and under-utilisation of equipment in the commercial sector. When there was no incentive to conserve costs, nor any need to restrict consumption, rivalry had to find another outlet. It did so in the quantity and quality of provision. But, as prohibitive legislation has become more relaxed, insurance policies can now be structured to attenuate moral hazard. The risk and the level of pay-out can be defined with that in view. Usually this requires subscribers to bear some of the cost in the event of a claim through, say, the introduction of co-payments, co-insurance or deductibles (recent inno-vations include 'savings accounts' attached as a joint product to the policy designed both to help finance deductibles and to reinforce, *ex ante*, the signal that a deductible transmits). Other competitive third-party payment schemes such as health maintenance organisations (HMOs) have also appeared. Patients pay in advance for care for a defined period irrespective of the quantity consumed. Physicians receive either a salary or a share of the profits after costs have been paid. The incentives are not to over-provide (or profits fall), nor to skimp on treatment (or semi-cured patients will return), but to provide it efficiently (or patients will seek an HMO with cheaper rates or better cover when contracts come up for renewal).

The problems of moral hazard may even be at their worst in a totally state-funded, no-charge system such as the British National Health Service. In particular, the long-term moral hazard implications of such insurance coverage can be especially disturbing. A report in *The Economist* (4 June 1994) stated: 'NHS doctors and hospitals may be under strain in some poorer areas... largely because the health of the local inhabitants is poorer, not because the NHS is spending less per head there'. This is readily understood from the first law of demand. It is cheaper for the poor and the unemployed to give up working time and to queue for care than it is for high-income earners. Since there are no other direct costs to the patient, one would expect, all other things being equal, that the poor and the unemployed would report sick more frequently. Even if the incidence of illness was identical, the price of buying and consuming healthcare to them is lower. But the report went on to indicate that it is not simply reported sickness that was higher. So too were 'objective' indicators such as infant mortality, likelihood of death in middle age and susceptibility to diseases such as cancer and heart conditions. Such indicators were diverging further from their respective UK means than they had in 1948. These are measures of health that are not susceptible to short- but to long-run moral hazard.[6] The poor eat less fresh fruit and vegetables and they consume more junk food. They take less exercise, are less health-conscious and smoke significantly more. Unhealthy lifestyle choices reflect the moral hazard of a tax-funded health insurance scheme.

None of this, of course, is surprising. Moral hazard, short- or long-run, is an inevitable function of any insurance. Epstein (1997, pp. 52-59) argues, however, that the long run hazard costs are greater with social insurance. He contrasts *casualty* with *social* insurance. Casualty insurance allows people to exchange a stream of premium payments for an increase in their aggregate utility or satisfaction. The utility increase comes from the smoothing out of their flow of wealth, irrespective of whether their health status is good or bad. The insurance transaction provides anticipated gains to each and every insured person who voluntarily participates. In casualty insurance markets higher risks require greater premiums, and these are voluntarily paid because the insured person believes it to be in his best interests to do so. Indeed many modern health insurance plans encourage clients to engage in healthy lifestyles by awarding discounts on long-term gym contracts, participation in healthy diet programmes and so on. This can change a client's risk profile and in turn result in him paying a lower premium for his health insurance. But, as in any commercial market, for any good or service, there will still be exclusions of those unwilling or unable to pay the cost of the premium for coverage.

Social insurance conversely avoids this outcome by mandating inclusion and coverage for all. Moreover, attainment of this complete coverage invariably requires also a redistribution of income. Cross-subsidisation across groups will occur, and the relative prices faced by consumers will change. In the case of the NHS, the money price has fallen to zero or close to zero at the point of consumption. There is nothing special in the healthcare market to refute the two laws of demand. Epstein (p. 59) states, 'some reduction in overall physical fitness will [then] follow from the increased subsidies of healthcare. As the price of ill-health goes down, the willingness of individuals to take health risks will increase'. Redistribution is thus achieved at the cost of mandating coverage and increasing moral hazard.

Adverse Selection

Mandating coverage and socialisation of health insurance are advocated not only for redistribution purposes but also to avoid the transaction costs of adverse selection. Adverse selection occurs when there is asymmetric information. Mandatory coverage is often argued for to overcome the associated problems of market 'failure' or collapse. The argument goes that younger, healthier, less risky individuals will either drop out of the insurance market or will purchase cheaper forms of coverage. If that happens the system of cross-subsidy between the sick and the well will be undermined. This last claim (implying that the sick will be left uncovered) is then a major argument for curbing private healthcare. It is, say the critics, made worse by the 'cherry-picking' desire of insurers to insure only good risks, and so to refuse cover to poorer risks. Again this sounds like a market 'failure'. But, of course, if priced accurately, a 'good' risk is not more profitable than a bad one. Pricing and managing risk is, after all, the function of insurance—not merely the mechanical payment of medical bills. In fact, since the demand for casualty insurance exists throughout one's lifetime, provided cover is accessible throughout life, there is no cause for concern. But how sound is the premise on which the above discussion is based?

Consider the following schema illustrating four alternative market situations:

		Is Risk Observable?		
		No		Yes
Can premiums be varied?	No	i) Community rating inefficiencies	ii)	Cherry-picking
	Yes	iii) Adverse Selection attenuated	iv)	Competitive behaviour

Quadrant (iv) is the competitive optimum where insurers can price freely according to the observed requirements of patients. Higher risk clients (often the elderly and hence wealthier groupings) would pay higher premiums for similar benefits than would younger (and usually poorer) patients. Some insurers would no doubt develop life-long plans involving pre-funding for later in life, with the elderly then paying lower premiums. In either event the outcome is identical and represents the most efficient and equitable form of financing. Quadrant (iii)—representing adverse selection—applies to cases where risk cannot be observed, and asymmetric information exists, with the insured knowing more than the insurer about the probability of ill health. Average premiums must therefore initially be charged to all. But low-risk patients will soon opt out of purchasing cover because the average premium—for them—is too high for good value. Such clients, by definition are unknown to the insurer *ex ante*, unlike patients who can be identified by demographic parameters such as age or gender or occupation group. Note it is the low-risk patients who cannot get cover with adverse selection present, since the insurer must charge an average premium covering the cost of healthcare expenditures for the average patient. In theory that average premium must rise and continue to rise as ever more (relatively low-risk) people drop out of the market because it does not provide value for money. But insurers can and do attenuate this threat of market collapse by offering a range of policies or plans with higher deductibles, or that contain conservative and tightly managed care elements. Low-risk patients (known to be such to themselves, but not to the insurer) will tend to opt into such plans thus revealing themselves voluntarily, while high-risk patients will tend to avoid such offers. In short, there is a spontaneous tendency, in the absence of regulation to the contrary, to move towards quadrant (iv).

So adverse selection is not a problem. But the belief that it is may well be a problem. Regulators often react to competitive behaviour by outlawing choice of insurance plans (particularly those offering less complete coverage). This forces insurers to charge a uniform or community rate to all, as they would with genuinely unobservable risks. They will, therefore, attempt to move to quadrant (ii) and 'cherry-pick' only those clients with identifiable (and low) risks. This is not only administratively costly, it is undesirable socially, as insurers attempt to appeal only to those with particular health records or who belong to specific age or gender groups. This opens the way to a further attack from the regulators who now wrongly allege that the market has failed because of adverse selection issues. They respond by mandating 'open enrolment' so that prospective clients cannot be refused cover, to prevent 'cherry-picking' quadrant (iv). The situation becomes inefficient and illogical. Insurers who have inherited or created a client base with low risks—for whatever reason—become relatively profitable. Those who have a higher-risk base of clients, unable to raise premiums or turn away risks, face losses and bankruptcy. The next bureaucratic step is to order the industry to set up a risk equalisation fund. Profitable insurers must contribute to these funds to cross-subsidise the loss-makers. The incentives for firms to be creative and efficient in catering for the needs of their client-base are virtually removed. (This applies to both the currently profitable, and, since their losses will be met, the currently unprofitable as well.) Indeed, incentives can become perverse. Some insurers may try to 'cherry-pick' on the one hand, and over-provide benefits on the other. They will aim to serve market niches with low-cost patients, offering lavish benefits; and if a loss is made, *ex post* they can argue their patients were indeed high-cost and cross-subsidisation is required.

The motives behind such laws designed to curb the costs of adverse selection are clearly misplaced. They outlaw precisely the techniques used to overcome the adverse selection problem. Insurance firms compete in two ways. They participate in normal price rivalry by keeping premiums low whatever the risk level of the client. Second, they fight against information asymmetry and struggle to prevent clients 'insinuating their way into too favourable a risk-class'. In that sense, says Epstein (p. 122), insurers are successful if they 'prevent redistribution of wealth from healthy to sick customers'. Rather the function of insurers is efficiently to redistribute premiums from the lucky to recompense the unlucky. Worse, these laws tend to exist in environments such as the USA where health insurance is often linked to employment. Employer-based insurance plans usually receive favoured treatment from the tax system. That results in more individuals being insured and insured more completely than would happen in a voluntary environment. And that concern then exists side-by-side with its converse, *viz.*, that some people remain uninsured, particularly the unemployed, the retired and the poor.

5.3 Poverty and Fiscal Inequities

If adverse selection is not a problem and if community rating (to tackle this non-problem) simply encourages short- and (worse) long-run moral hazard, what are the real issues of concern relating to voluntary production and consumption of healthcare? The remaining problem, not yet discussed, is that of fiscal inequalities and their perverse consequences. And, not unrelated, there is the concern that the poor will receive inadequate care, or provision. Even if one is a self-confident, self-assessed, low-risk individual today, there is always the fear that tomorrow one will become a high-risk individual. Moreover, the possibility of finding out (or being found out) that one is a high-risk individual, tends also to coincide with loss of coverage. Most private health insurance is employment-related. The individual can suffer the 'double whammy', when really ill, of losing his job—that is, his income—and his health insurance at one and the same time. But if fear of job loss and risk category change is a problem, if concerns about altruistic externalities and the less fortunate are strong, is there any policy change which can improve the workings of the healthcare market?

The answer lies in getting rid of the fiscal arrangement that distorts (i.e. lowers) prices for health insurance by a substantial percentage in most countries. The result of that distortion is a significant tendency to insure excessively. This offsets problems of adverse selection, but increases moral hazard. The cause is legislation that disregards and fails to count employer contributions to health insurance coverage as part of employee income. This in effect allows employers to purchase health insurance on behalf of their employees using their before-tax income, rather than forcing employees to purchase it themselves with after-tax income. The marginal tax rate of the employee thus determines the size of the implicit subsidy government provides for the cost of private healthcare. Payment of employees' healthcare contributions is part of the cost of hiring. They are a legitimate business expense against profits before tax. But they should also be regarded as a part of employee remuneration for purposes of computing his tax liability.[7]

To disregard this logic has resulted in tax treatment that is neither efficient nor equitable. It is inefficient because it encourages consumption of healthcare cover well beyond the point where the costs of obtaining extra cover equal the value of the marginal benefits received. Price signals are badly muffled. Demand increases and prices rise. Also, where employment is rising and more and more people are being afforded cover annually, the impact on price through growing demand is continuous. It is also inequitable. Horizontal equity requires equal treatment for all at the same real income level. Tax deductibility of premiums in the hands of the employer means a person pays lower taxes simply because his employer pays for his medical insurance. Vertical equity requires some degree of progressivity in the tax system. Tax deductibility of contributions in the hands of employers provides a higher subsidy for those in higher marginal tax brackets.

5.4 A Way Forward

One way to remove these distortions is to regard the payment of medical insurance contributions by employers as a fringe benefit to employees and to subject the payment to a fringe benefits tax. An alternative is to neutralise the distortions by permitting the tax privileges to continue, but to extend them across the population by means of a monetary tax credit or voucher provided for all who fail to qualify for the tax deduction. The tax credit could be provided to everyone, including the unemployed and others who do not receive employer-paid health insurance contributions. A third option is to combine elements of the first two by implementing a fringe benefits tax and complementing it with a voucher or cash benefit for the poor. The objective in each case is to encourage individuals to choose as patients how much they wish to pay for healthcare cover. Employees and others would have the incentive to bargain for 'freedom to shop'. And, with the fringe benefit tax option, inflationary expenditures on healthcare would be discouraged. In sum, these options would enhance the incentives for self-responsibility. State financing of healthcare would not disappear. The cash or vouchers to be provided for the indigent would remain a large item of state expenditure. State provision of healthcare similarly would not vanish. Its extent—shrinkage or growth—would depend on how and where patients or their agents decide to purchase care. Plurality, diversity and competition in both financing and provision would result. And the poor would have access to healthcare.

The recommendation on tax reform might seem to have one potential disadvantage. The economies of scope which multi-plan employer group schemes enjoy, enabling them to attenuate adverse selection problems, might disappear. But it is likely that the market process would evolve some alternative. One would be that medical plans could come to be offered as joint products with other personal and family insurance (e.g. car, fire, theft, housing property and life insurance). Stable groups with both economies of scope and scale would appear in ways they are discouraged from doing at present. Financial instruments such as savings and borrowing plans for house purchase and education fees might also be bundled into such packages according to individual household and family needs.

Markets, subsidiarity and self-responsibility therefore all have their place in the optimal provision of healthcare. Traditional reasons why they are inappropriate have been found wanting. Indeed these traditional objections (adverse selection, moral hazard, monopoly, lack of equity and efficiency), to the extent that they exist, have often been either intensified or introduced into the system by government action itself. There has been and continues to be enormous self-delusion on the part of the 'men of system'. A good example is the original Beveridge Report (1942) which resulted in the establishment of the NHS. There it was predicted that healthcare costs in the UK would fall, not rise. The argument went that healthcare, if provided free at the point of consumption, would eliminate 'arrears' in ill-health. Then, due to universal access to comprehensive care, a healthier population with no sub-normal health would make fewer demands. The NHS would be a self-eliminating expense. Enoch Powell, Health Minister in the early 1960s, called this a 'miscalculation of sublime proportions'. When there is an expectation that everything that can be done should be done and done 'free', demand will explode.

But why has it proven so difficult in political practice to make the case for markets in healthcare? In very few countries is commercial provision the norm. In the UK there is an aura of 'untouchability' around the NHS. Healthcare apparently does precede rights in the minds of many. Comtian solidarity-by-compulsion with its accompanying absence of personal responsibility is apparently more attractive to many than is the subsidiarity of private property and personal freedom with its accompanying absence of private security. As in social welfare, there appears to be widespread approval for reduced responsibility for the individual. This has come about not for reasons of inadequacy in the principles of voluntary exchange to provide mutually beneficial solutions. Indeed, the above discussion has illustrated that a market-based approach may well be optimal, quite apart from being aligned with the principles of Natural Law.

Perhaps we are still influenced by Karl Marx. Marx fully understood the principles of contractual freedom of exchange, and of the rights of life, liberty and property (*vide* the epigraph to chapter 7). But Thomas Sowell (1985, pp. 44-46) showed how he believed that the freedom to exercise these rights was delusory, 'in reality [it was] the perfection of [man's] slavery and his inhumanity'.[8] In 1845, Marx (with Engels) rejected the view that freedom was limited only by the requirement to avoid harm to others. He thought that the freedom of the Natural Law was a 'mere formal freedom' from constraints. He would ask: what good is freedom if it does not mean the 'material freedom' to do? What is the point if the resources, or the health status, 'the positive power' required to 'assert ...true individuality', is absent? In essence the Marxian view, in the context of this chapter, would coincide with the assertion that healthcare precedes (natural) rights. The Marxian view would see healthcare as a 'positive' right or a merit good.

But 'formal freedom' can be established; 'material freedom' can only be pursued. And this side of Nirvana, it can never be attained. Furthermore, formal freedom, based on the principles of natural rights, private property and voluntary exchange, brings us closer to achieving any desirable material ends we wish to pursue. And it does so without damaging the principle of subsidiarity, or replacing appropriate solidarity with Comtian solidarity-by-compulsion. The role of the state should be restricted to the achievable not, however well intentioned, to harming the principle or the detail of the Natural Law (as this chapter and chapter 4 have illustrated respectively, with the examples of social welfare and the healthcare market). Popper (1966, Vol. 1, p. 110) argued:

> I demand that the fundamental purpose of the state should not be lost sight of; I mean the protection of that freedom which does not harm other citizens. Thus I demand that the state must limit the freedom of the citizens as equally as possible and not beyond what is necessary for achieving an equal limitation of freedom.

And to ensure that we are not misled by Marxian arguments that pursuit of 'material freedom' justifies suspension of 'formal freedom' Popper goes on (Vol. 1, p. 161):

> The Utopian approach (i.e. policies aimed at achieving a grandiose long-term goal) can only be saved by the Platonic belief in one absolute and unchanging ideal together with two further assumptions, namely: (a) that there are rational means to determine once and for all what that ideal is. And (b) what the best means for their realization are. But even Plato himself and the most ardent Platonists would admit that (a) is certainly not true.

6

Markets in a University Culture?

A university should be a place of light, of liberty, and of learning.

Benjamin Disraeli, 1873*

A university... will study every question that affects human welfare, but it will not carry a banner in a crusade for anything except freedom of learning.

President L. D. Coffman, 1936†

Education is a right, not a privilege.‡

There is a classic subsidiarity/solidarity tension within universities. For some reason, their role in providing a place for the individual pursuit of learning, and their function as a provider of post-school education for upwards of half the population, do not rest easily together. Economists are supposed to understand the linkages of human action with organisational design. Yet only a few apply this expertise to the university as a firm or to education as a market. This chapter is prompted partly by that deficiency. But more importantly, after having experienced several decades of student unrest on campuses on three different continents, I want to ask if there are some deep-rooted, regulatory distortions in the market which initiate and maintain the dissatisfaction evident in university life.[1] If so, can we identify them and suggest how they might be attenuated? Universities, after all, are both the repositories of our knowledge and understanding of the Law of Nature, as well as prime sources of further discovery. The chapter begins with a generic history of universities. Then the debate in South African tertiary education is briefly described: this is a region with which I am currently familiar, and the issues have similarities with those argued over elsewhere. Third, an analysis is provided of tertiary education as a market and the university as a firm. Finally, I suggest alternative forms of funding

---

*   Disraeli, B., *Hansard*, 8 March, 1873.

†   President L. D. Coffman, University of Minnesota, *Journal of the American Association of University Women*, 1936.

‡   Campus graffiti, University of the Witwatersrand.

for both students and universities, and make a case for greater deregulation of higher education.

6.1 Whence They Came

Universities trace their roots back to the Greeks. Long before peripatetic stars like Jeffrey Sachs or Milton Friedman jetted from lecture stipend to consultancy fee, Protagoras (*circa* 485-415 BC) toured from place to place. The Sophists, lacking other means of support, charged for instruction. And Bertrand Russell (1961, p. 94) writes how it:

> ...was usual [for others]... to found a school, which had some of the properties of a brotherhood; there was a greater or smaller amount of common life, there was often something analogous to a monastic rule, and there was usually an esoteric doctrine not proclaimed to the public...

The best known of these was the Academy, established near Athens in the garden of that name *circa* 388 BC. Plato, a man of substance, did provide tuition free of charge, and believed himself superior to those who levied fees. However, neither in Greece nor later, in Rome, did government tend to subsidise the instructors (*vide* Walden, 1970, and Bonner, 1977). The activities of the Academy covered fields as diverse as mathematics and botany, philosophy and astrology. Greek cultural and educational values flourished and spread to Rome. There, Cicero applauded the pursuit of knowledge for its own sake. Cardinal Newman (1915, p. 85) cites Cicero's assertion that:

> ... as soon as we escape from the pressure of necessary cares, forthwith we desire to see, to hear, to learn; and consider the knowledge of what is hidden or is wonderful a condition of our happiness.

A tension developed as universities created an elite. Esoteric doctrines, not proclaimed to the public, requiring the effort—and ability—of seeing, hearing and learning what is hidden, are not the stuff of populist democracy. Furthermore, such a liberal approach may seem somewhat impractical. Indeed, Newman (p. 88) argued that the professions, however intellectual, cease to have a call on the appellation 'liberal' as soon as they have ends in view. He included medicine: the 'most popularly beneficial'; law: the 'most politically important'; and theology: the 'most intimately divine' as potentially non-liberal areas of study. This does not make the pursuit of a liberal education in career-oriented fields impossible. But it does make striving for the essence of knowledge difficult to conceptualise, confine and, for that matter, to justify from a liberal perspective. Newman (p. 89) quotes Aristotle, who taught at the Lyceum:

> Of possessions, those rather are useful which bear fruit; those *liberal which tend to enjoyment*. By fruitful I mean, which yield revenue; by enjoyable, where *nothing accrues of consequence beyond the use*.

(Emphases in original.)

Education for its own sake may sound strange to modern, pragmatic ears. So too it did to Romans like Cato the Elder. Unhappy with Grecian influences in Rome, Cato saw no purpose if the output of the pursuit was simply knowledge *per se*. As Newman (p. 68) put it, Cato 'despised the refinement or enlargement of mind of which he had no experience'. This lack of empathetic approval is understandable, even if difficult to condone. Inability to generate empathy and support from wider society, however, led to the closure of the universities. In the end, the practical men of Rome, with not a little help from religious bigotry, killed off the elite (because different or not understood) communities of scholars. The Academy, after nearly 1,000 years, was forcibly shut down by Justinian I. Hypatia's school in Alexandria was destroyed when a mob, perhaps encouraged by Cyril the Archbishop, lynched its leader. In our terms, she might be called the earliest female Vice-Chancellor. Hypatia was immortalised in the novel of that name by Newman's evangelical adversary, the Rev. Charles Kingsley. With these acts, noted Russell (p. 78), 'the Dark Ages descended upon Europe'.[2]

A second wave of institutions specialising in the pursuit of knowledge appeared outside of Christendom. The schools and universities of the Saracens emerged from the Ganges to Granada. Influenced by the teachings of Mohammed that too much organisation leads to corruption, the Saracen institutions, united by a common language, Arabic, emphasised learning, not teaching. Standard courses did not exist. Classes were held openly, and anyone who wished could stop, listen and, if he desired, pick a teacher, discuss a curriculum and agree on a fee. Formal graduation was unknown, and students quit when they had learned what they believed they wanted to know. The Saracens studied and built on the works of Galen, Aristotle and Euclid (*vide* McInery, 1993), and absorbed and improved upon knowledge from Asia. (The Greeks and Romans knew of, but ignored, 'Arabic' numerals. The Saracens adopted them—from the Hindus—and added to them the mathematically invaluable zero.) These institutions of higher learning also fell to violence and intolerance (*vide* Draper, 1876). Saracen civilisation was attacked and disrupted. In some places it was destroyed, and in others it stagnated. The Crusaders moved in from the North, the more lasting ravages of the Inquisition appeared in the West, whilst the Turks, having first overwhelmed Byzantium, came in from the East.

Modern universities evolved from a third wave of academies. These, the *studia generalia*, arose out of efforts to educate the clergy beyond the level of cathedral and monastic schools. Like the Saracen foundations, they were open to students from all geographical backgrounds, and in their earliest days the colleges or universities in any one city were simply private societies formed for mutual protection and support in a foreign land. In 1158 Frederick Barbarossa granted scholars in Bologna privileges such as trial before one's peers. In the thirteenth century corporate bodies emerged, *universitates studii*. These were ultimately recognised by civil or ecclesiastical authority although initially they had little corporate property. Their administrative powers were weak and they were subject to the loss of dissatisfied students. Thus Cambridge was commenced when disaffected scholars moved from Oxford in 1209, and 20 years later Oxford benefited from a migration from Paris. Nevertheless, peer assessment was often at risk. Oxford found this out in 1376 when it had to reject the Pope's claimed jurisdiction over John Wycliffe. His lectures on 'Civil Dominion', or what we now call property rights, were offensive to the ecclesiastical hierarchy.

After the Reformation, universities continued to be founded by the Church, Roman or Protestant, both in Europe and the Americas. From the establishment of Harvard (1636) until late in the nineteenth century, universities and colleges in the USA (as in Europe) were 'small institutions devoted to supplying ministers and gentlemen with a moral education not directly related to careers' (McCormick and Meiners, 1988, p. 424). However, by the late nineteenth century universities began to evolve towards their modern (and less liberal) form. Some characteristics of division of labour and large-scale organisation were imported from industry. Universities established specialised staffs organised into departments, collected into faculties administered by a dean, deans reported to vice-chancellors, who reported to councils of trustees. The format became prevalent and was emulated elsewhere—the Tokyo Imperial University (1877) and Peking National University (1902).

After millennia of institutional evolution, universities entered the second half of the twentieth century to find themselves in a crisis situation. Some modern Catos saw their activities as lacking relevance, while latter-day Cyrils viewed them as subversive. Japanese universities were subject to substantial student unrest in the 1960s and 1970s, as were United States campuses, while the turmoil in France in 1968 helped bring down a President. South African upheavals coincided with political change in the 1980s and '90s. Is there a common denominator to such discontent, aside and apart from society-specific politics? The continuation of discontent in North America post-Vietnam, in France after the fall of de Gaulle, and in the 1980s and 1990s on campuses as dispersed as those of Australia and the UK, suggests there is.

Professor Harry Johnson (1968) was one of the first to articulate the underlying economic generators of discontent. In the UK at the time, he wrote, unrest generally had been directed at increasing student control of the universities and secondarily at influencing government. These targets arose from what Johnson called the increasing 'democratisation' of universities since 1945; the increasing assumption by government of funding responsibilities; the governance structures of the universities themselves; and the increasing affluence of individuals, reflected in the rising value of people's time. Democratisation, meaning here enormously increased enrolments, had altered the function of the university from providing (in Johnson's words) a 'meal ticket' for an elite job to merely providing a 'hunting licence'. Staff, aware that they were no longer teaching the potential elite, refocused their efforts from teaching to research and consulting where (their) academic time could be put to (in their eyes) more valued uses. A 'disequilibrium' arose between what students wanted and what staff delivered. This disequilibrium, he claimed, was reinforced by the assumption of government fiscal responsibility for the tertiary sector, which resulted in occasional distributions of largesse interspersed with lengthier impositions of tight budgetary constraints on the institutions, on staff and on student funding. Governance structures of the universities reinforced these tendencies. They stifled the academic entrepreneurship that might have helped the system change. New educational and technological opportunities were not grasped. No incentives existed to adjust.

Thus, for example, since universities are bureaucracies, decisions on resource allocation, rewards and penalties are taken by bureaucratic methods, not by market tests. Entrepreneurial individual members of staff become frustrated. Moreover, students face similar obstacles. Success in inducing change depends on skilful use of consultation and representative processes behind the scenes. This is not an area where short-term members of the community (students) can be expected to have a comparative advantage. Yet that short term (three to four years) has a very visible high cost to them. They are foregoing both immediate earnings and the freedom to live out their day-by-day adult lives in a work-place and at tasks of their choice. This is done in stark contrast to their closest comparator adult group, contemporaries not in the university system. Protest will then often appear to them as a cheap means of inducing change or expressing dissatisfaction. Further, since rank and seniority are strongly correlated in universities, younger staff members are often tempted to ally themselves with students. In South Africa the situation is further complicated, indeed exaggerated, by racial differences in both the staff and student bodies. A whole university community can then appear to be fragmented on an ethnic basis.

6.2 The South African University Environment[3]

Between 1988 and 1993, a mere six years, student enrolment in South Africa grew by 23 per cent to over 232,000 full-time equivalents. For many institutions this understates the intensity and length of time the process of Johnson's 'democratisation' had been going on. (The official term in government circles is the more accurate, if less attractive term, 'massification'.) Thus the University of the Witwatersrand, Johannesburg, between 1983 and 1988 had already increased enrolment by some 3,000 students. African enrolment growth far exceeded growth rates for other ethnic groups. That figure went from 26 per cent of the total in 1988 to 39 per cent of the total in 1993. Johnson's dichotomy, 'hunting licence' rather than 'meal ticket', is hinted at by the nature of the subjects students enrolled for. In the historically black universities 67 per cent of students in 1993 enrolled for languages, social sciences, education, law and psychology. In the system as a whole, psychology was replaced in the top five (accounting for 60 per cent of enrolments) by commerce. Some of these categories are employment-linked, but the bias towards 'arts' as opposed to 'science', towards 'continued time at school' with an uncertain future career, rather than definitive 'occupation-oriented apprenticeships', is clear. Certainly, enrolment choices are determined partly by the nature of historic and politically determined high school preparation. Nevertheless, Johnson's notion of 'democratisation' with no guarantee of elitist employment after graduation is as valid a description of South African universities at the century's end as it was of universities elsewhere in the 1960s. This process of 'massification' is coupled with an excessive 'drift to the arts'. It was noted that:

> ... three year degrees in the South African system were never intended to provide... fully employable graduates... but... to give students skills and ways of

thinking creatively in order to prepare them for further study... the drift to the arts'... contains within it the very grave risk of producing a class of people who cannot find employment *which they believe* to be commensurate with their qualifications...'

(Emphasis added.)

The second of Johnson's identifiable generators of discontent—the increasing assumption by government of funding responsibilities—may, but should not, sound strange to South African ears. There '[f]unding was initially meant to be almost entirely provided by the state. The subsidy formula... specified that 80 per cent of funding would be provided, and that universities would have to find [only] the additional 20 per cent.' In fact Johnson's point on this issue was rather that state funding resulted in an erratic 'stop-go' flow of funds with consequent distorting effects on the incentives received by members of universities. The South African situation is simply a starker version of that. 'Full application of the state-funding formula has never actually happened. Every year... the state contribution has fallen short of the 80 per cent... by a larger amount... so that by 1995 it had fallen to 50 per cent.' This is less than the national university salary bill. The consequences of this slump in government appropriations have included inevitable cut-backs on library resources and staff. These cuts have been made in step with increasing student enrolments and, in some universities, increasing expenditures from their other income sources on subsidising students from poorer, 'disadvantaged' backgrounds. A Committee Report of University Principals from 1987 showed that in that year a professor was earning in real terms what a lecturer had earned in 1970— 'and there is no reason to think that this decline has not continued'. Under such circumstances it is not surprising that many academics have moved overseas, into the private sector, and into more lucrative employment in the public sector. Johnson's argument that declining real incomes increases the opportunity cost of those remaining in university employment is obviously valid in this context as well. Remaining staff members have an incentive to focus less on teaching (and, it may be added, less on basic research) and more on highly applied research or consulting linked to monetary rewards or fees for performance. Such activities are often more in the nature of off-campus part-time employment (at very low cost to the outside employer). The linkage of quality research with quality teaching is weakened. The disparity Johnson identified, between what students want and what staff deliver, is exacerbated.

A World Bank Report (1993), *Higher Education: The Lessons of Experience,* chronicles events in universities elsewhere in Africa. The similarities in the

135

symptoms are discouraging. The difference is only that the disease is more advanced elsewhere. The Report states:

> Uganda's Makarere University and the University of Dakar in Senegal were for many years after independence two of Africa's premier public universities. Today their facilities have deteriorated and the quality of instruction provided is profoundly threatened—the consequence of political and economic turmoil combined with chronic underfunding and misallocation. In Uganda... low salaries have transformed academic work into part-time employment for many staff. In addition, many of the residence halls are accommodating students far in excess of their physical capacity. The University of Dakar, originally designed for 3,500 students, enrolled nearly 20,000 students in 1991. There has been a gradual decline in the physical infrastructure... because of the lack of resources and maintenance... The University of Dakar spends five times more money every year to buy medicines for its students and their families than it does to purchase books or periodicals for the library...

South African university budgets have not yet been cut so dramatically, but the parallels are there. Not least is the fact that the transition of South Africa to majority rule occurred some 30 years after the colonialists departed from countries to the North. Universities claimed the assistance of the State in the process of transformation from colonial to African institutions. The long-term consequences, now being played out, were unfortunate. Mahmood Mamdani (1994) described the process of state intervention as follows:

> The local staff demanded equity and justice. As a minority in universities, it called on the newly independent state to spearhead the battle for justice in national universities. The expatriate staff, often the majority inside these universities, stood their ground on the principle of autonomy... the contest was resolved by the state stepping in, as the guarantor of social justice... We celebrated, but not for long. Soon, in the name of accountability, the state altered the mode of governance of universities. Collegiality was replaced with bureaucracy, and peer review by management. As we came to confront state-appointed vice-chancellors, state-appointed deans and state-appointed heads of departments, we discovered the importance of university autonomy... Several decades later (at a symposium on academic freedom) a key demand in the resulting Kampala declaration was for university autonomy... The first lesson of the African experience is the importance of university autonomy. Autonomy from vested interests, whether official or private, is a prerequisite for learning that is not afraid of it own consequences.

It is paradoxical, disappointing, but perhaps not surprising, that even with this evidence available, senior management at the University of the Witwatersrand later stated that, in relation to state dependence equal to approximately 50 per cent of total income, '[we] urge that this decline (from its target of 80 per cent) be arrested and reversed'. If Johnson (1968) is correct, that high and unstable government funding results in 'disequilibrium' within the university, and if a funding shortfall exists, then it seems quaint, even probabilistically, to believe that increasing the importance of the already dominant funder would stabilise cash flows over time. To believe that success in obtaining such an increased budget from the fiscus could be achieved without inviting state oversight (even if initially benign) flies in the face of the evidence. After all, in the past, when South African universities attempted to operate counter to the policies of a much less popular government than is currently in power, political interference was still substantial.

Experience, evidence and argument suggest there are problems with state funding of universities. What are the alternatives? In real life the polar opposite to state provision is market provision. A main function of economists is to study markets. This is the approach taken in the next section of this chapter.

6.3 The Economics of University Discontent

This topic can be approached at three levels: the industrial economics of universities; the labour market for academics; and the demand for university education. We look at each, *seriatim*.

Industrial Organisation

Most organisations have to produce for profit. They are constrained by the environment to do so. If they fail, the firm (or its management) is forced out of business. In the long run survival depends on satisfying consumer demand and doing so cost-effectively. On occasion production is monopolised, with certain well-known and undesirable side-effects, such as inefficiencies and high prices. But provided newcomers can enter the industry the consequences are either short-lived or unimportant. On still other occasions, when there are several firms, these autonomous units can come together as a cartel, and act 'as if' they were a monopoly, and collude on production quotas, prices, product specifications and terms of employment. George Stigler (1966, pp. 230-36) argued that the existence of a cartel was of little concern since the policing costs necessary for successful collusion would be so high that cartels would crumble as members 'chiselled'. Or if not, then again new entrants would come into the industry

137

and take business from the colluders. However, if *government* reduces the policing costs and bars new entry then there will be social costs resulting from the now suddenly effective cartel. And this will operate both in the short and in the long runs.

Many national university systems form such a government-backed cartel (for example, in the UK and South Africa). New entry is effectively barred. The size of the government subsidy to existing institutions itself represents a substantial financial impediment to external entrants. The right to confer degrees (granted in South Africa by the Private Acts which awarded each university its own charter) effectively blocked new direct competition. In the late 1980s, when the privately owned Midrand Campus attempted to co-operate with Rhodes University by opening a joint venture, awarding Rhodes degrees to be taught in what was then the Transvaal, the Minister of Education quickly invoked the Universities Act which restricted Rhodes entrepreneurship to its statutory 'seat' of Grahamstown and East London. In the UK the history of the University of Buckingham is one of success in attaining a Charter, but only after dogged persistence against established opposition stretching over a decade

Competition, of course, is not a tender plant. And if territorial rivalry (as in the Rhodes case) between cartel members is barred, it will emerge in other forms. Perceptions of university attractiveness to potential students vary. Thus students seek out universities they believe to be better—at least in their eyes. Since funds (government subsidies) follow student demand, more successful universities will benefit at the expense of less successful ones (in the eyes of the consumer). The persistently less successful will either have to go out of business or alter the nature of their business (their product—even if still nominally defined by charter—could, for example, alter). That, of course, is no way to run a cartel. And the South African (CUP) Committee of University Principals[4] (1995, p. 28) made this very clear. They proposed that:

> ... in contrast to the present procedures where student demand... determined the size of the system... the planners should calculate... (that size). After this the available places must be divided between the institutions...

In other words, production quotas should be set further to facilitate maintenance of the cartel. If a university exceeded its allocation and over-enrolled (p. 27) 'it would [no longer] earn additional subsidies'. If it under-enrolled it would earn less.[5] Of course, the cartel then recognised that these possibilities might prompt individual institutions to compete, or 'chisel', by altering their own fees, or by changing the nature or attractiveness to students of the degrees they offered. So the CUP emphasised that fees should only be altered bearing 'the norm of equity in mind... those identified by a means test should have the option of financial assistance'. And if the quality of the product is to be altered by raising admission standards, then academic support programmes should be available. In a nutshell, behaviour deviating from the cartel rules would be made costly. To strengthen the cartel even further the CUP proposed that any new subsidy formula be based on a detailed analysis of universities' 'actual cost structures that result from realistic staff-to-student ratios'. If some universities have higher costs because they have a higher proportion of laboratory-based teaching or of postgraduate students, then 'the independent variable' in the formula equation 'should be qualified to take these into account'. As a consequence it would 'not be necessary *to apply the formula differently to different universities... this should be strongly guarded against* (emphasis added).

This is all too predictable from the cartel theory of industrial economics. Not only do cartel members wish to inhibit entry, to minimise chiselling and to hamper product competition, they also want to limit the likelihood of cartel breakdown through cost-side competition. The formula (cost-based) should be applied uniformly to encourage uniform costs.[6] This 1995 proposal was made in the light of the breakdown in the mid-1980s of national salary structures for university staff. It is now possible for universities to bid against each other for high calibre personnel in ways not possible some years ago. The logical (cartel) reaction is a return to national scales. This has not yet occurred, although it will be worth examining future responses of the teachers' unions, *viz.*, the academic staff associations. Ostensibly they exist to increase the real income of their members. They should, therefore, resist any reversal of policy. It is not simply uniform costs the cartel wished to achieve, but uniform costs based on 'realistic' staff/student ratios. Again, product competition (e.g. innovative teaching methods requiring more or less staff per student) is discouraged. Those requiring more staff receive no additional subsidy. Whilst innovations requiring fewer staff do indeed provide budgetary benefits to the university concerned, they will not be pursued to their full potential. The university can neither expand as a consequence nor appropriate for residual owners[7] the benefits of either cost reduction or enrolment expansion.

139

The Labour Market for Academics

Here industrial economics overlaps with labour economics. The lack of residual ownership results in a manifestation of the agency problem[8] in the market for academics. How can rewards and penalties be structured so that the incentives of universities (and their staff) are aligned appropriately with those of their students? Long before the language of modern agency theory, Adam Smith noted (*WN*, p. 764):

> The discipline of colleges and universities is in general contrived not for the benefit of the students, but for the interest, or more properly speaking, for the ease of the masters. Its object is, in all cases, to maintain the authority of the master, and whether he neglects or performs his duty to oblige the students in all cases to behave to him as if he performs it with the greatest diligence and ability.

The peculiar element in the university labour market that permits or facilitates this type of slack or on-the-job consumption is that of security of tenure. Once confirmed in his post it is rare if not impossible for an academic to be removed other than for acts of 'gross moral turpitude'. *De facto* (even if not *de jure*) job security is often defended on the grounds that it is essential to protect a scholar should his pursuit of truth offend the orthodox. That, of course, begs the question as to whether 'truth' is a product requiring analysis different from that of other products. Further, does the scholar have to be employed by the 'orthodox'? The existence of innumerable sellers in the marketplace for ideas suggests the answers to both questions are negative. (Newspapers, churches, political parties, fictional and non-fictional writings, the cinema, management consultants and internet 'bloggers' typify a mere handful of such sellers and employers.) Universities are unique in their privileged monopoly status of conferring degrees on the young (after instruction) and in the employment relationship they have with their staff. This employment relation is the result less of a desire to protect the pursuit of truth and more a consequence of the absence of direct residual ownership on the market's supply side and inadequate use of the price mechanism on the demand side.

Alchian (1977, p. 201) puts it as follows: 'Without a private profit-seeking system and without full-cost tuition, the demand for tenure increases and the cost of granting it appears to change because the full costs are not imposed on those granting it'. For a non-profit organisation such as a university, the cost to a governing Council of granting requests for tenure is low. There are no residual claims that have to be forfeited if the request is granted. In general, ways will be sought to keep internal management hassles and labour conflicts to a minimum. Employment policies will evolve which are more oriented towards decision-maker gratification than towards productivity. After all, as Alchian (p. 186) notes, firing a person is always 'an unpleasant task, but in a profit-seeking business it is even more unpleasant not to fire them.' In a non-profit organisation a blind eye will tend to be turned towards 'unpleasant tasks'. By extension, when there is no residual from which to argue for increased salaries, for example because the staff member can claim to have contributed to achieving organisation objectives, then job security becomes a relatively attractive request to put forward.

Because taking 'profits' home in the form of increased salaries is difficult, academics and decision-makers also seek other ways to appropriate any 'surplus'. More time is devoted to community 'statesmanship', for example, than in a profit-seeking setting. On the other hand, if employment policies reflect administrative ease rather than productivity considerations, then employees without the ability to meet the subjective preferences of the employer but who are interested in meeting the ostensible objectives of the organisation will seek to protect themselves from the hiring, firing and employment policies which have evolved from the decision-maker's utility function. They will play 'by the rules' that do earn tenure and promotion. Some might argue that such self-protecting activities of the employees could result in a countervailing force bringing the organisation's objectives back into line with market preferences, but three arguments tend to negate this. First, to the extent that senior management incentives are inefficient because of the absence of profit, this is even truer for those operating at one further remove from the holding of residual rights, *viz.* the junior to middle-rank academics. Second, the decision-maker will tend to accept whatever employment policy has the least cost to him. Third, the employee will seek a policy providing high benefits within *his* preference ordering (formally—his utility function). Consider how this plays out in the tenure setting.

Job security provides staff with an employment contract with the university administration that is similar in many ways to an insurance policy. It is subject both to moral hazard and asymmetric information. (These terms are familiar from chapter 5.) Insurance is essentially a gamble. Younger staff will accept lower guaranteed salaries earlier in their careers in the hope that they will over-collect in the later stages. That part of the gamble is purely actuarial. But what of the moral hazard and adverse selection issues? A university, after confirmation, can be disappointed with an unproductive employee but can do little. A productive employee, conversely, may also surprise—but he can quit and go elsewhere. Because of this asymmetry the employer will offer a lower guaranteed, life-time salary than would equal expected productivity.

Several groupings suffer from the inefficiencies and perverse consequences of this insurance contract. Consumers (students and others who call on universities as suppliers of education and knowledge) are an obvious example. But certain sections of the university staff also bear disproportionate costs. Those who prove to be more productive will receive less over their lifetimes than those who are below average in productivity. The latter, of course, continue to earn more than they would have without job security. The consequence is a disincentive to all to perform well. This disincentive is reinforced by a penalty on job mobility. The already overpaid are relatively unlikely to find alternative employment, while the underpaid have to incur the costs of convincing potential employers that they are worth the risk of hiring.

There is worse. If participative, democratic procedures provide senior administrators with a quieter managerial life and result in sub-optimal agreements on job-security, they also provide academics themselves with an alternative career activity to teaching and research. It would be expected that those academics who do not possess a comparative advantage in teaching, research or consulting would gravitate to universities where decision making is relatively more democratic than autocratic. Within any given university, similarly, it would be expected that such staff members would participate in university governance more intensively than their peers. Casual empiricism suggests this is so. More scientifically, in a survey of 166 universities and economics departments in the USA, McCormick and Meiners (1988) found formal empirical support for the first of these propositions. Autocratically run universities were more productive than more democratically run institutions. To be precise, allowing staff to control one additional decision (a 6.16 per cent rise) was associated with a 2.77 per cent fall in articles per staff member published in leading journals. At the level of intake quality, McCormick and Meiners examined the Scholastic Aptitude Test Scores (SATS) for all disciplines, not merely economics. A sample of 133 universities showed that those with less democratic governance structures attracted better students. Universities allowing staff control over one more decision appeared to attract first year entrants with a SATS score of 0.2 per cent lower on average.

Older, better universities, with more brand name capital (associated with publications, quality alumni and a quality current student body) can charge higher fees, offer higher salaries to attract more productive staff, have larger libraries, are more successful in inviting quality students to enroll, and have more 'appropriate' staff/student ratios, i.e. appropriate in enrollees' eyes. The question McCormick and Meiners leave unanswered is why some universities are more democratic than others. Alchian's view that governance will be sub-optimal is confirmed. But why are there variations in the level of sub-optimality? Fama (1980) provides a possible answer. The critique of McCormick and Meiners is directed at the *method* of governance, not the time spent thereon. Democratic governance involves voting, lobbying, committee meetings and minute circulation or reporting to non-committee members and constituencies. Autocratic governance does not incur these costs to the same extent but it still requires time. Fama's model of internal markets for managers in profit-seeking firms is analogous. Managers monitor those above, below and on a par with themselves on a continuous basis. Academics call this peer review. More peer review will take place if the governance structure does not destroy its marginal value. Thus if the democratic process is replaced by the autocratic, more time will be spent reading one another's papers, discussing the merits of hiring, firing and promoting colleagues, ruminating over curricula and having informal talks with superiors—all in small, non-transparent groups and without formal record-taking.

Interestingly, McCormick and Meiners discovered that there is a negative relationship between membership of the American Association of University Professors (AAUP) and staff productivity, irrespective of the governance style of the university. Furthermore, the AAUP is a strong lobby for democratic decision-making, and democratically governed universities tend to have larger AAUP memberships. As a corollary, universities with a high percentage of self-perpetuating boards of trustees (councils) are associated with less democratic decision-making.

A leading British university administrator[9] noted that 'universities neither want nor need a complicated administrative framework'. (And democracy is complex.) The impact on South African universities of attempts to transform council membership, to making proceedings more democratic, to involving all stakeholders, including the 'gardener' caucus, in decisions ranging from vice-chancellorian appointments to exclusions of individual, failing students can be judged more clearly in the light of this discussion.

The Market for Students

But what of the third element in this discussion of university economics: the market? What of Smith's concern for students? What about Alchian's concern over lack of full-cost tuition? The situation is exaggerated if customers (students) do not pay cost-related tuition fees reflecting also their demand for university education. If there are other sources of income (e.g. government subsidies) which are relatively routinely available, and whose availability is only very loosely linked—if at all—to institutional performance in satisfying market requirements, then it is even more rational for university decision-makers to devote resources to activities unrelated to the direct task of encouraging consumers to reveal their true wants, or, once revealed, to meet them.

Education demand is 'different' in several ways. The consumer—the student—is part of the production process. This severely limits the time available to exercise effective demand. For a student meaningfully to express discontent during the production/consumption process is very costly. The low-cost alternative to withdrawal and re-registration elsewhere is protest, whether linked or not to any other underlying cause of dissatisfaction. Furthermore, if the product is but little valued anyway, harming it by protest behaviour will also be perceived to impose little personal cost. Since the money-price charged for tuition is substantially below what the market-clearing money-price would have been, this results in many (and more) students having valuations of the product which, at the margin, are far below the full costs of tuition. Prior to registration producers must devise alternative rationing devices other than price (fees), such as school performance, age, selection committees' preferences and even government-imposed yardsticks of social engineering. (In the USA, the UK and South Africa race and social class are typical examples of such centrally-induced discrimination.) Resources are thus allocated in ways other than would be achieved by the impartial, impersonal price mechanism. Personal characteristics of applicants and the preferences of selectors come into play. And as Sir Alan Peacock[10] argued: '... the more the allocation rule ignores the preferences of consumers, the more animosity there will be between consumer and allocators'.

All of the consequences that arise when student valuations of the product exceed perceived costs are intensified when demand for university education is increasing. This can occur when secondary education becomes more widespread, when racial barriers to universities are removed, or demographically if a larger than normal birth cohort moves through the

144

system. In addition demand will rise if the proportion of the qualified population leaving secondary school rises, and/or if it is perceived that the opportunity cost of foregoing such education is increasing—whether in terms of foregone returns on human capital (graduate salaries) or in terms of a higher probability of unemployment. So where should we look for solutions?

6.4 Towards Proprietorial Academies

A common argument put forward as to why government and society should continue to bear all of the direct and indirect costs discussed above is that there are externalities in university education. Government subsidies of fees (and all of the attendant indirect costs of discontent) and regulatory control of the system are worth bearing because society benefits in the future from a university educated population. These benefits would not otherwise be forthcoming since no person would pay for such an education since he himself does not capture these genuine social benefits. The fallacy here is that most graduates do indeed capture most of the benefits of higher education in their own higher incomes after graduation. This then begs an equity question. Why should the tax-paying bus driver of today pay for educating tomorrow's lawyer? An argument can really only be made, not for subsidy to students, but for access to loans, assuming today's student cannot borrow either from parents or commercial lenders. This is a likely scenario only for indigent students pursuing very low-paying career paths.

How can access equity be maintained when the young have differing levels of current wealth stocks? How can consumer preferences be aligned with the limited allocation of enrolment places? Or to put it in the words of Natural Law, how do we maintain stability of possession, consensual transfer of title, in an environment where both benevolence and prudence are moderating factors? What property rights require stabilisation? How can they be consensually transferred? In the field of tertiary education, what policies are prudent and benevolent? The broad inference drawn so far is that there should be closer linkages between students as consumers, and universities as producers. The ideal would be to grasp the advantages of proprietary organisations with residual claims. That may be difficult to achieve in a short span of time, but steps towards that goal can be taken. In particular, a more meaningful cash nexus between consumers and producers can be established. It is clearly not oxymoronic to analyse universities as firms, operating in markets, and hence to view them from an economic perspective. In fact, it may be a necessary preliminary, a *pour parler se tirer d'affaire*, for resolving the problems.

Historically, after all, universities were not *de facto* government establishments. Today many are. Yet the situation is not universal. In the USA many of the best universities were and remain private establishments. In the UK the University of Buckingham is now two decades old (although it had to fight hard to overcome the objections of established universities to the grant of the statutory right to award degrees). In Taiwan more than half of the 320,000 students at degree-awarding institutions attend private universities. In Australia, the private Bond University in Queensland is now successfully established. In South Africa 500,000 students attend private colleges in the non-degree awarding sector. A substantial number of them are being coached for degrees offered by local or by foreign universities (state and private). Monash University operates commercially self-sufficient branch campuses in Johannesburg and in Singapore. In the very early 2000s the following universities, although barred by South African law from operating directly in the country, used locally based sub-contractors for the provision of tuition and classroom facilities: Heriot Watt, Newport, London, Southern Cross, Hertfordshire, Brunel, London City, Thames Valley, Wolverhampton, Strathclyde and de Montfort. Clearly, absent regulation, willing suppliers and demanders are available for the operation of a proprietorial tertiary sector.

To facilitate the growth of this market only two positive legal steps need be taken. Barriers inhibiting potential entrants from competing in the market should be removed. And, as a corollary, so too should any financial obstacles to students. Thus any tertiary educational establishment in a country should be permitted to award degrees—this would help meet the revealed demand for more educational outlets whilst channelling it towards legal domestic institutions, reducing the inefficiencies and foreign exchange costs as producers and consumers strive to get around existing cartel-protecting laws. There is no danger that this would dilute the value of existing degrees. A degree from a 'good', well-known institution would still be universally acknowledged as being superior to one offered by the University College of Advanced Technology and Liberal Arts in Hicksville. As always, brand names economise on information costs. And nothing destroys a brand name more quickly than a poor quality product. The incentive for producers is to preserve the (intangible) capital asset of a good reputation.

The second recommendation is more contentious but has considerable support in the literature. It runs as follows: to the extent that commercial providers of loans fail to meet demand from financially poor but academically qualified applicants, government should provide or guarantee financing of full-cost fees. All poor students who wish to pursue post-secondary education would then be eligible for a full-cost covering loan to spend at the institution of their choice. The loan would be repayable through the tax authorities, who are, after all, specialist, low-cost collectors of moneys. This would minimise default and facilitate making repayments on an income-contingency basis. The loan would carry a real and compound rate of interest from date of graduation. If it did not, there would otherwise be strong incentives to prolong study and inequities would arise. (For example a school teacher on a modest salary would have to begin repaying immediately, while a law graduate doing articles would, on an even lower salary, perhaps repay nothing for several years, continuing to borrow interest-free at government expense, before ultimately repaying from a very much higher salary than the school teacher.) Loans would be renewable only on the basis of approved performance. The loan amount would depend only on the borrower's preferences, with ceilings linked to where the student was studying (i.e. to the fees set by the university of his choice). The loan scheme would be self-financing, with an interest rate high enough to meet administration costs, defaults, academic failure, or later, unanticipated, income-lowering events during employment necessitating deferral or non-payment.

With these conditions it is hard to understand why government intervention would be required in the first place. Private financing of university students might well occur sufficient to meet all the demands of all students willing and able to study at academies willing and able to provide places. Commercial organisations want to make loans. They want to continue financial relationships with their clients long after graduation. And academies also exert pressure on lenders to lend since they want to ensure that their students receive adequate financing for their studies. Furthermore, so do employers. For study areas in demand by employers, but in supply-short areas by student numbers, employers are often providers of study funding. In fact, the current financial background of the student, poor or rich, will be of little interest to such lenders. So why do writers in this area suggest that government be involved, either as a provider or as a guarantor of student loans?

Adverse Selection—Again

E.G. West (1994, p. 23) identified one 'market failure' in particular: the adverse selection problem. He rightly dismissed it as unimportant. But why do critics advance this as a serious counter-argument to the concept of study financing-by-loan? West explains that since any loan scheme is a form of insurance pool there is the theoretical possibility that only bad risks will borrow. Likely re-payers will self-select out of any commercially sound government-backed scheme. They will reason that their interest repayments are too high. They have to cover the interest and capital repayments of those who default (i.e. of the unsuccessful student, of those with unfortunate post-education life-events, and of the dishonest). Certainly interest rates must be high enough to make any scheme self-financing, and also high enough to meet the real borrowing rate faced by the lender, whether state or private. Nevertheless, if good-risks do self-select out of the scheme, interest rates would have to rise to cover the costs of the remaining, higher, average levels of default. The next best group of 'risks' would then also leave the pool, and interest rates would have to rise again, and so on until the scheme collapsed. But recall our earlier discussion on health insurance in chapter 5. Adverse selection only exists as a problem because of information asymmetry when the insurer (or lender) does not know who the bad or good risks are. He sets an average (premium) rate of interest to account for defaults, which does not represent good value for the 'good risk' borrowers. The cycle then commences as described. But in the case of student borrowers unobservable risk is not linked to either current poverty, or potential income after graduation. The first of these factors is observable to a lender, and the second depends partly on subject matter studied and associated with career choice, which can be predicted with as much accuracy by the lender as by the borrower. Nor is unobservable risk linked to gender, or age, or academic credentials on entry to university, or to curriculum choice, or to institution of study. All of these are observable variables, and if significant can be factored in to the interest rate charged. There is no information asymmetry and thus there is no adverse selection problem. It is doubtful, therefore, that student financing of the type described above necessarily requires state provision. The private sector could perfectly well meet the demands. It is not hobbled by the transaction cost of adverse selection.

Given these two provisos, easy consumer and provider entry into the marketplace for tertiary education, state university cartels and many of their undesirable side effects would be dramatically weakened. The long-term requirement for a continuing subsidy to existing universities would fall away. Recommendations aimed at keeping such cartels intact would become redundant. The costs of attempting to monitor and maintain cartel discipline would wither away. To illustrate such monitoring costs, take, for example, the recommendation aimed at homogeneity of admission criteria by the CUP (1995, pp. 39-40). In its attempt further to minimize product differentiation in state universities, it suggested replacing the then existing criteria of school performance, mature age and Senate discretion by 'a nationally accepted system of determining learning potential'. The temptation to compete on price (fee) terms would then be minimised by raising the costs of each institution since 'each university [would have to] grant access to a significant number of under-prepared students and give them the necessary support'. This was to be coupled, as we saw, with uniform subsidies for all universities. Yet there is an inevitable tension. Imposing cartel rules on a heterogeneous group of suppliers combined 'as if' they were a monolithic unit is inevitably fraught.[11] Some will probably try to break ranks. Allowing new entrants increases that likelihood.

The tertiary system would then evolve in a heterogeneous fashion responding to student demand, nudged here and there by private sector employers encouraging enrolment for particular professions or for particular types of training, or, for that matter, for particular types of student. Colleges or institutions with a comparative advantage in bringing the under-prepared school-leaver up-to-speed for degree courses would emerge. The inefficiencies which currently exist on some conventional campuses as university administrators impose directives on staff to engage in academic support for which they are unfit by training or predisposition would no longer be incurred. Institutions would have to compete ever more intensively for funds, for students and for academics. Staff rewards, management patterns and staff usage would become more flexible. And the paradox of the simultaneous clamour by many academics for the right to free speech but irritation if the now dominant funder (government) threatens to reduce support when they express 'undesirable' views would be resolved. He who pays the piper usually wishes to call the tune; a plurality of funding sources is the only way to avoid the threat of resource flows being curtailed if the university teacher broadcasts opinions not universally acceptable. Those who wish to pursue or to offer a liberal education (for purely personal enjoyment with 'no end in view') will continue to be able to do so; indeed it will be a choice open to all without financial barriers. And students will be better taught, whether in liberal or in professional fields. The incentives of instructor and pupil will be aligned. As Smith put it (*WN*, p. 764), education outside of government-funded institutions is 'generally the best taught. When a young man goes to a fencing or a dancing school, he does not always learn to fence or to dance very well but he seldom fails of learning to fence or to dance'.

What of resources and teaching in low-demand subject areas? Might such disciplines not wither through lack of resource support? There are two reasons why not. One is that outside funders may well subsidise such areas for philanthropic reasons because they offer external benefits to society. (Although, as noted, such externalities are not as great as is sometimes thought.) The corollary to external benefits is the presence of economies of scope (a jargon term implying lower costs or greater effectiveness throughout the institution, that is, internal benefits existing *because* the university provides a broad diversity of subject or disciplinary offerings). Good universities, with high research outputs, attracting high quality students, are good because they successfully exploit these economies. It is cheaper to produce some goods jointly rather than separately. A small enrolment music department, for example, by its very existence, can attract students to enrol at an institution in unrelated courses because of the potential for them to benefit from its output other than in their formal curricula. Leading research universities encourage interaction between scholars of different disciplines, and between student and teacher. Only by doing so, they find, can they maintain their teaching quality and their total research output. Their fees, their attractiveness to students, to staff and to outside providers of funds will reflect this. No one paradigm can cover the optimal blend, but movement away from state dominance provides opportunities for pluralistic response. The result will be a coordinated, higher education system, appropriately diversified. The co-ordinating mechanism would be the market place. What is meant by 'appropriate diversification' would be similarly determined; that is, by the scholars and their students. Comtian solidarity-by-compulsion would be replaced by an appropriate level of subsidiarity.

7

Concluding Thoughts

[Political problems] can be properly solved only by a recasting of society on an organic or pluralist basis...a regime no longer based on the self-propagating power of money...but on the human value and aim of work where the class struggle introduced by capitalist economy will have been surmounted along with this economy itself...

Jacques Maritain, 1943*

Natural Law: *in classical economics the embodiment of the belief that the natural order of economic matters is inherently simple, harmonious and beneficient. A free market, relieved of all monopolistic restraint, was conceived in the long run to serve the interests of all alike and therefore the greatest good of the greatest number. By what Adam Smith called the 'simple principle of natural liberty' the operations of the market were thought to produce prices as low as was consistent with maintaining the flow of goods and services yet yielding enough return for the effort expended to ensure their continued production.*

Everyman's Dictionary of Economics, 1975†

Economists have a predisposition to assume that a rising national income is an end in itself. Certainly there are benefits from economic growth, but we should be aware how limited these are. Smith (*WN*, p. 99) made the case for economic growth as follows:

> ... it is in the progressive state, while the society is advancing to the further acquisition, rather than when it has acquired its full complement of riches, that the condition of... the great body of the people, seems to be the happiest and most comfortable. It is hard in the stationary, and miserable in the declining state. The progressive state is in reality the cheerful and the hearty state to all the different orders of the society. The stationary is dull; the declining, melancholy.

---

*   Maritain, J., *The Rights of Man and Natural Law*, New York: Charles Scribner, New York. 1943. p. 90.

†   Seldon, A. and Pennance, F.G., *Everyman's Dictionary of Economics*, London: J.M. Dent, 1975.

People tend to measure their well-being against either their peers or their immediate family, its history and its prospects. In a situation of growth people realise they are better off than they or their parents have been, and that their children in turn will do still better. There is more room for contentment and less for jealousy when all see their conditions improve. Aspirations tend to be satisfied and continuous improvement diminishes the desire to be ahead of one's fellows. Further, most people are risk averse, so upward improvements in wealth, although welcome, provide a degree of contentment less than would be the dismay generated by an equivalent fall in material welfare. So economic downturns are not desirable. In short, there is a strong material and psychic case for growth as brought about by a continuous rise in the volume and value of mutually beneficial exchanges of private property. But this argument also has limits. Smith wrote (*WN*, p. 190) that:

> With the greater part of rich people, the chief enjoyment of riches consists in the parade of riches, which in their eyes is never so compleat as when they appear to possess these decisive marks of opulence which nobody can possess but themselves.

Competitive materialism can produce desires that, *ipso facto*, cannot be gratified. If economic growth results in increasing numbers of people demanding goods that by their very nature are scarce, then people will not feel better off. They will be dissatisfied and frustrated. They will have the money to buy, but not the opportunity to purchase and acquire. Hirsch (1976) termed such goods 'positional'. The richer we become the more likely it is that the material goods we seek will prove unobtainable. The concept of positional goods is simply an extreme reminder that self-actualisation requires more than material possessions and increasing wealth. Only an appropriate stock of spiritual capital, held by each at the individual level, not economic growth, can quench the thirst generated by otherwise insatiable demands. This is a lesson that is well known, even if it is not always fully understood (*vide* Christ's words to the woman at the well in Jn. 4:13).

In our own quest better to understand this we have examined how the Natural Law has evolved from pre-Christian Greece to the present. The key question raised was how man with both intellect and free will should live. Aquinas answered that we ought to conform to the Natural Law of the Creator, in whose image we are made. Jacques Maritain, the French Catholic philosopher, claimed that Natural Law expresses both what is natural in the world, and what, by all, is known naturally. Moreover, fully

152

to appreciate and understand this natural reality requires us to draw upon our reason and from all human disciplines from the sciences to poetry and mysticism. This essay has not been so ambitious. We have asked rather what the discipline of purposeful human action, economics and exchange, has to tell us as we attempt to conform to the Law of God? Even this limitation has problems. In chapter 2, we saw how Rommen and Piedra (Catholics) and Rushdoony (a Protestant) blamed Grotius as the initiator of a process that, in their eyes, resulted in the rejection of Natural Law. They viewed the thinking that developed post-Grotius as replacing God. The second epigraph to this chapter, a dictionary entry, certainly does provide support for this concern. The Creator is nowhere mentioned.

However, in our discussions on economics and its development alongside Natural Law we did not adopt that interpretation. Instead, we showed how an understanding of Natural Law had evolved continually from Aristotle's understanding of private property, to Grotius' ident-ification of the *suum*, 'one's own', to Locke's trinity of 'Life, Liberty and Estates', and to Pufendorf's explanation of occasions when commonly held property and publicly provided goods were natural and appropriate. From there we saw how Francis Hutcheson described the Moral Sense, and its integration with benevolence, self-love and the right to contract with others, as evidence of the essence of Natural Law and its Creator. Smith developed this theme. The desire to engage in mutually beneficial, voluntary exchange of private property is an innate propensity of man. And the associated contractual rules and expectations relating to promise and justice have become a normal part of modern commerce. Hume regarded these rules as belonging to the Laws of Nature. They are not the products of human design. They are the empirically discovered best, and natural, practices that emerge from human action.

A related and more overt tension derived from the virulently anti-Christian writings of economists such as Mises and Knight. They would have been, if not in full agreement, certainly sympathetic to the social and economic ideas of the Scottish Enlightenment. But their anti-Christian views were difficult to pin down. Clearly they were not believers. But that is an issue of grace and a matter of faith. More specifically they were both champions of economic and of political freedom. But these objectives are not incompatible with Christianity. Leaders of the religion, however, have shifted their emphases over time. That has provided opportunities for critics such as Mises and Knight to argue (wrongly) that Christianity is antagonistic towards personal and economic freedoms. One such shift with far reaching effects was what Fogel, the economic historian, termed the 'Third Great Awakening'. From this emerged the development of the Social Gospel and the political outcome of an increasing role for the State. Knight and Mises deplored expansion of the state's role on both moral and pragmatic grounds. They believed personal freedom was thus curtailed, and man's material welfare damaged.

Mises, Maritain and Market Socialism.

Mises believed socialist policies resulted in a decline both of material welfare and individual liberty. He was correct in general terms. On one specific issue, however, he erred. In *Socialism* (p.184) he argued that the joint stock corporation (the legal form of most modern businesses) was an artificially created, privileged legal entity. As a consequence it could readily be co-opted to carry out the wishes of those who had granted it its alleged privilege: *viz.* the state. Further, because the managers of large corporations are often not the owners, it would be easy for government to push any active opposition to one side. Mises's fellow Austrian, Joseph Schumpeter (1950, pp. 141-42), agreed. He too criticised the legally sanctioned division of labour between risk-bearing capitalists and business administrators for having pushed 'into the background all... the institutions of property and free contracting... that expressed the needs of economic activity'. Historians (e.g. Hessen, 1987) have now shown to the contrary: that the joint stock company with limited liability is a creature of private agreement, not a creature of the state. It is a freely negotiated example of contractual specialisation and is a device for greater efficiency in meeting private wants. To Schumpeter the modern firm was rather a shirking of responsibility, complete with 'absentee ownership' (p. 142) which because nobody was 'left... to stand for it' would evolve into a state-controlled bureaucracy.

Are joint stock corporations, commonly regarded as pillars of capitalism, actually the precursors of syndicalism? 'The transition from the managerial system of mature capitalism to the managerial system of the planned socialist commonwealth [can] be smoothly effected' (*HA*, p. 707). Mises and Schumpeter, of course, had both been affected by their closeness to Germany before they emigrated to America. Schumpeter worked in Bonn prior to Harvard. In Germany the corporation was somewhat different from the product of free contracting that had emerged in the British and American economies. Lal (2005, pp. 66-67) explains some of the contrasting features. First, German corporations were actively encouraged (as opposed to passively permitted) to grow and dominate in their home markets. Bismarck, in the 1870s, erected protective trade barriers to shelter agriculture and encouraged domestic industries, not least iron and steel. The National Liberals broke from Bismarck on these issues, but they were based on the longstanding German intellectual influence of Frederic List. List was a keen proponent of the German economic unity that began with the *Zollverein* or customs union of 1834 and culminated in Bismarck's Germany of 1871. List had little time for the 'natural liberty' of the Scottish Enlightenment, its 'individual economy'. Satisfying individual wants, he argued, would not secure the comforts or necessities of life for all. For List, the basic economic unit was not the individual; it was the nation. Accordingly he proposed treaties strictly to regulate international trade, in order to in turn protect the development of key 'infant' and indigenous industries.

A second difference in the nature of the corporation in Germany was the two-level system of corporate control. The 1870 law *allowing* free incorporation *imposed* on firms the obligation to have a management board responsible for day-to-day decisions, but also a supervisory board consisting of various stakeholders. Other than owners, these included interest groups such as banks, cartel members, local politicians and trade unions. Into this syndicalist atmosphere, in the late 1880s, Bismarck introduced the *obligation* that firms be socially responsible by providing social insurance to employees and providing a formal voice to workers on company boards, 'co-determination'. Much of Bismarckian corporatism was recreated in the so-called 'social market' economy opted for by Germany in the years after 1945. As Lal (p. 67) expressed it, 'old habits die hard'.

With these differences in mind, Mises' and Schumpeter's concerns are more understandable. Their worries relate to state ownership of capital, or to the more insidious breaches of consensual contracting that occur when 'stakeholders' other than shareholders intrude on decisions relating to the allocation of financial capital.[1] Mises (p. 707) claimed it was then easy for neo-socialists to argue that:

> ... there is a better pattern of socialism [than abolition of market exchanges] available. It is possible to instruct the managers of the various production units to conduct the affairs of their unit in the same way as they did under capitalism... with the same care and attention. The only difference will [be] the fact that the fruits of their endeavours will enrich the whole society, not the shareholders. For the rest they will buy and sell, recruit and pay workers, and try to make profits in the same way they did before. Nothing will change except

the ownership of the capital. Society will be substituted for the shareholders, the people will henceforth pocket the dividend. That is all.

The persuasive aspect of this viewpoint is its apparent comprehensibility. It assumes away the problems of information and incentives that the market signals of prices and profits tend to resolve. It exemplifies the approach of the inventory clerk, not that of the economist. The inventory clerk (more grandly—the 'social planner', the 'man of system') looks at the current consumption of goods and services in an economy. He compares it with current capacity and concludes that if capacity exceeds consumption or *vice versa*, for any given industry or firm, there is a surplus or shortage. In accordance with his policy preference he then advocates measures to maintain or remove the presumed overcapacity or shortage. The economist does not prejudge the market in this way. He does not presume to know, beforehand, whether a corporation has over- or undercapacity. He does not presume to know, before the event, whether a standardised product or a heterogeneous range of goods would be the consumers' favourite and the most profitable for producers. Nor does he presume to know, in advance, the most efficient form of corporate, administrative or industrial organisational structures for manufacturing some products. By contrast, the inventory clerk and the politician who listens to him believe they do know. And they will take decisions that do not reflect consumer preferences or producer insights.

Governments are frequently tempted, as Mises feared, to engage in 'industrial policy', which usually means nothing more-nor-less than a deliberate attempt at piecemeal socialisation. Such policy aims at intervening in normal market evolution. It involves government intervention in business practices. It can vary widely: from tariff protection to export subsidies; from decentralisation strategies to 'kick-starts'; from encouragement of 'strategic' industries to protection of 'national champions'; and from price controls to outright nationalisation. Smith warned strongly against it (1776, p. 456):

What is the species of domestick industry which his capital can employ, and of which the produce is likely to be of the greatest value, every individual, it is evident, can, in his local situation judge much better than any statesman or lawgiver can do for him. The statesman, who should attempt to direct private people in what manner they ought to employ their capitals, would not only load himself with a most unnecessary attention, but assume an authority which could be safely trusted, not only to no one single person, but to no council or senate whatever, and which would nowhere be so dangerous as in the hands of a man who had folly and presumption enough to fancy himself fit to exercise it.

156

There are other reasons why Mises was concerned that a 'better pattern of socialism'—the control, direct or indirect, of the managers of joint stock corporations by government rather than by capitalists—was undesirable. Politicians and bureaucrats, no less than anyone else, pursue their own self-interest. They do so in an institutional environment that makes it all too likely that their efforts will be at the expense of the public. The role of *information* has already been mentioned. The price mechanism provides private financiers with the information about shortages and surpluses they need for their decisions. They also have an *incentive* to use this information that government officials do not have. The latter have no property rights in the gains created from a profitable trade. Nor do they suffer directly the losses from error in misdirecting the flows of capital or labour. They will not be alert to the best opportunities and will be less likely to exercise caution in the face of unpromising opportunities. This is quite apart from the phenomenon of *rent seeking:* the use of government power by interest groups and individuals to obtain special privileges for themselves.

Jacques Maritain, the French Catholic philosopher, contributed— somewhat unhelpfully—to this debate on the role of the corporation in the economy. His book *The Rights of Man and Natural Law* was reviewed by Frank Knight (*FR*, pp. 312-57). Maritain rightly, in Knight's view, condemned socialism, communism and totalitarianism in economic and political matters. He argued (cited in *FR*, pp. 338-39) that the concept of the 'planned economy' should be replaced with the idea of the 'adjusted economy'. 'Collectivisation', in turn, should be modified to 'associative ownership of the means of production'. Knight says (p. 339) these phrases suggest 'radical economic reorganisation'. Yet they are so vague 'it seems impossible to make out what [Maritain] has in mind'. Maritain goes on to insist that the temptations of 'corporatism' and of 'state corporatism' should be avoided. Knight did not pass specific comment on this. Yet he would certainly have agreed. State corporatism, after all, is simply the Italian fascist idea of the 1930s. That is, the so-called social partners of big business, labour unions and government come together to hammer out an 'industrial policy'. However, although Maritain condemns this, he emphasises that the 'corporatism' he condemns is very different from the idea of 'corporation' presented by Pius XI in the encyclical *Quadragesimo anno*. Knight was clearly not convinced of Maritain's absolution of the encyclical from the temptations of state corporatism. (Nor, as we saw in chapter 3, was Mises.) Knight complained that nowhere did Maritain explain why the two were distinct. A clue to Knight's scepticism of

Maritain's economic credentials is provided when he quotes Maritain (*FR*, p. 339): 'a just wage... is not a piece of merchandise subject to the mere law of supply and demand'. Again, in chapter 3 we saw how and why Mises strongly disagreed with those who advocated the 'just price and just wage' concepts. Knight (p. 340) was equally frustrated and wrote:

> It is probably useless to point out [to Maritain] that 'supply and demand' is the only possible way of apportioning men and other productive agents to their tasks, between different enterprises or within any enterprise, in such a way as to produce what consumers want or to produce anything effectively.

Government direction of industry, attenuation of property rights and price and wage regulations were for Knight (and Mises) socialist, even fascist ideas that were joined at the hip.

They were right. But the energies they used in attacking Christianity were misdirected. Similarly, the criticisms levelled by Rommen and others at the Scottish economists should have had more appropriate targets. Benevolence and concern for one's fellow man were always key components of Christianity. The Scots regarded them as essential parts of the Law of Nature. In the decades after the Scottish Enlightenment a productive balance between social cohesion, solidarity and subsidiarity was observed and displayed, not least by Christian groups. But this was not the case with the writers of French Enlightenment. To them the Natural Law was seen as merely the product of human reason and the General Will. By the time of Comte the notion of solidarity-by-compulsion had apparently resolved any tension between social cohesion and subsidiarity. Thereafter, particularly at times of economic stagnation, the practical impact of the French Enlightenment (together with the political fall-out of the Social Gospel movement) was seen in the shift from co-operatively and privately funded health and welfare insurance, towards the tax funded, social security state.

But as time went by it became apparent that solidarity-by-compulsion had not resolved the social cohesion/subsidiarity tension. Lower level institutions such as trade unions, friendly societies, cooperatives, families and other groupings have seen a diminution in their importance as either funders or providers (or both) of the various forms of insurance and care required in times of need. Paradoxically, individualism at the lowest level has been permitted to flourish as never before. A subsidiarity in behavioural lifestyle choice has become possible and prevalent. What has emerged may be perverse and contrary to Natural Law. But its prevalence should not surprise. It is a fundamental law of economics that if something falls in price, more of it will be consumed. This applies to any good, including what many would consider 'bads'. For example, ill-health, unemployment, fatherless families, hedonism, irresponsible individualism, selfishness and reported physical disabilities are all phenomena that become cheaper to consume when they, or the behaviour that leads to them, were collectively funded, universally available on request, and free of charge at the point of consumption. The corollary is that the alternatives become relatively more expensive. Hence less of them, the alternatives, will be consumed. The outcome is increased inequality between people in their holdings of spiritual assets such as the ethic of benevolence, a sense of discipline, of self-esteem, of a work ethic, and of a vision of opportunity to achieve better things. People often then lose meaning in their lives, feel socially estranged and hopeless.

It is not surprising then that theologians and economists are concerned about the negative impact of the welfare state on subsidiarity properly understood. To the concerned, it then becomes imperative somehow to equalise the stocks people hold of spiritual capital. Christianity and the Natural Law have vital roles to play in this egalitarian process.

It was suggested that, perhaps for the first time, economic growth has provided us with the means to achieve a more equal distribution of spiritual capital in society. Fogel, studying economic and social trends over America's last century, identified the possession of discretionary time as a principal achievement realised by economic advance. More time enables each of the better endowed to share spiritual capital with the less fortunate. This sharing is unlike financial giving. That is largely a zero sum game (what one gives equals what the recipient gets). Sharing spiritual capital is a positive sum activity, more akin to trade. Both parties feel better off. Further, helping another to expand his stock of spiritual capital does not diminish the stock of the donor. Spiritual capital is non-rival. Like a Pufendorf-style public good, the stock available does not diminish on consumption or on transfer. Economic growth has provided us with the time in which sharing of spiritual capital can occur.

The motive for sharing, however, has nothing to do with economic growth. It is, as it always has been, provided by caritas. Christian love in action, which is both benevolent and prudent, which is enhanced by closeness and tempered by distance (to paraphrase Smith), which is prompted by emotion, deepened by concern, shared at a cost—even if only that of time, and confined within the framework of Natural Law, is, for the believer, the only way to optimise his lifestyle. But we commented earlier that not all transferees will want to 'get and use' freely offered spiritual assets. The Prodigal Son took a long time to return to his senses. Caritas implies not only concern and empathy, but also persistence in the exercise of concern. Persistence, of course, may not be enough. Persuasion may also be required, but given free choice, Original Sin if you like, many will still fail to perceive the benefits to be gained by switching out of a lifestyle of self-centred hedonism. If persistence and persuasion prove to be inadequate, then another tactic is pre-emption.

Consider again economic growth. Economic growth always involves change. And change disrupts and hurts. Empathy for others implies concern for the hurt. For example, even if two groups of people are both better off at a macro level because of consensual trades there may be some *sub-groups* who are worse off, at least temporarily. To illustrate, take the following oversimplification. The rise of China in international trade has provided foreign producers in some industries with significant additional demand. Foreign consumers have benefited similarly from a significant and hence price-lowering increase in total world output of some goods. But there are four sub-groups of 'losers'. At least for a period of transition, some foreign manufacturers, workers and capitalists, will see a reduction in demand for their output as consumers switch to Chinese products. And some Chinese producers will be similarly displaced by importation into China of foreign goods. Conversely some consumers in each of the two trading groups will also be superficially and temporarily worse off. There are those who must now pay a higher price than before because of the reduction in supply caused by a diversion of goods from home to export sale. This illustration, with its 'losers', even if we refined it for all the additional complexities of reality, does not lessen the truth that enormous net benefits arise from truck, barter and exchange. The issue for the concerned is how to lessen the costs of the frictions of change for the individuals who have been forced to bear them.

The answer is to pre-empt suffering by being alert to individual hurt arising from change. Caritas demands pre-emption and alertness to need. Spiritual capital can then be shared, frictions reduced and hurt alleviated. On the other hand, it is harmful and misguided to presume superior wisdom and to try to eliminate the frictions by halting the process of consensual exchange. And this remark, as we now know, can be generalised. In earlier chapters we looked in some detail at each of welfare, healthcare and education. In each case there were apparently good reasons why private provision through the market was inappropriate. The market allegedly 'failed' in these areas, or transactions costs were so high that an

160

optimal volume and value of consensual exchange contracts would not take place. In each case the objections were shown to be invalid, or to have, on closer inspection, little or no support from economic reasoning. Moreover, particularly in healthcare and education, subsidiarity is almost discounted when the state is provider. An appropriate level of subsidiarity is withdrawn from individuals, families, and other organisations in order to compel an inappropriate kind of solidarity at state level. Innovation, diversity, freedom and choice are thus diminished. And society's stock of spiritual capital shrinks.

Frank Knight, that outspoken atheist, summarised as follows:

> If more religious faith can create a greater degree of serenity and confidence, without sapping the springs of action, that is a consummation devoutly to be wished, both on its own account and as a condition favourable to effective action itself... *It is imperative to understand the relation between morality and intelligence, and the provision of adequate means...* 'True religion', we submit, is a matter of the right emotional attitude toward the problem as a whole, and an energising faith that study and rationally directed effort will lead to its solution.

> (*FR*, p. 216. Original emphasis.)

If the above pages prompt more 'study and rationally directed effort' by the theologically minded towards a better understanding of market economics then they will have achieved part of their purpose. Similarly, their objective will be served if economist readers are prompted to adopt 'the right emotional attitude' to discovering the proper balance between solidarity and subsidiarity. Diversity of individual choice, innovation and social cohesion can only be achieved in the market place, subject to Natural Law, and not the law of party. Conversely, contrary to the libertarian ethic and to the views of some tough-minded free-marketeers, only caritas coupled with a satisfactory redistribution of spiritual capital can complete and fulfil the Natural Law.

Bibliography

Acton, Lord, 1985, Essays in the History of Liberty, Vol. I in J. Rufus Fears (ed.), *Selected Writings of Lord Acton*, Liberty Classics, Indianapolis, Ind.

Alchian, A., 1977, *Economic Forces at Work,* Liberty Press, Indianapolis, Ind.

Aristotle, 1925, *The Nicomachean Ethics of Aristotle,* Sir David Ross (ed.), Oxford University Press, World Classics Edition, 1954.

_____, 1959, *Politics,* John Warrington (ed.), J.M. Dent & Sons, London.

Baird, C.W., 1988, 'The varieties of right to work: An essay in honour of W. H. Hutt', *Managerial and Decision Economics.*

Baumol, W.J., 1995, *Healthcare as a Handicraft Industry,* Office of Health Economics, London.

Beveridge Report, 1942, *Report on Social Insurance and Allied Services,* HMSO, London.

Beveridge, William, 1948, *Voluntary Action,* Allen and Unwin, London.

Bonner, S.F., 1977, *Education in Ancient Rome,* Methuen, London.

Buckle, Stephen, 1991, *Natural Law and the Theory of Property, Grotius to Hume,* Clarendon Press, Oxford.

Bullock, A., 1991, *Hitler and Stalin, Parallel Lives,* Harper-Collins, London.

Burke, Edmund, (1790), *Reflections on the Revolution in France,* reprinted as Vol. 2 of *Select Works of Edmund Burke,* (1999), Liberty Fund, Indianoplis, Ind.

Burtt, Edwin A., 1939, *The English Philosophers from Bacon to Mill,* The Modern Library, Random House, New York, NY.

Coase, R.H., 1937, 'The Nature of the Firm', *Economica.*

_____, 1976, 'Adam Smith's View of Man', *Journal of Law and Economics.*

Committee of University Principals (CUP), 1995, Submission to the National Commission on Higher Education, Pretoria.

Draper, J.W., 1876, *A History of the Intellectual Development of Europe,* Harper and Brothers, New York.

Enthoven, A., 1988, *Theory and Practice of Managed Competition in Healthcare Finance,* Elsevier Science, New York.

Epstein, R., 1997, *Mortal Peril*, Addison Wesley, Reading, Ma.

Fama, E., 1980, 'Agency Problems and the Theory of the Firm', *Journal of Political Economy*.

Ferguson, Adam, (1767), *An Essay on the History of Civil Society*, reprinted 1995, Cambridge University Press, Cambridge.

Fogel, Robert W., 2000, *The Fourth Great Awakening & The Future of Egalitarianism*, University of Chicago Press, Chicago, Ill.

Frech, H., 1996, *Competition and Monopoly in Medical Care*, American Enterprise Institute, Washington.

Friedman, Benjamin M., 2005, *The Moral Consequences of Economic Growth*, Alfred A. Knopf, New York, NY.

Friedman, David, 1987, 'Just Price' in Eatwell, Milgrave and Newman (eds), *The New Palgrave: A Dictionary of Economics*, Macmillan, London.

Gray, N., 1979, 'John Stuart Mill: Traditional and Revisionist Interpretations', *Literature of Liberty*, II. No. 2, 7-37.

Green, David G., 1993, *Reinventing Civil Society: The Rediscovery of Welfare Without Politics*, Choice in Welfare Series No. 17, Institute of Economic Affairs, London.

_____, 1993b, 'The Voluntary Reconstruction of Civil Society in Post-Communist Countries', *Journal des Economistes et des Etudes Humaines*, Vol. IV, 675-703.

Griffiths, Brian, 1982, *Morality and the Market Place*, London, Hodder and Stoughton.

Hayek, Friedrich A., 1944, *The Road to Serfdom*, Unversity of Chicago Press, Chicago, Ill.

_____, 1960, *The Constitution of Liberty*, Routledge and Kegan Paul, London.

_____, 1967, *Studies in Philosophy, Politics and Economic*, Routledge and Kegan Paul, London.

_____, 1973, *Law, Legislation and Liberty*, Vol. I, Routledge and Kegan Paul, London.

_____, 1978, 'Competition as a Discovery Procedure' in *New Studies in Philosophy, Politics, Economics and the History of Ideas*, University of Chicago Press, Chicago, Ill.

_____, 1988, *The Fatal Conceit: The Errors of Socialism*, Routledge, London.

Henderson, D., 2001, *Misguided Virtue: False Notions of Corporate Social Responsibility*, Institute of Economic Affairs, London.

Hessen, R., 1987, 'Corporations' in *The New Palgrave: A Dictionary of Economics*, Macmillan, London.

Himmelfarb, Gertrude, 1985, *The Idea of Poverty: England in the Early Industrial Age*, Vintage Books, Random House, New York.

_____, 1990, *On Liberty and Liberalism, The Case of John Stuart Mill* (First published in 1974 by Alfred A. Knopf), Institute for Contemporary Studies, San Francisco, Ca.

_____, 2004, *The Roads to Modernity: The British, French and European Enlightenments*, Alfred A. Knopf, New York, NY.

Hirsch, F., 1976, *The Social Limits to Growth*, Harvard University Press. Cambridge, Ma.

Hume, David, 1985, *Essays: Moral, Political and Literary* (ed. Eugene F. Miller, first published in 1741, with additions to later collections up to, and posthumously beyond, the author's death in 1776), Liberty Classics. Indianapolis, Ind.

_____, 1911, *A Treatise of Human Nature*, Vols. 1 and 2 (first published in 1739 and 1740), J.M. Dent, London.

_____, 1962, *Enquiries Concerning the Human Understanding and Concerning the Principles of Morals* (ed. L.A. Selby-Bigge), first published in 1777), Clarendon Press, Oxford, UK.

Hutcheson, Francis, 2004, *An Inquiry into the Original of Our Ideas of Beauty and Virtue* (first published 1725), Liberty Fund, Indianapolis, Ind.

_____, 2002, *An Essay on the Nature and Conduct of the Passions and Affections, with Illustrations on the Moral Sense* (first published 1728), Liberty Fund, Indianapolis, Ind.

Hutt, W.H., 1936, *Economists and the Public*, Jonathan Cape, London.

Johnson, H.G., 1968, 'The Economics of Student Protest', *New Society* (November).

Kirzner, Israel, 1979, *Perception, Opportunity and Profit*, University of Chicago, Chicago, Ill.

_____, 1982, 'Uncertainty, Discovery and Human Action' in Israel Kirzner (ed.), *Method, Process and Austrian Economics: Essays in honor of Ludwig von Mises*, D.C. Heath, Lexington, Mass.

_____, 1985, *Discovery and the Capitalist Process*, University of Chicago Press, Chicago, Ill.

Knight, Frank H., 1935, *The Ethics of Competition*, University of Chicago Press, Chicago, Ill.

_____, 1982, *Freedom and Reform*, Liberty Press, Indianapolis, Ind.

Lal, Deepak, 2005, *Trade and Industrial Policy: Classical Liberalism and the New Dirigisme*, Chambers of Commerce and Industry South Africa, Johannesburg.

Leube, Kurt R., 2003, *On Some Unintended Consequences of the Welfare State*, Occasional Paper 14, Free Market Foundation, Johannesburg.

Lewis, C.S., 1963, *The Four Loves*, Fontana, Glasgow.

Lindsay, C.M., 1980, *National Health Issues: The British Experience*, Roche, Nutley, NJ.

Locke, John, 1953, *Two Treatises of Government* (first published 1690), 2nd edn, A.C. Fraser (ed.), Dover, New York.

Maine, Sir Henry Sumner, 1986, *Ancient Law* (first published 1861), Dorset Press, United States of America.

Mamdani, M., 1994, 'A Reflection on Higher Education in Equatorial Africa: Some Lessons for South Africa', a paper presented to the Conference of the CUP: The Future Role of Universities in the South African Tertiary Education System.

Marris, R., 1964, *The Economics of Managerial Capitalism*, Macmillan, London.

McCormick, R.E. and Meiners, R.E., 1988, 'University Governance: A Property Rights Perspective', *Journal of Law and Economics*, 31:2.

McInery, R., 1993, *Aquinas Against the Averroists: On There Being Only One Intellect*, Purdue University Press.

Mill, John Stuart, 1947, *On Liberty* (first published 1859), AHM Publishing Corporation, Arlington Heights, Ill.

Mises, Ludwig von, 1922, *Socialism*, English edition, Liberty Press, Indianapolis, Ind.

_____, 1949, *Human Action*, Henry Regnery, Chicago, Ill.

Mossner, E.C., 1977, 'Hume and the Legacy of the Dialogues', in G.P. Morice (ed.), *David Hume Bicentenary Papers*, University of Edinburgh Press, Edinburgh.

Murray, Charles, 1984, *Losing Ground: American Social Policy 1950-1980*, Basic Books, New York.

_____, 1996, *Charles Murray and the Underclass: The Developing Debate*, Choice in Welfare, No. 33, Institute of Economic Affairs, London.

Musgrave, R.A. and Musgrave, P.B., 1989, *Public Finance in Theory and Practice* (5th edn), McGraw Hill, London.

Nelson, Robert H., 2001, 'Frank Knight and Original Sin', *The Independent Review*.

Newman, J.H., 1915, *On the Scope and Nature of University Education*, Everyman, Dent, London.

North, Douglass C., 1990, *Institutions, Institutional Change and Economic Performance*, Cambridge University Press, Cambridge.

Novak, Michael, 1991, *The Spirit f Democratic Capitalism* (originally published 1982), second and British edn, Institute of Economic Affairs, London.

Nozick, Robert, 1974, *Anarchy, State and Utopia*, Basic Books, New York, NY

Otteson, J.R., 2000, 'Adam Smith: Moral Philosopher', *Ideas on Liberty*.

The Oxford Companion to Christian Thought, 2000, Adrian Hastings, Alistair Mason and Hugh Pyper (eds), Oxford University Press, Oxford.

Piedra, A.M., 2004, *Natural Law: The Foundation of an Orderly Economic System*, Lexington Books, Lanham, Md.

Plato, 1871, 'The Dialogue of Plato', Benjamin Jowett (transl.), *Encyclopaedia Britannica*, 1952.

Popper, K., 1966, *The Open Society and its Enemies* (5th edn, originally published, 1942), Princeton University Press, Princeton, NJ.

Preston, R.H., 1986, 'The Legacy of the Christian Socialist Movement in England', in W. Block and I. Hexham (eds), *Religion, Economics and Social Thought,* The Fraser Institute, Vancouver, Canada.

Pufendorf, S., 2003, *The Whole Duty of Man, According to the Law of Nature* (originally published in 1735), Liberty Fund, Indianapolis, Ind.

Rawls, J.A., 1972, *Theory of Justice,* Harvard University Press, Cambridge, Ma.

Rommen, H.A., 1947, *The Natural Law* (1998 English edn), Liberty Fund, Indianapolis.

Rothbard, Murray N., 1976, 'New Light on the Prehistory of the Austrian School' in Edwin G. Dolan (ed), *The Foundations of Modern Austrian Economics,* Sheed and Ward, Kansas City, Kansas.

Rushdoony, Rousas John, 1973, *The Institutes of Biblical Law,* The Craig Press, Nutley, N.J.

Russell, B., 1961, *History of Western Philosophy,* Allen and Unwin, London.

Saunders, P., 2002, *What Future for Welfare?,* Occasional Paper 11, Free Market Foundation, Johannesburg.

Schumpeter, J.A., 1950, *Capitalism, Socialism and Democracy,* Harrap, New York, NY.

_____, 1954, *A History of Economic Analysis,* Oxford University Press, New York.

Scruton, R., 1994, *Modern Philosophy,* Sinclair-Stevenson, London.

Shinn, Roger, 2000, 'Entry on Reinhold Niebuhr' in *The Oxford Companion to Christian Thought.*

Smith, Adam, 1976a, *The Theory of Moral Sentiments* (originally published 1759), Liberty Press, Indianapolis, Ind.

_____, (1762-3, 1766), *Lectures on Jurisprudence* (1978 edn), R.L. Meek, D.D. Raphael and P.G. Stein (eds), Oxford University Press, Oxford.

_____, 1976b, *The Wealth of Nations* (originally published 1776), Glasgow edn, Oxford University Press, Oxford.

Sowell, T., 1985, *Marxism*, William Morrow, New York.

Spencer, Herbert, 1884, *The Man Versus the State* (reprinted 1982), Liberty Fund, Indianapolis, Ill.

Stigler, G. J., 1966, *The Theory of Price* (3rd edn), Macmillan, New York.

Vaughn, Karen Iversen, 1980, *John Locke. Economist and Social Scientist*, University of Chicago Press, Chicago, Ill.

Walden, J.W.H., 1970, *The Universities of Ancient Greece*, Libraries Press, Freeport, NY.

Wasley, T.P., 1997, *What Has Government Done to Our Healthcare?*, Cato Institute, Washington DC.

West, E.G., 1976, *Adam Smith: The Man and His Works*, Liberty Press, Indianapolis, Ind.

_____, 1994, *Britain's Student Loan System in World Perspective*, Institute of Economic Affairs, London.

.

2: Natural Law and Property Rights

1   The wording is that of the *World Development Report 1996*, p. 1.

2   The word 'daimonion' does not appear in the Oxford English Dictionary. However Rommen originally wrote in German and the word is probably that of his translator. Nevertheless the meaning is clear from the context. Moreover the *OED* indicates that 'daimon' in English is a direct transliteration of the Greek 'divinity, one's genius or demon'. 'Conscience and its voice as divinely implanted in the individual, and reflecting the ultimate values of the divinely created order' may not be an inaccurate translation of Rommen's meaning.

3   Aristotle also dismisses Plato's recommendation that the family be abolished and that men and women should have identical roles in society, *ceteris paribus*, if the only difference between the two is that of child-bearing capacity. That, after all, is the rule in the animal world. Of course, even in the original argument as stated, other thing are not quite equal, Socrates and modern feminists notwithstanding. Aristotle argues 'it is ridiculous to conclude from the analogy of brute beasts that men and women should pursue the same occupations; for a brute beast has no household duties' (1264b).

4   In *De re publica*, III 13, Cicero wrote: 'True law is right reason in agreement with nature; it is of universal application, unchanging and everlasting; it summons to duty by its commands, and averts from wrongdoing by its prohibitions. And it does not lay its commands or prohibitions upon good men in vain, though neither have any effect upon the wicked. It is a sin to try to alter this law, nor is it allowable to attempt to repeal any part of it, and it is impossible to abolish it entirely. We cannot be freed from its obligations by senate or people, and we need not look outside ourselves for an expounder or interpreter of it. And there will not be different laws at Rome and at Athens, or different laws now and in the future, but one eternal law will be valid for all nations and all times, and there will be one master and ruler, that is, God, over us all, for he is the author of this law, its promulgator, and its enforcing judge. Whoever is disobedient is fleeing from himself and denying his human nature, and by reason of this very fact he will suffer the worst penalties, even if he escapes what is commonly called punishment.' (Cited in Rommen, 1998, p. 21.)

5   Cited in Rommen, 1998, p. 22.

6   Cited in Maine, 1861, pp. 37-38.

7   Cited in Rommen, 1998, pp. 31-32.

8   See the entry on 'Cicero' in *The Encyclopaedia Brittanica, Macropaedia*, 15th edition Vol. 4, 1976, p. 610.

9   The Scholastics were that group of scholars and thinkers working in Europe from the end of the first millennium. St Anselm of Canterbury is often viewed as the initiator of their efforts. They attempted to synthesise, organise and classify the traditions which had been handed down by the Greek and Roman philosophers and lawyers, together with patristic theology. The need for this became ever more apparent as Christianity spread to the 'uneducated barbarians' in the north, while in the lands of the former Empire orderly government and traditions were under threat of decay or of outright loss.

10 In *Summa theologica* (II-II, 66, 2) Aquinas simply repeated the Aristotelian arguments for private as against common property: *viz.* additional care, increased productivity, reduced shirking and less quarrelling. Aristotle had also argued that private property permits charitable giving. Aquinas strengthened this by citing I Timothy 6:17-8. 'Command those who are rich…to be generous and willing to share.'

11 Grotius wrote *Mare Liberum* in 1609. In this work he defended the freedom of access to the seas, which unlike land, could not be 'used up', and hence was not subject to the Natural Law of protecting the *suum*.

12 West (1976, pp. 42-49) also notes that Hutcheson was the first teacher in the University to give up lecturing in Latin. He had an animated manner of walking up and down among his students which was 'revolutionary' in its day. After three years Smith won a scholarship to Oxford. There was no Hutcheson there! Smith later complained in the *Wealth of Nations* that the system of payment at Oxford (from endowment income rather than student fees as at Glasgow) resulted in an incentive structure for teachers which encouraged indolence among the teaching staff, reinforced in turn by strict college discipline over students. Smith left Oxford before his scholarship expired. West does offer an additional explanation for Smith's discontent. He was at Oxford during the 1745 Rebellion when Charles Edward Stuart attempted to regain the throne. There were many Jacobites at Oxford. Smith, to the contrary, never made any secret of his strong opinions in favour of the Glorious Revolution which had deposed Charles' grandfather James II.

13 The 'approbation' of others need not be by ourselves. Hutcheson, pre-empting Smith, also uses the phrase 'any Spectator or Observer'. (See, as one example, Hutcheson, 1728, p. 173).

14 Wolfgang Leidhold, in his Introduction (p. xv) to Hutcheson (1725) notes that this act of will is consistent with Christian love. Christian '*benevolence* is not an emotion or a feeling'. Christ's command to 'love your neighbour as yourself' would be, says Leidhold, 'a very strange commandment: a feeling cannot be commanded'.

15 Hume's most obvious work of sceptical agnosticism is his *Dialogues Concerning Natural Religion*. This work, written in 1759, was held back 'from motives of prudence' (Burtt, 1939, p. 584) for posthumous publication in 1779. In these Socratic style *Dialogues* one can presume the writer Pamphilus, the pupil, to represent Hume. If so, he clearly rejects orthodox dogma as represented by Demea. But his own sympathy seems to lie with the philosopher Cleanthes who rebukes the sceptical Philo thus: 'take care; push not matters too far: allow not your zeal against false religion to undermine your veneration for the true'. (Hume, *Dialogues*, reprinted in full in Burtt, *op. cit.*, p. 761).

16 Hume requested Smith to take on the task of posthumous publication of the *Dialogues*. When Smith refused, Hume asked his publisher William Strachan to do so, with the proviso that if Strachan failed to act within 30 months of Hume's demise, Hume's own nephew, David, would take on the task. In a letter to Strachan, announcing Hume's death, Smith described Hume 'as approaching as nearly to the idea of a perfectly wise and virtuous man, as perhaps the nature of human frailty will permit'. (See Eugene Miller's Foreword, pp. xi and xii, and Smith's letter, p. xlix in Hume's *Essays, Moral, Political and Literary*,(1985).)

17 Buckle (1991, p. 1) quotes Hume's well-known footnote: 'This theory concerning the origin of property, and consequently justice, is in the main, the same with that hinted at and adopted by Grotius.' The footnote is present in *Enquiries Concerning Human Understanding and Concerning the Principles of Morals*. The two *Enquiries* were originally published in 1748 and 1752 respectively as 'restatements in more popular form' of the two volumes that comprised *A Treatise on Human Nature*. (See Burtt, *op. cit.*, p. 583 and A.D. Lindsay's Introduction to *A Treatise*, p. vii.) Perhaps the allusion to Grotius in the *Enquiries* was an attempt to gain a public acceptability which the more austere *Treatise* failed to generate.

18 In his *Dialogues* Hume writes of biological evolution rather in the manner he approached the evolution of social institutions (Burtt, 1939, pp. 723-33). It is Philo speaking: 'matter [may] be susceptible of many and great revolutions, through the endless periods [and the] incessant changes... seem to intimate some general transformations. [Or else there would be] total deformity and confusion... Chance has no place...Everything is surely governed by steady, inviolable laws.' But did each animal or season have its own god? Philo next subjects polytheism to his Darwinian 'survival of the fittest' arguments. The point here is not Philo's scepticism (which Cleanthes later rebutted). The issue is that Hume saw discovery and evolution as crucial sources for establishing the truth both in the institutional world in which we live as well as in the natural world of animals and plants. Hayek (1967, p. 119n) points out that while Hume's view of evolution in general obviously preceded the work of Charles Darwin, Darwin's grandfather Erasmus was strongly influenced by Hume, and

that channel is the most likely to have had a strong bearing on the thoughts of the later Darwin.

19 Recall the narrator of the *Dialogues*, Pamphilus, was most inclined to agree with the philosophical Cleanthes. (Other authorities on Hume, however, such as Mossner (1977), identify Hume with Philo, the Sceptic.)

20 'Just as it is wrong to withdraw from the individual and commit to the community at large what private enterprise and industry can accomplish, so too it is an injustice, a great evil, and a disturbance of right order for a larger and higher organisation to arrogate to itself functions which can be performed efficiently by smaller and lower bodies... Of its very nature, the true aim of all social activity should be to help individual members of the social body, but never to destroy or absorb them.' Paul XI, *Quadragesimo Anno*, 1931, s79. Cited in Rommen, *op. cit.*, p. 194.

21 Piedra (2004, p. 51) condemns the Scottish Enlightenment for its 'misunderstanding—if not rejection—of Natural Law'. He singles out Hume, Ferguson and Smith (the 'founder' of the 'English [*sic*] Classical School' for particular condemnation. In addition, Piedra attacks (pp. 14-18) philosophers of the French Enlightenment, from Voltaire to Rousseau to Comte. Here he has more cause. They rejected God, placed their faith entirely in Reason and assumed, in their search for Utopia, the essential goodness of man. The canny Scots did not embrace atheism, and assumed rather self-interest tempered by benevolence. Reason could be used, given these assumptions, in order to understand human behaviour, but also to deny that a Utopia could be reached if only a 'man of system' could be found.

3: Rationalism and Caritas

1 Tolstoy, after his conversion (*c.* 1880), believed that Christ left five commandments for life: do not be angry; do not lust; do not bind yourself by oaths; resist not him that is evil; and be good to the just and the unjust. He came to believe private property should be condemned because ownership was secured by force. Organised government should also be opposed since it maintained itself through coercion. He wrote several essays on these themes. In 1901 he attempted to divest himself of his own property, but after pressure from his family, legally transferred his estate to them. (*Encyclopaedia Britannica*, Vol. 18, pp. 483-86, 1976.)

2 Mises' pupil Murray Rothbard wrote in a similar vein (1976, p. 62): '...Aquinas and other theologians denounced "covetousness" and love of profit, mercantile gain being only justifiable when directed at the "good of others"; furthermore Aquinas attacked "avarice" as attempting to improve one's "station in life"'.

3   Mises, (1922, pp. 383-84) also gave the example of the Church Father, St John of Chrysostom in Constantinople. Chrysostom strongly advocated mimicking the practice of the Jerusalem congregation in order to provide an 'inexhaustible' fund to aid the poor.

4   Michael Novak was Vice-Chairman of the Lay Commission on Catholic Social Teaching and the US Economy. In 1984 the Commission produced its Report, *Toward the Future: Catholic Social Thought and the US Economy*. It is not improbable that this Report influenced the contents of the encyclical written by Pope John Paul II, *Centesimus Annus*, in 1991. This encyclical marked a break in the Church's teaching and attitudes towards enterprise capitalism. Prior to 1991, the Church's official line had been expressed in two encyclicals dating from 1891 and 1931: respectively these were *Rerum Novarum*, issued by Leo XIII, and *Quadragesimo Anno*, issued by Pius XI.

5   Here, perhaps, I fail faithfully to paraphrase Novak's intent. His actual words (p. 14) are 'a polity respectful of the rights of the individual to life, liberty and the pursuit of happiness'.

6   Griffiths, as a man of the Book, could have expanded further on the Separation of Realms. For example, on the Mount of Temptation (Matt. 4) the devil offered Jesus several attractive earthly alternatives (alternatives which can also be tempting to individual men). These were the power to turn stones into bread, the kingdoms of the world, and the superhuman ability to leap unharmed from the pinnacle of the temple. The seductive attractiveness of power over other human beings, at no danger to oneself, coupled with the miraculous ability costlessly to provide the necessities of physical life, are the lodestones of socialists everywhere and always. Jesus rejected these political and earthly temptations on spiritual grounds. (Matt. 4: 4, 7 and 10.) The temptations related to a Separate Realm. Succumbing to the temptations would have endorsed a theocratic command economy. This Jesus conspicuously refused to do. (The writer is grateful to James Wood for first introducing him to this exposition.)

7   Novak here approaches with alarming proximity the views of Mises and Knight. As examples of counter-natural Christian counsels he cites the loving of enemies and the turning of the other cheek. They no doubt had somewhat different interpretations from Novak, but Knight regarded such instructions as 'mush', while Mises said they implied recommendations including self-imposed 'castration'.

8   Novak's emphasis on pluralism in unity, which he epitomised by using the doctrine of the Trinity, is sufficient ground for this assertion.

9   See *TMS*, pp. 155-75, 437 and 467-85. West, in his Introduction to *TMS* states: 'Smith insists that a balance is required among [the] three subsets of virtue', p. 27.

10 See Coase (1976, pp. 538-39). He notes, along with Jacob Viner, that Smith tended to use phrases such as the Architect of the Universe, or the Director of Nature and 'other circumlocutions' as 'evading [the] giving [of] an answer' to the question of whether he accepted a personal God as creator.

11 See Otteson (2000). He summarises the outcome of the process, the self-command, as 'very non-Freudian'. See also the quotation from Keynes on the first page of the Introduction *supra*.

4: Caritas and Social Welfare

1 See the entry on Lassalle by Tom Bottomore in the *New Palgrave Dictionary of Economics*, Vol. 3, London: Macmillan, 1987, p. 134.

2 Cited by Mises in *Socialism, op. cit.*, p. 278.

3 An early milestone in anti-self-help legislation history was the prosecution in 1834 of the Friendly Society of Agricultural Labourers. The judge, attempting to suppress the growth of trades unions, found the members of the society guilty of administering an unlawful oath. The oath (common amongst friendly societies) was simply a pledge of loyalty to other society members and a promise not to disclose society affairs to outsiders. The six Tolpuddle Martys, as they became known, were sentenced to seven years transportation and entered the history books. After a public outcry in 1836, the Martyrs were granted a free pardon and are today regarded as suffering pioneers of trades unionism. It would be equally correct to view them as victims of government opposition to mutual aid in health and welfare funding.

4 Friedman claims (2005, pp. 243 and 491) that this was 'in response to economic *growth'* (emphasis added). Certainly, unlike the other welfare state initiatives, this one did not occur during a period of stagnation. National income was rising. But per capita *consumption* was stable or declining because of government's continuation of wartime austerity programmes.

5 Not only did the friendly societies foster mutual self-help, they encouraged individual responsibility. New members of the Ancient Order of Foresters (which had 620,000 members by 1910) at their Ceremony of Initiation had to heed the following words: 'In your domestic relations we look to find you, if a husband, affectionate and trustful; if a father, regardful of the moral and material well-being of your children and dependants; as a son, dutiful and exemplary, and as a friend, steadfast and true.' (Cited in Green, *op. cit.*, p. 48).

6 The argument was well put by William (Lord) Beveridge in 1948 (pp. 58-60). It is a heavy irony that Beveridge's political memorial is the universalist British welfare state. He wrote: '...in a field already made into a State monopoly, those

dissatisfied with the institutions that they find can seek a remedy only by seeking to change the Government of the country. In a free society and a free field they have a different remedy; discontented individuals with new ideas can make a new institution to meet their needs. The field is open to success or failure; secession is the midwife of invention.'

7   We noted, *supra*, how Locke wrote in part to justify the Glorious Revolution of 1688-9. Jefferson, in the Declaration of Independence, wrote: 'We hold these truths to be sacred and undeniable; that all men are created equal and independent, that from that equal creation they derive rights inherent and inalienable, among which are the preservation of life, and liberty, and the pursuit of happiness.' Substitute 'Estates' or 'property' for the 'pursuit of happiness' and these could be the words of Locke. Alternatively, infer 'Estates' from 'life' and the words are simply an expansion of Locke.

8   The leading *philosophes* of the French Enlightenment contributed to the *Encyclopédie*, compiled by Diderot from 1751 to 1772. In 1756, Adam Smith, in the *Edinburgh Review*, described it as promising 'to be the most compleat of this kind which has ever been published or attempted in any language'. Yet Diderot's philosophy was far removed from that of Smith.

9   The fact that this notion did not square with the premise that man had no free will was not untypical of Holbach's inconsistent writings.

10 When Mill wrote *On Liberty* in 1859 he had moved so far from Comtian solidarity-by-compulsion that he was exalting the individual and condemning society. He summarised (1947, pp. 4-5) the book's main purpose as follows: '[W]hen society is itself the tyrant...enslaving the soul...the practical question [is] where to place the limit...[on social control].' Mill's work was a protest not just against government, but against all the groups in society that can impede, whether by laws, rules, opinions or suasion, the decisions or actions of the sovereign individual. Mill answered his own question (p. 12) indicating that each individual should have 'liberty of thought', 'liberty of tastes and pursuits...without impediment from our fellow creatures, so long as what we do does not harm them, even though they should think our conduct foolish, perverse and wrong', and 'within the same limits...freedom to unite'. Later (p. 75) he indicated that individuals have to 'bear their share' in upholding the authority of society to protect these individual freedoms. This is a far cry from the Mill who so enthusiastically supported and expanded on Comte. Mill thus displayed in one lifetime ambivalence and schizophrenia towards liberty and authority. See also Gray, 1979 for a discussion of the 'Two Mills'.

11 Cited from a letter written by Churchill when President of the Board of Trade to Prime Minister Asquith, 29 December, 1908.

12 From the *Christian Century*, 23 July, 1930.

13 Rent-seeking is the technical term for attempts to transfer or shift wealth towards oneself in technically unproductive fashions. (One party loses what the other gains.) It is distinguished from profit-seeking activities and trading, where wealth is created through exchange, and both parties benefit.

14 Solidarity-by-compulsion has permitted a perverse, spontaneous order within planned societies. The self-interest of bureaucrats and politicians prompted the promises of care in order to obtain the resources to fund the transfers (and finance their careers). The self-interest of voters provided them with political support. The self-interest of individuals resulted in ever more imaginative uses of state transfers. The consequence, says Leube, is that 'we witness the erosion of the family as the all important core of any social integration... which among many other purposes serves as the decisive meeting place for family members, the altruistic care is no longer provided' (p. 14). 'Owing to the [resulting] excessive tax burden... both parents are forced to work... schoolchildren are mostly viewed as a burden when they return...earlier than mid-afternoon'. In turn (p. 15) '... these developments require collective welfare institutions to take over the former "household production"'.

15 The 'underclass' is not a uniquely British or American problem. It has appeared recently in South Africa. Before the introduction of the universal franchise in 1994, state welfare was available for the elderly and indigent. But the list of 'needs' for which benefits are available has now been extended. Patekile Holimisa, an African National Congress MP, wrote (*Business Day*, 5 June 2003): 'Prior to 1994 youngsters who would be seen at old-age pension payout stations would be those who accompanied their frail and sickly grandparents...You still see a number of young women—girls in fact—at these social grants pay stations. But most of them come to receive their share of the state social benefits [as] recipients of foster-grants or child-support grants. Snide remarks are often passed that these girls deliberately get pregnant so that on the birth of their children they benefit from these social grants. Such assumptions are supported by statements that there is no reason for them to fall pregnant in the first place in the light of government's related policies... condoms... are freely available in local clinics. Where they choose to be reckless, contraceptive pills are also freely available at the same clinics. When they take none of these precautions... government policy and laws allow them to terminate the pregnancies... [but] the more children they have the more money will come into the household... The time has come to put an end to this unnecessary tension between human rights and good morals.'

16 Fogel's 'self-realisation' (a term also used by Frank Knight) appears to be similar in meaning to the concept of 'self-actualisation' in the 'hierarchy of human needs' as first described by the American psychologist Abraham Maslow (*d.* 1970).

17 This warning was written prior to the boredom of work generated by the large-scale factory system of the Industrial Revolution. It was also written prior to widespread formal education. It was education, not welfare, that Smith wished government to be involved in.

18 Jimmy Carter, former US President, often cited Niebuhr's words that 'the sad job of politics is to bring justice to a sinful world'. (*vide* Shinn, 2000.)

19 See the comment by Smith (*TMS*, p. 369) at the opening of this chapter on benevolence.

20 Knight (*FR*, p. 211) notes it 'is particularly indefensible in the case of dependent persons to treat economic performance as the measure of moral desert, *or of socially imperative income... the family is in many respects more real as a social economic unit than is the individual*'. (Emphasis added.)

5: Competition in Healthcare

1 This section draws on Baird (1988).

2 In present day South Africa, to take just one example, we can see the implications of the anti-Lockean position. A duty to supply is mandatory. There is conscription. Health professionals (doctors, pharmacists, nurses and so on) must do a 'compulsory period of service' in a post and at a place, of government's choosing before they can enter the normal labour market. Alan Bullock (1991) characterises such a policy as emanating from the 'twin cults' of *Volksgemeinschaft* and *Erlebnis*. [Alan Bullock (1991, pp. 320 and 362) has discussed the nature of governments who indulge in this type of 'compulsory service'. In Russia in the 1930s the gulags were established so that 'a population of slaves' could do 'socially useful work'. In Germany, at the same time, membership of the Deutsche Studentenschaft was made compulsory. Students had to do four months of 'labour service' and four months in an SA camp as part of the twin cults of *Volksgemeinschaft* and *Erlebnis* (work experience as opposed to academic stress on knowledge, *Erkenntnis*).] The result, of course, is pre-emptive emigration and a skills shortage, including emigration of complementary financial capital and managerial expertise as private South African hospital corporations sub-contract work from the NHS, which, for reasons similar in principle, has its own problems of a shortage of resources relative to demand.

3 The reasons could be that the least serious cases are treated first, or because those with the greatest pathological likelihood of response are given preferential care, or because all are treated simultaneously, but the intensity of therapy at low levels of expense is so superficial that only the least serious cases or the most pathologically responsive are cured.

4   The exceptions to this argument are related to public health issues such as clean water, sewerage, health education and programmes such as immunisation, directed against communicable diseases. (Furthermore, a little thought will make it obvious that even these are not 'pure' public goods. For example, clean water can be metered and free-riders excluded, and an immunisation programme is not non-rivalrous, as vaccines are limited in supply).

5   As a monopoly is a single seller, who can raise price by restricting output, so a monopsony is a single buyer who can hold price down by restricting purchases.

6   The first law of demand states that, as price falls, the quantity consumed increases, and *vice versa*. The second law of demand states that in the longer term the quantity consumed increases even further, and *vice versa*. This is because the passage of time permits us to change our structural behaviour pattern. Thus a fall in the petrol price results in more petrol being used immediately, as we use our cars more. In the longer term we may buy 'gas guzzlers', pushing up our petrol consumption even further.

7   The system as described is common to most countries with large commercial healthcare sectors. The origins of the system in the USA lie in the attempts by employers to attract workers from each other during World War II, a time of labour shortage. Since wages were controlled they had to make their bids more attractive by offering tax free perquisites such as health insurance.

8   Thomas Sowell (1985, p. 46) quotes from *German Ideology* and from *The Holy Family*. These were joint works by Marx and his colleague Engels in 1845-46 and in 1845 respectively. In the former they write: '...only in the community...is personal freedom possible'. In the latter they argue that freedom from the constraints of others is a delusion. 'Indeed, the individual considers *his* own freedom the movement, no longer curved or fettered by a common tie or by man, the movement of his alienated life elements, like property, industry, religion, etc.; in reality, this is the perfection of his slavery and his inhumanity.'

6: Markets in a University Culture?

1   Few participants in European university life in the 1960s and 1970s were unaffected by Daniel Cohn-Bendit (Danny the Red) in France, Rudi Dutschke in West Germany and Tariq Ali in Britain.

2   Russell devoted not a little space to Hypatia. He rightly included this tragedy on the southern shore of the Mediterranean in European, not African history.

3   This section draws on the Submission to the National Commission on Higher Education, prepared by the University of the Witwatersrand, July 1995.

4 The CUP consisted of all 21 heads of each of the then extant universities. It was a statutory body with its origin in an Act of 1916, since modified by the 1955 Universities Act. Its self-declared purpose (CUP, 1995, p. 148) was to be 'the collective voice of *those responsible to execute policy decisions made by government*' (emphasis added). As, like Britain, the binary system distinguishing between universities and technikons (polytechnics) has evolved, the CUP has been replaced with a committee comprising the heads of all of these tertiary institutions.

5 The cartel was successful. This recommendation was adopted and is now part of government funding policy.

6 The cartel's success in lobbying for government support is also provided by a *Discussion Document* produced by the National Commission on Higher Education (NCHE, 1996). Institutions will again be funded against a formula. The formula proposed (p. 133) will vary by registration of 'approved' numbers of students, in 'approved' programmes, proceeding at 'normative throughput rates', given 'normative prices unrelated to 'actual costs' (supply) or actual enrolments (demand) above approved levels. Funds will no longer follow students. This recommendation is now law.

7 In normal commercial firms there are shareholders, known in economic jargon as residual owners since their rewards are not contractually predetermined. This contrasts with employees (who earn a wage), or of lenders, or of owners of land or buildings (who respectively earn interest or rent). Residual owners receive dividends varying with the success of the enterprise. Success is measured by producing goods or services of a quality that consumers approve of and at a price they are prepared to pay. If the enterprise fails they are at risk of a total loss of their share of ownership. Some shareholders or their representatives form the board of directors that is thus motivated to ensure success. Failure to ensure satisfactory dividends would result in the Board's dismissal. The university equivalent of a council or of a board of governors has no such incentive or penalty structure.

8 An agency problem exists when an owner or principal employs another, an agent, to help the principal achieve his objectives. Since the agent does not have the same objective as the principal, the agency problem is that of incurring costs to align the goals, or the incentives of the two. One such agency cost is the activity of monitoring the agent. Another might be an agreement to share residual rewards. Company directors have to overcome this problem when they employ mangers. But when there is no residual ownership by principals, the agency problems can be very large.

9 Ralf Dahrendorf, Director of the London School of Economics (though I have lost the source).

10 Cited in Culyer, A.J., 'A Utility Maximising View of Universities', *Scottish Journal of Political Economy*, 1970.

11 In the UK several universities formed the 'Russell Group' to lobby for the ability to levy differential fees. Non-Russell group universities were either more content to follow the then government line of continuing with a zero fee policy, or were satisfied with the finally adopted maximum (effectively uniform) fee. But even within the Russell Group, diversity emerged. Edinburgh and Oxford experienced changes of Vice-Chancellor and both broke ranks. In the former the zero fee exemption ruled by the Scottish Parliament was adopted with some enthusiasm, while in the latter, serious thought is being given to opting out from the state subsidy system altogether and to becoming a private, non-state university which can set a fee structure of its own choosing, subject to student willingness to pay.

7: Concluding Thoughts

1   One of the latest trends in this area is to argue that businesses run their affairs in the interests of 'stakeholders', and that their activities be audited on a 'triple bottom line' basis to assess how well they have met the goal of 'corporate social responsibility' by economic, social and environmental yardsticks. An excellent critique of this movement is provided in Henderson (2001). Corporations are, of course, free to structure their governance systems as they will. They also choose to employ their resources as they will. Corporate social responsibility spending is not unusual, and can be assessed, when engaged in voluntarily, as having been judged to be an activity taken in the company's best interest. The problem with the corporate social responsibility movement is its wish to impose legislative obligations on corporations that they would not voluntarily adopt. 'Stakeholders' as auditors or decision participants are, after all, unlikely to embody the wishes of consumers, workers, owners, suppliers, lenders, managers, or even the wider population as represented by the impartial legal framework within which the company operates. Each of the latter already has a satisfactory explicit or implicit contract with the corporation. These mutually beneficial, consensual contracts vary with the situation. Any standardised legal imposition or requirement placed on corporations to compel the taking of actions, which would not otherwise be taken, will reduce the volume of such contracts in the economy. Such a law would reduce both contractual freedom and wealth. In poorer countries employment opportunities would be suppressed.

Index

Abraham, 23

Acton, J.E.D-A., Lord, 92

adverse selection, 118, 122-7, 148

agency costs, 118-9, 140, 179

Alchian, Armen, 140-1, 143-4

alertness (entrepreneurial), 2, 8, 24-5, 30, 103-4, 158, 160

American Economic Association, 52, 79

Aquinas, St Thomas, 2, 13, 19-22, 25, 40-1, 43, 55-6, 58-9, 64, 152, 170, 172

Apollo, 2, 102

Aristotle, 4, 10, 13-6, 18-9, 23, 31, 33, 39, 43, 56, 131, 153, 169-70

Atlee, Clement, 83-4

Augustine, Bishop of Hippo, 18-9

Baumol, W.J., 114

benevolence, virtue of, 5, 32-4, 39, 43, 66-7, 70, 74-5, 78-9, 81, 84, 87-8, 94, 97, 99, 103-5, 145, 153, 158-9, 170, 172, 177

Bentham, Jeremy, 32

Bevan, Aneurin, 119

Beveridge, William, Lord, 84, 127, 174

Biblical references,

Gen., 62

Gen. 13, 23

Ex., 36

Ex. 22:1, 41

Lev. 19:9, 60

Lev. 19:35-7, 60

Lev. 25:30, 60

Deut. 6:7-9, 69

I Sam. 8:3-19, 42

I Sam. 10:19, 42

I Sam. 12:14-5, 42

Matt. 4, 173

Matt. 4:4, 7 and 10, 173

Matt. 5:30, 54

Matt. 5:34-6, 105

Matt. 6:33, 48, 97

Matt. 19:30, 47

Matt. 20:1-16, 50

Matt. 20:26, 47

Matt. 24:3, 74

Matt. 25:14-30, 49-50

Matt. 25:31-46, 74

Mark 12:31, 49

Luke 15:17, 102

Luke 14:26, 66

Luke 16:1-12, 61

Luke 9:60, 47, 54

Jn. 1:1, 15

Jn. 4:13, 152

Acts 2:44-5, 61

Acts 4:32-5, 61

Acts 5:1-10, 61

Rom. 2:12-16, 17

I Cor. 9:24-7, 63

I Cor. 13: 4-8, 103

II Thess. 3:10, 49

I Jn. 3:17, 103

Rev., 62, 70

Rev. 21:1, 61

Bismarck, Otto von, 76-8, 92, 155

Blue Cross/Blue Shield, 120

Bonner, S.F., 130

Booth, Charles, 83-4

Buchanan, James, 72

Buckle, Stephen, 21-4, 26, 171

Burke, Edmund, 69, 81-2, 89-90, 94

Byzantium, 132

Caesar, 48, 63

Canavan, Francis, 90

capitalism, 56, 62-4, 68, 154-5, 173

capitalist, 46, 57, 76, 151, 154, 157, 160

Capone, Al, 32

caritas, 2, 4, 8, 18, 45-6, 48-9, 56, 60, 62, 64-8, 70-2, 74-5, 93, 96-7, 103-4, 159-61

cartels, behaviour of, 137-9, 146, 148-9, 155, 179

Catechism of the Catholic Church, 96-7

181